Comparative Youth Justice

Comparative Youth Justice

Critical Issues

Edited by

John Muncie and
Barry Goldson

Los Angeles | London | New Delhi
Singapore | Washington DC

First published 2006

Reprinted 2009

SAGE Publications Ltd
1 Oliver's Yard
55 City Road
London EC1Y 1SP

SAGE Publications Inc.
2455 Teller Road
Thousand Oaks, California 91320

SAGE Publications India Pvt Ltd
B-1/I 1 Mohan Cooperative Industrial Area
Mathura Road
New Delhi 110 044

SAGE Publications Asia-Pacific Pte Ltd
33 Pekin Street #02-01
Far East Square
Singapore 048763

British Library Cataloguing in Publication data

A catalogue record for this book is available from
the British Library

ISBN 978 1 4129 1135 1
ISBN 978 1 4129 1136 8 (pbk)

Library of Congress control number 2005935709

FSC
Mixed Sources
Product group from well-managed
forests and other controlled sources
Cert no. SGS-COC-2482
www.fsc.org
© 1996 Forest Stewardship Council

Typeset by C&M Digitals (P) Ltd., Chennai, India
Printed on paper from sustainable resources
Printed in Great Britain by TJI Digital, Padstow, Cornwall
Text pages are FSC certified

Contents

List of Contributors

Trevor Bradley is Lecturer in Criminology, Institute of Criminology, Victoria University of Wellington, New Zealand.

Chris Cunneen is the New South Global Professor of Criminology at the Faculty of Law, University of New South Wales, Australia.

Mark Fenwick is Associate Professor at the Faculty of Law, Kyushu University, Japan.

Sophie Gendrot is Professor of Political Science at the Centre for Urban Studies, University of Paris-Sorbonne, France.

Barry Goldson is Senior Lecturer in Sociology at the University of Liverpool, England.

Barry Krisberg is President of the National Council on Crime and Delinquency, Oakland, California, USA.

Tapio Lappi-Seppälä is Director of the National Research Institute of Legal Policy, Helsinki, Finland and Professor of Criminology and Sociology of Law, University of Helsinki.

Lesley McAra is Senior Lecturer in Criminology at the Centre for Law and Society, University of Edinburgh, Scotland.

John Muncie is Professor of Criminology and Co-Director of the International Centre for Comparative Criminological Research at the Open University, England.

David Nelken is Distinguished Professor of Legal Institutions and Social Change at the University of Macerata, Italy and Distinguished Research Professor of Law at the University of Wales, Cardiff.

Johan Put is Professor in Youth and Social Law at the Catholic University of Leuven, Belgium.

Russell Smandych is Professor of Sociology at the University of Manitoba, Canada.

Juan Tauri is a Criminologist and Doctoral Candidate a the Auckland University of Technology, New Zealand.

Jolande uit Beijerse is Lecturer in Criminal Justice at Erasmus University, Rotterdam, The Netherlands.

René van Swaaningen is Professor of Criminology at Erasmus University, Rotterdam, The Netherlands.

Lode Walgrave is Emeritus Professor in Youth Criminology at the Catholic University of Leuven, Belgium.

Reece Walters is Senior Lecturer in Criminology at the University of Stirling, Scotland.

Rob White is Professor of Sociology and Head of the School of Sociology and Social Work at the University of Tasmania, Australia.

Editors' Introduction

This book is a companion volume to *Youth Crime and Justice: Critical Issues*, edited by Barry Goldson and John Muncie and published simultaneously by SAGE. Together they are designed to encourage critical reflection on contemporary juvenile justice reform not only in England and Wales but across various western jurisdictions.

This volume, *Comparative Youth Justice: Critical Issues*, identifies major international shifts in juvenile justice policy and practice. There is a widespread assumption that the penal population of children and young people is growing worldwide amidst a burgeoning USA inspired 'culture of control'. Through various measures of 'adulteration', young people are also now assumed to be more likely to find a decline in their special status as in need of care and protection and more in need of punishment through which they will be made responsible for their own actions. However, such developments stand in some opposition to numerous counter movements which seem designed to further rather than diminish children's rights. Of note is the 1989 UN Convention on the Rights of the Child (UNCRC) which stresses the importance of incorporating a rights consciousness into juvenile justice reform by, for example: establishing an age of criminal responsibility relative to developmental capacity; encouraging children's participation in decision making; providing access to legal representation for children; protecting children from capital or degrading punishment and ensuring that arrest, detention and imprisonment are measures of last resort. Above all, the Convention emphasises that the well-being of those aged under 18 should be a primary consideration. The UNCRC has been ratified by 192 countries. As a result, it may be singularly misleading to claim that an ethos of child protectionism has all but disappeared from juvenile justice.

International statistical comparisons of the operation of youth and juvenile justice systems are now routinely gathered by the likes of the United Nations, The Council of Europe and the International Centre for Prison Studies based at Kings College, London. In particular they focus on comparing counts and rates of youth custody. This may appear uncontroversial but such data is not always easy to recover or to interpret and none can claim to be beyond dispute. Most of the chapters in this volume indeed lament the absence of reliable statistical records in their own jurisdictions. Even when data exist, the collection of penal statistics is continually dogged by the problem of strict comparability before any academic interpretation of exactly what 'difference' signifies can take place. The classification and recording of crime varies and different countries have developed different judicial systems for defining and dealing with young offenders. Different means are used to record imprisonment. What is classified as penal custody in one country may not be in others though regimes may be similar. Not all countries collect the same data on the same age groups and populations. None seem to do so within the same time periods. Linguistic differences in how the terms 'minor', 'juvenile', 'child' and 'young offender' are defined and operationalised further hinder any attempt to ensure a sound comparative base. In itself, it is significant that the term 'youth justice' has become preferred over that of 'juvenile justice' in many jurisdictions. However even with these caveats in mind the degree to which nation states jealously preserve distinct criminal justice systems as a means of retaining independent sovereignty seems to be borne out by a quite remarkable divergence in the recourse to youth custody worldwide.

To address comparative issues, statistical and descriptive measures and accounts, even when accurate, are of only limited value. Of late, a number of edited texts have appeared which have begun to unravel national differences but rarely do these go much beyond describing the historical emergence and the powers and procedures of particular jurisdictions. Tonry and Doob's (2004) *Youth Crime and Youth Justice: Comparative and Cross-National Perspectives* includes chapters on Canada and New Zealand, as well as various European countries, and discusses the relevance of welfare, age limitations and the emergence of separate systems. Winterdyk's (2002) edited collection, *Juvenile Justice Systems: International Perspectives*, covers 18 countries and is, to date, the most comprehensive, whereas Bala et al.'s (2002) *Juvenile Justice Systems* restricts itself to North America, Australasia, and the UK. Nevertheless, comparative knowledge of international systems generally remains sketchy and conclusions tentative. What is required are detailed analyses of the politics of policy formation in different jurisdictions. This edited collection is designed to address the way in which global convergent trends become translated, inflected or hybridised in particular national, regional and local settings. To gain a deeper understanding of international convergence/diversity, each chapter in this volume addresses such key critical issues as degree of compliance with international law, extent of repenalisation, adulteration, and tolerance, and the impact of experiments in restoration and risk management.

The choice of case studies included here has been informed by our previous comparative work (Muncie, 2002; 2005; Goldson, 2004). In particular the USA is, worldwide, often perceived as the pinnacle of punitiveness characterised by labour camps, juvenile waiver, high rates of incarceration, failure to ratify the UN Convention and until recently the death penalty for children. Yet the USA also is at the forefront of many community based interventions involving sub-sidised probation, mentoring and community justice. How can such disparities be accounted for? England and Wales is often perceived as the most punitive jurisdiction in Europe with high rates of incarceration. Can it be viewed as a prime case of policy transfer from the USA with the import of risk profiling, electronic monitoring, mandatory sentencing and pre-emptive early interven-tion? Similarly Canada's recent youth justice reforms appear in part to emulate those of England and Wales while re-establishing that the principle of the pro-tection of society be uppermost. Do these amalgams of restorative, community and custodial measures based on risk profiling and risk management offer any hope for a more progressive future?

Once heralded as a beacon of tolerance and humanity, Holland has recently embarked on a substantial prison building programme linked to a tendency to expand pre-trial detention and to deliver longer sentences on conviction. Is this a classic case of European repenalisation? In France in the 1980s the Mitterand Government responded to a series of violent disturbances in Lyon and Marseilles, not by implementing more authoritarian measures, but by developing the Bonnemaison initiative of providing education and vocational opportunity and avenues for local political participation. Since the 1980s, however, the socio-economic conditions that produce youth marginalisation and estrangement seem to no longer be given central political or academic attention. Does a zero tolerance approach (emulating UK/USA developments and particularly evident since the disturbances of 2005) now mean that questions of security have taken precedence over those of repub-lican solidarity?

Restorative justice processes in New Zealand are now established in statute as the fundamental rationale for youth justice. Most academic and policy research speaks highly of various forms of 'conferencing' in impacting on re-offending (particularly for less serious violent offenders) and on ensuring that both victim and offender are the *key* participants and decision-makers in deter-mining any future action. Is this the most clear international case of progressive juvenile justice reform? Over the past decade, most Australian states have wit-nessed an intensification of intervention into the lives of young people, whether offenders or not. Two key themes have been the racialisation of juvenile justice and the criminalisation of children in poverty. However there is no one system of juvenile justice in Australia, rather a diversity of legislative powers across the 6 states, the Australian Capital Territory (ACT) and the Northern Territory. Notable are wide disparities in sentencing policy and custodial rates. The cases of New Zealand and Australia, as well as Canada, raise a series of issues sur-rounding the import of restorative approaches (particularly in police cautioning and shaming), the treatment of Aboriginal populations and the meaning of indigenous justice.

Belgium is often cited as being at the forefront of welfare protectionism and of restorative juvenile justice in Europe. In Belgium, all judicial interventions are legitimated through an educative and protective, rather than punitive and responsibilising discourse. How far is this under threat from a growing emphasis on offender accountability? Scotland has been operating with a welfare tribunal for the majority of under 16 year old offenders for the past 30 years. As such, child welfare considerations appear to hold a pivotal position for younger offenders and it has long been argued that they provide a credible alternative to the punitive nature of youth justice pursued in many other jurisdictions. However, how far do recent developments, such as the re-establishment of youth courts for 16 and 17 year olds, herald the beginnings of the decline of welfare?

An Italian cultural tradition of familial control has been traditionally linked to low levels of formal penal repression. In Italy, judicial discretion to pardon, discharge or divert cases has created a climate of relative penal leniency. The 'cultural embeddedness' of Catholic paternalism it is argued has provided the parameters in which a different purpose and meaning of punishment is understood. Why is Italy one of a few European countries to witness a *decrease* in juvenile incarceration in the past decade and with what consequences? In Finland the juvenile prison population has been reduced dramatically over the past 40 years. Finland is one of a very few countries to be able to claim that community penalties are given as direct alternatives (rather than as additions) to prison sentences. Part of this dramatic shift may be explicable by a conscious effort on the part of successive Finnish governments to formulate a national identity closer to that of other Scandinavian states. If so, is it then a pivotal example of decarceration? Japan has long been assumed to be a relatively 'crime free' and 'non-punitive' society. The protection of juveniles has long taken precedence over individual accountability. The juvenile offender is deemed as much a victim as a criminal. How far, though, can this vision of 'innocence' survive a growing politicisation of the 'youth crime' issue, as already witnessed in a series of reforms following a number of high profile cases of juvenile murders?

This volume is explicitly designed to address such issues. It is not simply an attempt to document national similarities and differences in Western youth and juvenile justice but to critically unpack their contradictions and inconsistencies: to delve below political rhetoric to how youth justice plays itself out in practice; to recognise the regional and the local as units of comparison as well as the more familiar nation state; and, most significantly, to understand better how the rights of children can be recognised and upheld. This is not, and never can be, a purely academic exercise. Comparative work is always done for a purpose. In our case it is a growing unease with the recurrent scapegoating of young people, the consolidating reliance on punitive interventions, and the further denial of children's rights. The diverse structures of juvenile justice explored in this volume should reveal that 'it does not have to be always like this'. This book is designed to promote change as well as critical reflection.

John Muncie and Barry Goldson
January 2006

References

Bala, N., Hornick, J., Snyder, H. and Paetsch, J. (eds) (2002) *Juvenile Justice Systems: An International Comparison of Problems and Solutions*. Toronto: Thompson.

Goldson, B. (2004) 'Differential justice? A critical introduction to youth justice policy in UK jurisdictions'. In J. McGhee, M. Mellon and B. Whyte (eds) *Meeting Needs, Addressing Deeds*, Glasgow, NCH Scotland.

Muncie, J. (2002) 'Policy transfers and what works: Some reflections on comparative youth justice', *Youth Justice*, 1(3), pp. 27–35.

Muncie, J. (2005) 'The globalisation of crime control: the case of youth and juvenile justice', *Theoretical Criminology*, 9(1), 35–64.

Tonry, M. and Doob, A. (eds) (2004) *Youth Crime and Youth Justice: Comparative and Cross-National Perspectives*: Crime and Justice volume 31 Chicago: Chicago University Press.

Winterdyk, J. (ed) (2002) *Juvenile Justice Systems: International Perspectives*, 2nd edition. Toronto: Canadians Scholars Press.

Rediscovering the Juvenile Justice Ideal in the United States

1

Barry Krisberg

An idea that changed the world

In the early 1990s I attended a conference in Bremen, Germany, that involved judges from around the world. I learned that the American juvenile court ideal was the dominant legal paradigm for handling wayward children in many nations in Africa, Asia, Europe, and Latin America. Most of the speakers talked about efforts in their countries to achieve a justice system for young people that emphasized compassionate and enlightened care for vulnerable children. Privately, many of the conference participants wanted me to explain to them why it appeared that the United States was abandoning this ennobling ideal and jumping on the bandwagon of more incarceration and more frequent prosecution of children in the adult criminal courts. Many of the judges from across the globe could not comprehend why the United States clung to the barbaric policy of executing people who had committed their crimes as minors. Some wanted to know why several US judges, especially representatives of the National Council of Juvenile and Family Court Judges, seemed to embrace new laws designed to 'get tough' on juveniles. These were very profound and disturbing questions.

At the dawn of the twentieth century, legislatures in Illinois and Colorado established a new 'Children's Court'. This new legal entity built on many earlier progressive developments and established an innovative justice system that sought to substitute treatment and care in lieu of a stark regimen of punishment for wayward youths. Law reform was pursued by a broad range of child advocates such as the famous American social activist, Jane Addams, crusading judges such as Ben Lindsey of Denver, Colorado, women's groups, and local bar associations (Platt, 1968; Krisberg, 2005). Over the next two decades, the new paradigm of justice for children spread throughout the nation. Although the new children's court never possessed adequate resources to fulfill its lofty mission, the intellectual promise of the juvenile court was virtually unchallenged for two-thirds of the twentieth century. America's leading legal philosopher, Roscoe Pound, proclaimed that '[T]he American juvenile court was the greatest step forward in Anglo-American law since the Magna Carta' (Pound, 1957). Equally important, although it escaped the myopic attention of many US scholars, the American juvenile court ideal was adopted by many other nations (Stewart, 1978).

The American juvenile court evolves

Beginning in the 1960s, the legal hegemony of the juvenile court faced some significant challenges. A series of legal decisions culminated in the landmark US Supreme Court decision, *In re Gault* (1968), which profoundly challenged juvenile justice in America. Writing for the Court, Justice Abe Fortis proclaimed that being a minor should not subject one to a 'kangaroo court'. The Gault case demanded that states provide guarantees of due process and equal protection in juvenile court proceedings. Later court decisions stopped short of requiring jury trials for juveniles (*McKiever v. Pennsylvania*, 1971) and continued to endorse preventive detention of juveniles (*Schall v. Martin*, 1984), but the movement towards a 'constitutionalized' juvenile court was ineluctable. The conception of a benign Children's Court that always acted in 'the best interests of the child' was replaced with new attention to the legal rights of minors.

Concurrent with the new legalistic focus in the juvenile court was a growing skepticism about the ability of the juvenile court to effectively respond to a variety of youth issues. The popularity of Labeling Theory (Becker, 1963) in academia brought new questions about whether the juvenile justice system did more harm than good. Sociologist Edwin Schur (1973) advanced the policy of 'radical non-intervention' – whenever possible, the state should not intervene into the lives of families and children. Within the juvenile justice profession there were proposals to divert as many youths as possible from the formal court system, and to decriminalize those behaviors known as juvenile status offenses such as truancy, running away, curfew violations, and incorrigibility (Krisberg, 2005). In the early 1970s there also were widespread efforts to deinstitutionalize youths, moving them from secure detention centers and youth training schools to community-based programs (Scull, 1977). The most dramatic manifestation of this trend was the closing of all of the state juvenile facilities in Massachusetts in 1972 (Miller, 1991).

California was a national leader in attempting to decarcerate its juvenile offenders. The Youth Authority established a program in which counties were paid to keep youngsters in local programs and out of state facilities (Lemert and Dill, 1978). At the national level, these forces led to the enactment of the Juvenile Justice and Delinquency Prevention Act of 1974 (JJDPA).

The federal juvenile justice program

The JJDPA was considered landmark child welfare legislation and was passed by an overwhelmingly bipartisan vote. The JJDPA established a federal Office of Juvenile Justice and Delinquency Prevention (OJJDP) that had authority to conduct research, to provide training, and to make grants to states and jurisdictions that wanted to voluntarily comply with the JJDPA mandates. The new federal law required that participating states remove status offenders and dependency cases from secure confinement, and that juveniles be separated from adults by 'sight and sound' in correctional facilities. Four years later the JJDPA was amended to require that participating states remove minors from jails. Despite some expressed concerns that these major reforms would be too difficult for many locales, all but a very small number of states declared their intention to join the JJDPA.

Over the next several years, the OJJDP became the focal point for reforms of the American juvenile justice system. There was substantial progress made on all three major mandates of the JJDPA (Krisberg, 1996). Further, OJJDP launched a number of research efforts that substantially advanced the science of delinquency prevention and pointed the way to evidence-based juvenile justice programs (Krisberg, 2005). The annual appropriation of OJJDP grew from $5 million under President Gerald Ford to over $600 million during the Administrations of President Bill Clinton. In its early years, the OJJDP grew in its influence and stature under President Jimmy Carter and US Attorney General Benjamin Civiletti.

OJJDP's history was not without its trouble spots. President Ford actually wanted to veto the JJDPA, but in the aftermath of the Watergate scandals, he had little ability to overturn Congressional opinion. Presidents Ronald Reagan and George Herbert Walker Bush sought to eliminate funding for OJJDP, but the agency budget was restored by Congress. Both Presidents Reagan and Bush (the elder) appointed very conservative people to head OJJDP, several with limited or no qualifications for the job. One Reagan appointee proudly displayed a bumper sticker on his car that asked 'Have you slugged your kid today?'. A Bush appointee to OJJDP had a background in bible sales to religious schools, hardly a professional qualification. During these years there were highly questionable grants given to a former scriptwriter of the children's television program 'Captain Kangaroo' to study the link between cartoons in *Playboy* magazine and juvenile crime. Another dubious grant set up a center on school safety at Pepperdine University to be headed by a recently defeated Republican candidate for California

Attorney General. This center was plagued with questions about improper expenditures of federal funds on fancy furniture, inflated staff salaries, and limited examples of work products. Other grants were given to conservative legislative groups and other organizations that wished to eliminate the juvenile court. Federal monies were used to establish a center to find missing and exploited children. This center has not found a single missing child in over 20 years, although its budget continues to grow.

This period was a low point in terms of OJJDP's prestige in the juvenile justice community. Despite these problems, Congress tried to reign in the worst abuses in the federal juvenile justice program and required that most of the dollars be spent consistently with the goals of the JJDPA. Efforts in Congress to weaken the reform mandates of the JJDPA met with very limited success.

The appointment by President Bill Clinton of Janet Reno as US Attorney General brought a renaissance to the federal juvenile justice program. Guided by Reno's vision that delinquency prevention was the key component of combating youth crime, the OJJDP turned its attention to promoting research and programming to advance the Attorney General's goal to 'reweave the fabric of society' around vulnerable children and families. She was remarkably successful in persuading the law enforcement community that early childhood education programs and the prevention of child maltreatment were more important crime fighting tools than more prison beds.

The Congress substantially increased the budget of OJJDP via the Title V program that offered funding for improved prevention efforts and the Juvenile Accountability Incentive Block Grants (JAIBG) that funded a broad range of juvenile justice activities. While some of the purposes envisioned by the JAIBG legislation pointed to trying more children in criminal courts and ensuring more certain 'accountability' (the code word for punishment) for juvenile offenders, the leadership of OJJDP, with support of the Attorney General, encouraged jurisdictions to implement programs of 'proven effectiveness' that were in keeping with a more progressive than conservative view of juvenile justice.

Under Attorney General Reno, OJJDP was led by Reno's chief aide at the Dade County State Attorney's Office, Shay Bilchik. He brought an added focus on reducing the disproportionate presence of minority youth in the juvenile justice system, improving the conditions of confinement in juvenile corrections facilities, increasing delinquency prevention services, and strengthening the key linkages between juvenile justice and child welfare services. On leaving OJJDP, Bilchik took over the leadership of the Child Welfare League of America, a leading professional association in the child welfare field.

President George W. Bush returned to the earlier practice of appointing a head of OJJDP with virtually no experience on juvenile justice. Its new Administrator, Robert Flores, was a prosecutor and a legal advocate to punish child pornographers. The policy thrust of OJJDP moved more in the direction of programs involving missing and exploited children, faith-based programs, and mentoring. The OJJDP was no longer a high priority of the Attorney

General, as the national focus turned to preventing and responding to international terrorism after the attacks on the Pentagon and the World Trade Center. The administration proposed dramatic cutbacks in the OJJDP budget, and the Republican-dominated Congress was inclined to support these reductions. Concurrently, there was an increase in the amount of federal juvenile justice dollars earmarked by Congress to particular grantees. Thus, the discretionary ability of the OJJDP to set a policy agenda and to support reforms was severely restrained. The role of OJJDP in sponsoring research, disseminating statistics and other information, or providing technical assistance to juvenile justice agencies was sharply curtailed.

The Massachusetts revolution

Starting in the early 1970s, the state of Massachusetts shocked the world of juvenile justice by closing all of its secure congregate juvenile corrections facilities. In a gesture of historical symbolism, the first institution to be closed was the Thomas Lyman School, which was the first state-run juvenile correctional facility in the United States.

The commissioner of the Department of Youth Services (DYS), Jerome Miller, was initially brought in to clean up a range of scandals and abuses in the Massachusetts juvenile facilities. He attempted to implement new policies and practices consistent with 'therapeutic communities.' However, Miller soon discovered that the corrections officers were adamantly opposed to even modest reforms such as letting the youth wear normal clothing instead of prison uniforms, or not requiring that their heads be completely shaven. He decided to close the training schools completely and transferred nearly 1,000 youngsters to a newly created network of small community-based programs. As the young inmates of the Lyman School were loaded onto a bus that would take them to dormitories at the University of Massachusetts, where they were housed temporarily until being reassigned to community programs, one top Miller deputy proclaimed to the shocked guards, 'You can have the institutions, we are taking the kids' (Bakal, 1973; Miller, 1991).

Although Miller left Massachusetts after just two years as the commissioner of DYS, the Bay State continued to expand community-based programming and never reopened large juvenile institutions. Research by Harvard and the National Council on Crime and Delinquency (NCCD) showed that the Miller reforms had been successful (Coates et al., 1978; Krisberg et al., 1991).

Miller went on to implement more limited versions of his Massachusetts reforms in Pennsylvania and Illinois. Other states followed the new Massachusetts model. States as politically diverse as Utah, Missouri, and Vermont closed their training schools, expanding community-based programs. In the 1980s and early 1990s a number of states closed some of their larger congregate youth facilities, including Colorado, Indiana, Oklahoma, Maryland, Louisiana, Florida, Georgia, Rhode Island, and New Jersey. For a time it appeared that the Miller reforms would become the 'gold standard' for juvenile corrections. The federal OJJDP provided training and support to jurisdictions exploring the replication of the Massachusetts approach.

The barbarians at the gates

Then something happened. Rates of serious violent juvenile crime as measured by the National Crime Survey were relatively constant between 1973 and 1989, but these rates rose by over one-third and peaked in 1993. Arrests of juveniles for violent crimes and weapons offenses also climbed during this period (Snyder and Sickmund, 1999). This rise in violent crime among juveniles led some to predict that a new wave of 'super-predators' were reaching their teen years and would drive up rates of juvenile crime for the foreseeable future (Elikann, 1999). Conservative academics such as James Q. Wilson (1995) and John DiIulio (1995) led a small band of hysterical criminologists to predict the worst. Wilson suggested that there would be 30,000 more 'juvenile muggers, killers, and thieves'. DiIulio upped the ante claiming that there would be more than 270,000 more violent juveniles by 2010 compared with 1990. Other more mainstream criminologists such as Alfred Blumstein (1996) and James Fox (1996) joined in the youth crime jeremiad. DiIulio used the most incendiary language, warning of a 'Crime Bomb' created by a generation of 'fatherless, Godless, and jobless' juvenile 'super-predators' that would flood the streets of urban America (DiIulio, 1996: 25).

The media and the politicians jumped on the fear bandwagon. The public was warned about a generation of babies, born to 'crack addicted' mothers, who would possess permanent neurological damage including the inability to feel empathy with others. The scientific evidence supporting this claim was nonexistent. However, America was in the grips of a 'moral panic' that seemed to demand decisive action.

In over 40 states, legislation was introduced to toughen penalties against juvenile offenders and to make it easier to try children in criminal courts (Torbert et al., 1996). This resulted in a significant growth in the number of minors in adult prisons and jails. At the local level, school districts enacted 'zero tolerance policies' designed to make it easier to expel youngsters from school, and communities attempted to reintroduce curfews for juveniles, harsher penalties for truancy, and a range of measures designed to discourage gangs. Many urban schools required students to pass through metal detectors to attend classes. Some school districts began random searches of school lockers and increased the presence of police on campus groups. Passing a drug test was required for students who wished to participate in team sports or other school activities. The value of mandatory school uniforms was a subject of widespread public debate. National leaders of both political parties, including President Clinton, endorsed these stringent new policies. Every crime bill discussed during the Clinton Administrations included new federal laws against juvenile crime. Ironically, as the United States Attorney General sought to promote a wider and stronger social safety net for vulnerable families, the White House joined the chorus demanding a crackdown on juvenile felons that included more incarceration in both the adult and juvenile correctional systems.

Political leaders embraced the unproven value of 'boot camp' correctional programs for youths. The US Congress allocated tens of millions of federal dollars to encourage the expansion of 'boot camps' for juveniles and adults. Despite the reservations about these 'get tough' programs and the overwhelmingly negative evaluation findings, the 'boot camp' movement grew (Krisberg, 2005). But, as the media began reporting on young people dying in these programs due to harsh treatment and abuse, there was a slowing of the politicians' enthusiasm for military-style juvenile correctional programs. There was a rise in litigation against states that placed young people in these cruel and dangerous programs.

Another popular program involved bringing at-risk youngsters to visit prisons. These programs, known as 'Scared Straight', assumed that prison inmates would frighten the youth into law-abiding behavior by threatening them with the personal consequences of being in prison. These programs tried to extract a positive result out of the rampant physical violence and rape that occurs in US prisons. Once again, the careful research showed that 'Scared Straight' programs were completely ineffective. Still, the popular media and the politicians embraced these foolish programs as part of their posture of 'getting tough' with youthful offenders.

The much-feared generation of super-predators never showed up. After the peak year of 1993, rates of serious juvenile crime continued to plummet to historically low levels over the next decade. These declines occurred long before the tougher juvenile penalties were actually implemented. The mountebanks such as James Q. Wilson, John DiIulio, and Charles Murray had based their predictions on bad science, but they dominated and won the public policy battle throughout most of the 1990s. By the 100th anniversary of the founding of the juvenile court in the US, it looked like the famed children's court was near death and that the celebration would be more like a wake than a birthday party.

The American juvenile court ideal abides

Despite dire political circumstances, the American juvenile court experienced new life as the nation entered the 21st century. Several developments helped buoy the spirits of the defenders of the juvenile justice ideal. At the national level, the OJJDP helped sponsor two new ideas that helped many communities 'reinvent' the ideal of juvenile justice.

Balanced and restorative justice

The first of these conceptual frameworks was known as Balanced and Restorative Justice (BARJ). It envisioned a merger of the traditional focus on individual rehabilitation with increased involvement of the community and of victims in the juvenile justice process (Bazemore and Maloney, 1994). BARJ was initially proposed as a new paradigm to guide juvenile probation services, but it grew in appeal and was embraced by many jurisdictions and enacted into law in some states.

BARJ placed a renewed value on involving victims in the rehabilitative process. The aim of BARJ was to restore the victim and the community that had been changed due to the criminal behavior. By coming to terms with those who had been harmed, the youthful offender was also offered a way to restore his or her role in the community. Under the conceptual tent of BARJ were programs involving victim restitution, community service, peer and community panels to hear cases and choose dispositions, and programs designed to promote reconciliation between victims and offenders.

There is no body of research in the US that demonstrates the efficacy of BARJ in reducing youthful criminal behavior. However, this new approach represented a significant move away from the ideology of deterrence and incapacitation that had dominated American juvenile justice policy in the 1980s and 1990s. BARJ has also been tried by other countries, most notably the United Kingdom. Some in the UK suggest that balanced and restorative programs have merely been tacked on to systems that are primarily focused on punishment.

The expansion of BARJ in the US was greatly assisted by funding and training offered by OJJDP. As the federal juvenile justice program has shrunk, it remains to be seen if the rapid diffusion of BARJ will continue. Still, this new conceptual framework for the juvenile court has many adherents and is likely to be a feature of the American juvenile justice system for the foreseeable future.

The OJJDP Comprehensive Strategy

The second significant development in American juvenile justice as it entered the 21st century was the OJJDP Comprehensive Strategy for Serious, Violent, and Chronic Juvenile Offenders. The Comprehensive Strategy (CS) began as a modest policy proposal written by two top OJJDP officials, John J. Wilson and James C. Howell (1993). These federal officials sought to refute the dominant US Department of Justice policy that valued incarceration as the best approach to youth crime. Wilson and Howell briefly summarized a substantial body of research on pathways to serious, violent, and chronic juvenile offending, as well as studies on effective prevention and intervention programs. The CS asserted that prevention was the most cost-effective response to youth crime. Further, it held that strengthening the family and other core institutions was the most important goal for a youth crime-control strategy. They noted that there were a very small number of offenders who committed the largest number of serious juvenile crimes, and that the identification and control of these 'dangerous few' was key to reducing youth crime. The CS envisioned a complete continuum of services including prevention, early intervention, community-based programs for middle-level offenders, residential programs for the more serious offenders, and appropriate re-entry services. These services needed to be effectively linked using good case-management techniques and interagency collaborative approaches. The basic idea was to help communities build their youth service systems to provide 'the right service, for the right youth, at the right time'. Good community planning that involved data-driven and research-based programs and policies was viewed as key to the success of CS.

The CS was enthusiastically embraced by Attorney General Janet Reno and became the official policy position of the Department of Justice in all matters relating to youth crime. OJJDP supported NCCD and Developmental Research and Programs (DRP) to translate the original policy paper into a detailed guide for implementing the CS (Howell, 1995). Next OJJDP, in partnership with the Jessie Ball duPont Fund, created a pilot test of the CS in three communities. Over the next several years, the CS was implemented in nearly 50 communities across the United States with very positive results (Krisberg et al., 2004).

The Juvenile Detention Alternatives Initiative (JDAI)

A third major reform movement was launched by The Annie E. Casey Foundation in 1994. The goal of this effort was to reduce the overuse of juvenile detention facilities and to redirect funding toward more pertinent youth services for at-risk youngsters. The Casey Foundation also sought to improve the conditions of confinement for youths who were detained and to reduce the over-representation of minority youths in detention centers.

To accomplish these goals, the Foundation required that each community form a multi-agency task force to plan for better detention policies and practices. Similar to the OJJDP Comprehensive Strategy, the JDAI approach assumed that getting good data about youth being processed by the juvenile justice system, and building awareness of evidence-based practices, would lead to meaningful reforms of the juvenile justice system.

The JDAI approach included the development of improved risk screening for detention, expansion of non-secure detention options for most detained youths, and efforts to expedite the processing of cases through the juvenile justice process. The initial demonstration of JDAI took place in four urban areas, Cook County, IL; Multnomah County, OR; Sacramento County, CA; and New York City. Excellent results were obtained in Cook and Multnomah Counties in terms of reducing local detention populations, improving conditions of confinement, and reducing the proportions of minority youth in secure confinement. Measures of public safety showed that the JDAI did not compromise public safety, and may have actually reduced the numbers of youths that missed court hearings or committed subsequent crimes (Krisberg et al., 2001; Krisberg and Lubow, 2005). In the cases of Sacramento County and New York City, the JDAI reforms also produced the predicted positive outcomes, but changes in the political leadership of these sites led to a retraction of the JDAI programs.

The Annie E. Casey Foundation has expanded the JDAI program to scores of communities across the nation over the past ten years. Whereas the initial sites received seed funding from the Foundation to start the alternative programs, the later JDAI locales only received modest support to assist the local multi-agency collaboratives. The Foundation also offers some technical assistance and convenes annual meetings for the later JDAI sites. At the last such meeting in San Francisco, over 700 people from across the nation gathered to discuss ways to further reduce unnecessary juvenile detention. The original demonstration project has led to a vibrant national movement that continues despite little or no support from the United States Department of Justice. The Casey Foundation has produced high-quality replication manuals, a documentary on how JDAI can help communities, as well as a number of academic and professional publications.

The JDAI is an excellent example of how the core values of the American juvenile court continue to flourish despite an often hostile political and media environment. At its core, the JDAI reaffirms the basic commitment of the juvenile court to prioritize the best interests of the child, to strengthen family and community solutions to youth misconduct, and to emphasize humane treatment of the young rather than harsh punishment.

Conclusion

Despite regular examples of abusive practices that continue to plague American juvenile corrections facilities in many states, the juvenile court ideal continues to recover from the moral panic over 'super-predators'. The chorus is growing that rejects 'tough love' approaches such as juvenile correctional boot camps or 'Scared Straight' programs that use prison visits to allegedly frighten youngsters away from criminal lives (National Institutes of Health, 2005). Although these programs continue to exist, many jurisdictions have shut them down. Litigation on behalf of incarcerated youths is gaining headway in the courts, and even the conservative United States Department of Justice is pursuing civil rights violations against abusive juvenile facilities in many states. There is both the growing awareness of the mental health needs of youth in the juvenile justice system, and the beginning of efforts to better meet those needs. The most dramatic and positive development in 2005 was a decision of the US Supreme Court to end the practice of executing persons under the age of 18 at the time of their offense (*Roper* v. *Simmons*, 2005).

This good news does not minimize the severe problems of the American juvenile justice system. The juvenile court is, as always, underfunded and under-staffed to provide quality care for the large numbers of troubled youngsters that cross its portals. Young people still do not have anything resembling adequate legal representation in the juvenile court system. Too many young people are transferred to the criminal court system and languish in adult prisons. Services for young women and for children of immigrant families are inferior. Most important, children of color continue to dominate the lock-up facilities of the juvenile court system, and they receive harsh and discriminatory treatment. While the population of juvenile corrections facilities has not seen the explosive growth of the US prison system, the number of incarcerated youngsters continued to grow slightly, even as the numbers of juvenile arrests declined significantly over the past decade.

It is also troubling that the US is only one of two nations (with Somalia) that have failed to ratify the United Nations Convention on the Rights of the Child. President George Herbert Walker Bush opposed the international treaty based on the arguments of religious conservatives that the Convention would infringe on parental rights. Some wanted to continue to recruit minors for military service – a practice prohibited by the Convention. Further, there were concerns that the goal of reducing child hunger would create a new legal entitlement for impoverished children in this country.

President William Clinton signed the UN Convention, but under the US Constitution, the treaty must be ratified by two-thirds of the Senate to become law. Given the current majority of political conservatives in the Senate, ratifying the Convention is unlikely. Further, President George W. Bush has expressed a blanket opposition to signing onto international legal treaties in areas such as the environment, war crime tribunals, arms control, and some international trade agreements. It is highly unlikely that the UN Convention on the Rights of the Child will become part of US law in the near future.

The original development of the American juvenile court illustrated to the world the brilliant insight of British philosopher, Aldous Huxley, that improvements in civilization are more tied to advances in charity than in advances in justice (Huxley, 1937). Despite some hopeful new policy directions reflected by BARJ, the CS, and the JDAI, the future of American juvenile justice ideal is by no means a settled matter. Racial and class antagonisms, fear of immigrants, and ambivalence over the societal role for the young in the post-industrial world, will continue to fuel calls for 'crackdowns' on young offenders. Yet the ideals set forth by American reformers Jane Addams and Judge Ben Lindsey at the dawn of the 20th century are needed now more than ever as the United States faces the challenges of the new millennium.

References

Bakal, Y. (1973) *Closing Correctional Institutions*. Lexington, MA: Lexington Books.

Bazemore, G., and Maloney, D. (1994) Rehabilitating Community Service: Toward Restorative Service in a Balanced Justice System. *Federal Probation,* 58, 24–35.

Becker, H. S. (1963) *The Outsiders: Studies in the Sociology of Deviance*. Glencoe, IL: Free Press.

Blumstein, A. (1996) *Youth Violence, Guns, and Illicit Drug Markets: A Summary of a Presentation*. Washington, DC: US Department of Justice, Office of Justice Programs, National Institute of Justice.

Coates, R. B., Miller, A. D., and Ohlin, L. E. (1978) *Diversity in a Youth Correctional System: Handling Delinquents in Massachusetts*. Cambridge, MA: Ballinger.

Dilulio, J. J. (1995) Crime in America: It's Going to Get Worse. *Reader's Digest*, 55–60.

Dilulio, J. J. (1996) They're Coming: Florida's Youth Crime Bomb. *Impact*, Spring, 25–27.

Elikann, P. (1999) *Superpredators: The Demonization of Our Children by the Law*. New York: Insight.

Fox, J. A. (1996) *Trends in Juvenile Violence: A Report to the United States Attorney General on Current and Future Rates of Juvenile Offending*. Washington, DC: US Department of Justice, Bureau of Justice Statistics.

Howell, J. C. (ed.) (1995) *Guide for Implementing the Comprehensive Strategy for Serious, Violent, and Chronic Juvenile Offenders*. Washington, DC: US Department of Justice, Office of Justice Programs, Office of Juvenile Justice and Delinquency Prevention.

Huxley, A. (1937) *Ends and Means*. New York: Harper and Brothers.

In re Gault (1967) 387 US 1.

Krisberg, B. A. (1996) Should the Government Have a Major Role in Reducing Youth Crime? *Congressional Digest*, 75, 8–9.

Krisberg, B. A. (2005) *Juvenile Justice: Redeeming Our Children*. Thousand Oaks, CA: Sage Publications.

Krisberg, B., Austin, J., and Steele, P. (1991) *Unlocking Juvenile Corrections*. San Francisco: National Council on Crime and Delinquency.

Krisberg, B., Barry, G., and Sharrock, E. (2004) *Reforming Juvenile Justice Through Comprehensive Community Planning*. Oakland, CA: National Council on Crime and Delinquency.

Krisberg, B., and Lubow, B. (2005) *Assessing the Outcomes of the Juvenile Detention Alternatives Initiative*. Oakland, CA: National Council on Crime and Delinquency.

Krisberg, B., Noya, M., Jones, S., and Wallen, J. (2001) *Juvenile Detention Alternatives Initiative: Evaluation Report*. Oakland, CA: National Council on Crime and Delinquency.

Lemert, E. M. and Dill, F. (1978) *Offenders in the Community: The Probation Subsidy in California*. Lexington, MA: Lexington Books.

McKiever v. Pennsylvania (1971) 403 US 528.

Miller, J. G. (1991) *Last One Over the Wall: The Massachusetts Experiment in Closing Training Schools*. Columbus, OH: Ohio State University Press.

National Institute of Health. (2005) *State of the Science Conference Statement: Preventing Violence and Related Health-risking Social Behaviors in Adolescents*. Bethesda, MD: National Institutes of Health.

Platt, A. (1968) *The Child Savers: The Invention of Delinquency*. Chicago: Chicago University Press.

Pound, R. (1957) *Guide to Juvenile Court Judges*. New York: National Probation and Parole Association.

Roper v. Simmons (2005) 543 US 112 SW 3d 397.

Schall v. Martin (1984) 467 US 253.

Schur, E. M. (1973) *Radical Nonintervention: Rethinking the Delinquency Problem*. Englewood Cliffs, NJ: Prentice-Hall.

Scull, A. E. (1977) *Decarceration: Community Treatment and the Deviant – A Radical View*. Englewood Cliffs, NJ: Prentice-Hall.

Snyder, A., and Sickmund, M. (1999) *Juvenile Offenders and Victims: 1999 National Report*. Washington DC: US Department of Justice, Office of Justice Programs, Office of Juvenile Justice and Delinquency Prevention.

Stewart, V. L. (ed.) (1978) *The Changing Faces of Juvenile Justice*. New York: New York University Press.

Torbet, P., Gable, R., Hurst, I., IV, Montgomery, L., Szymanski, L., and Thomas, D. (1996) *State Responses to Serious and Violent Juvenile Crime*. Washington, DC: US Department of Justice, Office of Justice Programs, Office of Juvenile Justice and Delinquency Prevention.

Wilson, J. J., and Howell, J.C. (1993) *A Comprehensive Strategy for Serious, Violent, and Chronic Juvenile Offenders*. Washington, DC: US Department of Justice, Office of Justice Programs, Office of Juvenile Justice and Delinquency Prevention.

Wilson, J. Q. (1995) Crime and Public Policy. In J. Q. Wilson and J. Petersilia (eds), *Crime* San Francisco: Institute for Contemporary Studies Press. pp. 489–507.

Canada: Repenalization and Young Offenders' Rights

Russell Smandych

Introduction

In the past century Canada has seen the introduction of three different legislative regimes for administering juvenile justice, the 1908 Juvenile Delinquents Act (JDA), the 1984 Young Offenders Act (YOA), and the 2002 Youth Criminal Justice Act (YCJA) (Smandych, 2001). In the course of this legislative history, Canada has followed a pattern of legislative change that appears similar to many other Western countries, including England and Wales, Australia, and the United States. In each of these jurisdictions recent decades have witnessed earlier predominately child-welfare models of juvenile justice eroded and replaced with more legalistic and punitive 'justice' and 'crime-control' models of juvenile justice procedure. Despite evident similarities in the direction of recent juvenile justice developments across a number of countries, few efforts have been made to systematically compare the experiences of different countries (Bala et al., 2002), and even fewer attempts have been made to offer a cross-national comparative analysis of such developments written from a critical perspective (Muncie, 2005) that goes beyond the typically narrow-legalistic and reformist-technocratic discussions found in most publications (cf. Tonry and Doob, 2004). The aim of this chapter is to contribute to the comparative discourse on youth justice by offering a critical analysis of recent juvenile justice developments in Canada. This analysis takes into account the themes of repenalization, adulteration, risk management, restoration, and internationalization, and attempts to contribute to a discussion where Canadian juvenile justice practices stand on a continuum in relation to each of these evidently more global juvenile justice developments. In addition, I attempt to provide a more critical account that highlights, among other factors, some of the race and class implications of recent developments in juvenile justice in Canada; which is something largely missing from existing overviews of the Canadian juvenile justice system (cf. Winterdyck, 1997; cf. Bertrand et al., 2002; Doob and Sprott, 2004).

Moral panics and repenalization

'Moral panics' refer to specific periods in history when a particular type or group of individuals 'become defined as a threat to societal values and interests' (Cohen, 2001: 69), while 'repenalization' refers to 'a distinct hardening of attitudes and criminal justice responses to young offending' typically tied to the growth of politically right-wing law and order, or 'get-tough', thinking about crime (Muncie, 2005). The argument that moral panics and repenalization are more often directed at visible ethnic minorities and the poor is supported by evidence from the Canadian experience over the last two decades. While Canadian youth crime rates stabilized and began to drop in the 1990s, the media still found numerous opportunities to make it appear that youth crime was getting worse and that young criminals were getting more dangerous. Although all Canadian youth are collectively portrayed in this way, Schissel (1997) documents numerous media reports of the 1990s that perpetuated racialized, class, and gender-biased images of dangerous and out-of-control young criminals; producing 'decontextualized' stories of youth crime and young criminals, in which criminal behaviour – disproportionately reported to be that of Aboriginal and Asian youth – was blamed on poverty and inadequate parenting, especially in single-parent (typically female-led) families. It is no coincidence that Aboriginal youth are among the poorest of the poor in Canada (Canada, Statistics Canada, 2003a, 2003b), and that they are also vastly over-represented in juvenile justice processing and youth incarceration statistics (Green and Healy, 2003). In their study of the competing discourses of youth justice reform in the 1990s, Hogeveen and Smandych (2001) point to similar racialized and class-based images of youth crime and young offenders that emanate from the media and politicians. More recently, Hogeveen (2005: 74) has taken this analysis further, arguing that construction of an archetypal dangerous and 'punishable young offender was clearly evident in Canada throughout the late 1990s as politicians and the public debated solutions to the problem of youth crime. In the ethos of a "new punitiveness" that eschews any pretence of compassion toward serious offenders, the Federal Government signalled its intention to come down tougher on problematic youth'.

What have been the driving forces behind repenalization in Canada? Are recent trends in the criminal justice processing and imprisonment of juvenile offenders indicative of a continuing movement toward repenalization? To address these questions, it is necessary to retrace the circumstances that led to growing criticisms of the 1984 YOA and the move toward replacing it with new 'get-tough' federal legislation. Legislative and political power in Canada is divided between the Federal government, and the country's ten provinces and three territories. As part of this division of power, the Federal government has the sole responsibility to enact national juvenile justice legislation. However, it is the responsibility of provinces and territories to implement federally-enacted juvenile justice laws. Consequently, one of the realities of the Canadian situation is that each of the provinces and territories has a great deal of autonomy to decide how it will implement, or not implement, federal criminal legislation respecting young offenders.

When the YOA was implemented in 1984 it signaled a shift in the spirit of both adjudicating and governing erring youth, as envisaged by Federal politicians. No longer would 'the causes of delinquency' be the focus of legislation and experts, as was the case under the earlier child-welfare model, but now 'young offenders' themselves would be adjudicated and managed. Thus, with the enactment of the YOA, the 'young offender' became viewed as a deviant adolescent who was 'responsible for their actions and should be held accountable' (Canada, Young Offenders Act, Section 3). At the same time, however, it is equally important, although perhaps less well-known outside of Canada, that this legislated move toward a 'justice' model of juvenile court procedure was also undertaken in order to make Canadian juvenile justice legislation consistent with the new Charter of Rights and Freedoms enacted in 1982, which for the first time guaranteed 'all Canadians' constitutionally-defined fundamental legal rights (Bala, 1997). One inconsistency recognized by law reformers was that under the 1908 JDA the provinces had the power to decide on the upper age limit of children who would fall under the jurisdiction of juvenile courts (with this age varying from 15 to 17 depending on the province). The problem of inter-provincial variation in the assigned age of criminal responsibility was addressed in the YOA, and remains the same under the new YCJA, with courts given jurisdiction over youth from 12 to 17 years old. However, even with the move from a 'child-welfare' to a more legalistic 'justice' model that came with the enactment of the YOA, a dramatic amount of inter-provincial variation continued to persist, for example, in the rates of bringing cases into youth court, the use of custody, and the transfer of cases to adult court (Doob and Sprott, 2004). In addition, from the outset, youth court judges had the difficult task of attempting to balance the legislated need to hold young offenders more 'accountable' and 'responsible', with their judicial responsibility of ensuring that accused youth were afforded the 'enhanced legal rights' granted in the Charter and spelled out in the YOA. Not surprisingly, youth court judges and their decisions soon became a lightening rod for the attacks of law-and-order critics who complained that the YOA was 'soft on crime' and too concerned with protecting the rights of 'young criminals'. What ensued was largely a political battle for votes played out in the media, with most politicians involved in the campaign arguing the same line; that the YOA needed to be scrapped and replaced with 'tougher' more adult-like youth 'justice' legislation (Hogeveen and Smandych, 2001).

The processes of repenalization, defined as the hardening of attitudes and criminal justice responses to young offending, and adulteration, as the erosion of special measures designed to protect young people from the full weight of the law (Muncie, 2005), were in full-swing in Canada by the mid-1990s. This is reflected, first, in the young offender punishment trends and incarceration rates. As Hogeveen (2005: 81) notes, 'in 1997 Canada had an incarceration rate of roughly 1046 while the United States possessed an incarceration rate of roughly 775 per 100,000 youths aged 12 to 17. In addition, from 1991 to 1997 while the American rates for incarceration were remaining relatively stable, Canadian rates were steadily increasing'. It was also routine in the 1990s that many of the custodial sentences handed down in youth court were for relatively minor offences and that judges tended to hand out relatively short sentences; most of them being for property offences and minor assaults, and the majority of sentences (77%) being less than 3 months (Doob and Sprott, 2004: 216–17). At the same time that the use of custodial sentences was increasing, the use of 'alternative measures', or formalized programs by which young offenders were dealt with through non-judicial community-based alternatives, was shown to have been decreasing (Canada, Statistics Canada, 2000, 2004).

The shift toward treating young offenders more similar to adult offenders is also reflected, although not in a simple straightforward way, in amendments made to the YOA from 1986 to 1995 on sentencing and transfers to adult court. In 1986 a new offence was introduced in the YOA called a 'failure to comply with a disposition', which was aimed at making the Act 'look tough' on youth who failed to comply with the conditions attached to their non-custodial sentences. As Doob and Sprott (2004: 201) have recently pointed out, '[f]ourteen years later, this single offense would be responsible for 23% of the custodial sentences handed down in the country'. This 'get-tough' amendment was followed by others in 1992 and 1995, which increased the maximum sentences available in youth court for murder from three years in custody to a combined sentence of six years in custody and four years of 'conditional supervision in the community' (Doob and Sprott, 2004: 208). Amendments were also introduced in this period to make it progressively easier to transfer cases to adult court. This was done mainly by changing the 'test' followed by the courts in transfer hearings from one based on the 'interest of society ... having regard to the needs of the young person' (YOA, 1984, s. 16(1)), to one based on the 'paramount' importance of the 'protection of the public' (YOA, 1995, s. 16(1.1)) (cited in Bala, 1997: 276). Another related change introduced in 1995 was the creation of 'presumptive' offences for 16 and 17 years olds, which meant that if a youth of this age was charged with any of four serious violent offences (murder, manslaughter, attempted murder, and aggravated sexual assault) they 'would be "presumptively" transferred to adult court unless they successfully argued that the transfer should not take place' (Doob and Sprott, 2004: 213). Not without controversy, as we will see shortly, in the YCJA enacted in 2002 the notion of 'presumptive' offences was taken a punitive step further, by lowering the age to 14 years from 16 years and by adding a new category of other 'serious violent' offences, that if a youth was convicted of twice before, it would be presumed on the third conviction that an adult sentence be imposed. There is also evidence that during the years the YOA was in force young offenders received more severe sentences than adults for some similar offences (Sanders, 2000; Roberts, 2003). Why, then, despite the bifurcated nature of the legislation that was finally enacted, were media and political discourses surrounding Canadian youth justice reform in the 1990s predominantly 'punitive' in tone (Hogeveen, 2005)? The obvious reason for this is political expedience, as Doob and Sprott (2004: 214) aptly note in their discussion of the series of 'get tough' amendments made to the YOA in 1995: 'The political imperative is simple to describe ... it is easier to be "tough on crime" than to be smart about crime.'

The YCJA was finally proclaimed in force 1 April 2003, with many new ostensibly 'tough on youth crime' measures clearly aimed at placating the law-and-order lobby. However, something that was not predictable from the vast bulk of the preceding media and political discourse, but that was also contained in the YCJA when it was finally enacted, was a very explicitly-stated concern and detailed mandate for making greater use of alternative community-based 'extrajudicial' measures for dealing with less serious young offenders in order to meet Canada's commitment to respecting the United Nations Convention on the Rights of the Child (Barnhorst, 2004; Denov, 2004). Later we will look more specifically at how this second legislative agenda is reflected in the content of the YCJA. We will also see that the perennial Canadian problem of the potentially inconsistent and inequitable local implementation of federal juvenile justice legislation has not disappeared with the YCJA. Rather specific enabling provisions of the legislation relating to the bifurcated use of adult sentences and restorative-justice conferencing, along with other provisions, may even further intensify this problem.

Since both repenalization and adulteration were in full-swing in Canada by the mid-1990s, the introduction of a new supposedly 'tougher' legislative regime heralded in the YCJA actually represents more of a continuation of an already established trend than a radical departure from the past. In the next section, we look in more detail at specific provisions of the YCJA that reflect the further dismantling of traditional 'child-welfare' oriented juvenile court procedures that were originally designed 'to protect young people from the stigma and formality of adult justice' (Muncie, 2005: 39). In doing so, information is introduced to help the reader decide whether, with the implementation of the federal YCJA, Canada is getting any tougher, or any smarter, in the way it is approaching the problem of youth crime. However, before we turn to this, one other key development that occurred on the eve of the implementation of the YCJA must be mentioned.

In the lead up to the enactment of the YCJA, both right (conservative) and more left (social democratic) provincial governments opposed the legislation as either being still not 'tough enough' or a complicated 'rat's nest' (Rabson, 2003), while Québec, standing alone, opposed the legislation because it threatened to destroy what defenders claimed was the province's already well-functioning juvenile justice system (Hogeveen and Smandych, 2001; Trépanier, 2004). To further legitimate its claim of the disastrous consequences of implementing the YCJA, the Québec government launched a court challenge to the legislation in the form of a reference to the Québec Court of Appeal on the constitutionality of the impending Act; in response to which the Court of Appeal ruled that specific provisions of the Act concerning the imposition of adult sentences on young offenders and exceptions to protecting the privacy of accused and convicted youth violated the Canadian Charter of Rights and Freedoms (Anand and Bala, 2003; Québec, Court of Appeal, 2003). To date, the Federal government's response to the Québec Court of Appeal has been to state that at some point the Act will be amended to make it legally-consistent with its ruling, while a number of provinces have reacted with 'outrage' that Ottawa is going to water-down the key 'get-tough' provisions of the YCJA to comply with the Québec Reference decision (Benzie, 2003; Gillis et al., 2003a, 2003b). Consequently, from the outset, the YCJA has operated under a cloud of controversy and uncertainty about its future.

Punishing 'criminal kids' under the YCJA: from child-welfare to adulteration and risk management

From 'youth court' to 'youth justice court'

One sign of increased adulteration in the YCJA resides in the renaming of youth courts and the revamping of procedures to be followed in prosecuting cases. The YCJA provides for the creation of a new court called the youth justice court. Although many of the functions to be performed by this new court are the same as those carried out in youth courts under the YOA, the new youth justice court has also added newly defined responsibilities. In addition to allowing for the continuation of specialized courts to hear criminal cases involving youth, the YCJA stipulates that any superior court of criminal jurisdiction can be deemed a youth justice court for the purpose of the operation of the Act. A key reason for this added option is that under the YCJA a young person accused of committing a serious criminal offence has *the right to elect to be tried by a judge and jury* sitting in a superior court of criminal jurisdiction. This legal right to a jury in youth court trials did not exist under the YOA, except, after 1995, in the case of a youth charged with murder who could face a sentence of more than five years in prison if convicted (Bala, 1997). Granting young persons accused of committing more serious offences a right to a jury trial is only one example of how the YCJA treats criminally-accused youth more like adult accused criminals.

The adulteration of principles

The YCJA contains specific sections spelling out the general principles under-lying the legislation (Section 3), as well as declarations of principles regarding the use of extra-judicial measures (Sections 4, 5) and sentencing and committal to custody (Sections 38, 39). What is most significant about the declaration of the purpose of the YCJA (Section 3) is that it recognizes that 'the principal goal of the youth justice system is to protect the public'. As recent commentators, including Bala (2003) and Doob and Sprott (2004) emphasize, Section 3 of the YCJA should not be read simply as a sign that greater emphasis is being placed on deterrence or incapacitation, since the section also focuses on the need for the 'long term' protection of society through the 'prevention of crime' and 'rehabilitation and reintegration'. Moreover, these authors point out that in comparison to the YOA 'the various provisions of the YCJA that articulate principles and philosophy pro-vide a *clearer message* for those charged with the operation of the youth justice system and the making of decisions about individual young offenders' (Bala, 2003: 74, emphasis in original; Doob and Sprott, 2004). According to this argu-ment, these more clearly enunciated principles set a high standard of care to be adopted by youth justice officials empowered to enforce the YCJA, and thus con-sequently they 'have the potential to increase consistency in the youth justice system across Canada' (Bala, 2003: 74). However, given the nature of the actual enabling sections in the YCJA under-girding these somewhat lofty principles, this hope seems overly optimistic.

Adult sentences

Provisions of the YCJA regarding the use of adult sentences are probably the most complicated, and definitely the most controversial sections of the legisla-tion. They also perhaps most clearly demonstrate the over-optimism of the pre-diction that the YCJA may result in a more uniform youth justice system across Canada. When the YCJA was originally introduced for debate in the House of Commons, it contained a clause (in Section 61) on the sentencing of a youth con-victed of a 'presumptive offence' which stated that an adult sentence could 'be imposed on a young person who is found guilty of an offence for which an adult could be sentenced to imprisonment for more than two years' if it was 'com-mitted after the young person attained the age of 14 years'. However, in the amended Act passed in February 2002, this clause was replaced with one that allows much more room for discretion on the part of provincial governments to set the lower age, stating: 'The lieutenant governor in council of a province may by order fix an age greater than fourteen years but not more than sixteen years for the purpose of the application of the provisions of this Act relating to pre-sumptive offences' (Canada, 2002, YCJA, assented to 19 February). The impe-tus for the amendment came from the vehement opposition to punishing 14 year olds like adults that was voiced by opposition members of the Bloc

Québecois (Canada, 2000). This concession to Québec poses serious implications for the possible unequal application of the YCJA in different provinces and territories. Specifically, since each province and territory now has the option of 'opting' out of the application of Section 61, it is inevitable that for potentially exactly the same offence, some 14 year olds will be sentenced as adults while others will not.

Risk management

There are also numerous parts of the Act, from new front-end 'extra-judicial' and 'deferred custody and supervision' measures ('conditional sentences' in the adult system), to new back-end 'intensive rehabilitative custody' and post-release 'supervision in the community' (mandated offender treatment programs and parole in the adult system), that make the treatment of youth under the YCJA more similar to the treatment of adult offenders in regard to the increasing concern shown for predicting risk and managing potentially-recidivist offenders in the 'community' (Hannah-Moffat, 2005; Muncie, 2005). Again, however, since the exact manner in which any criminal law provisions affecting youth are followed is determined at the provincial level through discretion invoked by police, prosecutors, defense counsel, judges, and government justice and corrections officials, as well as an array of possible non-governmental 'community' participants, the YCJA will inevitably create many opportunities for 'substantive differences' in the treatment of 'at-risk' and criminally-convicted youth in different parts of the country (cf. Doob and Sprott, 2004: 236). Regardless, it appears that under the YCJA concern for the general welfare or 'best interests' of children has been made subordinate to concerns with holding young criminals more accountable (like adults) and managing them in custody and in the community through measures based on risk profiling and risk management. However, it needs to be pointed out that there is no clear rationale or principle included in the YCJA justifying the increased risk profiling and risk management of young offenders; but instead, it is more likely that the extent to which these features become part of the implementation of the YCJA will largely depend on how provincial and territorial authorities decide to interpret and apply the Act. At the same time, as we will see shortly, risk management techniques may often also co-exist at the local level in a complex fusion with forms of pretentiously less-punitive (Daly, 2002) community-based 'restorative' justice approaches.

Identifying 'criminal youth'

A final telling sign of both adulteration and increased concern for risk management in the YCJA resides in changes affecting the publication of information that reveals the identity of young persons. Although initially under the YOA access to information on youth court cases was tightly restricted, later amendments 'decreased the privacy protections afforded youths' (Bala, 1997: 213). These protections have been eroded further by provisions contained in Part 6 of the YCJA. Most importantly, Section 110(2) allows information about the identity of a young person to be made public, in cases (a) 'where the information relates to a young person who has received an adult sentence'; and (b) 'where the information relates to a young person who has received a youth sentence for an offence ... [defined as a] "presumptive offence"', while Section 110(4) allows a youth justice court judge, on an application made by the police, to permit 'any person to publish information that identifies a young person as having committed or allegedly committed an indictable offence, if the judge is satisfied that (a) there is reason to believe that the young person is a danger to others; and (b) publication of the information is necessary to assist in apprehending the young person'. In addition, the YCJA allows for a considerable amount of judicial discretion in this area, since Section 75(3), which relates to youth given adult sentences, states that a youth justice court judge 'may', alternatively, 'order a ban on publication of information that would identify the young person ... if the court considers it appropriate in the circumstances, taking into account the importance of rehabilitating the young person and the public interest'. Canada's leading legal-expert on youth justice, Nicholas Bala (2003: 386–87), points out that 'by allowing for the publication of identifying information about young offenders who have committed very serious offences but who are not subject to adult sanction', the YCJA represents a 'significant change to the publication regime of the YOA'. In its Reference Re Bill C-7, the Québec Court of Appeal (2003) obviously agreed with Bala (2003) on this point, and went further by ruling that it was clear that Sections 110(b), 75(3) and related provisions could be considered unconstitutional, and in violation of the Canadian Charter of Rights and Freedoms protection of privacy guarantees. Like its ruling against provisions dealing with 'presumptive' adult sentences of the YCJA in the same Reference, the controversy raised by the Québec Court of Appeal's ruling on sections of Part 6 of the YCJA is far from over (Anand and Bala, 2003).

From blaming to shaming? The restorative pretensions of the YCJA

While in the enactment of the YCJA the Federal government signaled that it is willing to promote more strict penalties for serious offenders, the YCJA also facilitates the expanded use of 'extra-judicial' measures (diversion, police warnings, family group conferencing, and mediation) for first time and non-serious offenders. Consequently, in order to assess whether Canadians are punishing tougher or punishing smarter, we also need to look, at least briefly, at these extra-judicial measures provisions.

The YCJA defines extra-judicial measures as any 'measures other than judicial proceedings under this Act used to deal with a young person alleged to have committed an offence'. Under this ambit, the YCJA contains explicit enabling clauses that allow for police and crown prosecutors to use warnings, cautions, *and referrals* (Sections 6, 7, 8, 9) as an alternative to judicial proceedings. In addition, it allows for the use of extra-judicial sanctions (Sections 10, 11, 12) with young persons whose offences are considered too serious to be dealt with only with a warning or caution, but not serious enough to warrant formal court proceedings. Related sections outline the role of youth justice committees (Section 18) in administering extra-judicial measures and provide for the creation of conferences (Section 19(2)) that have the mandate, 'among other things, to give advice on appropriate extra-judicial measures, conditions for judicial interim release, sentences, including the review of sentences, and reintegration plans'. The mandate given to community conferences is potentially extremely broad, since the YCJA (Section 19(1)) states that at any point in the processing of a young offender: a 'youth justice court judge, the provincial director, a police officer, a justice of the peace, a prosecutor or a youth worker may convene or cause to be convened a conference for the purpose of making a decision required to be made under this Act'. Also, the overall tone of the YCJA is one that discourages the use of custody for less serious offenders and, in turn, creates many new possible opportunities for the use of more restorative community-based diversion and sentencing options. For example, Section 39(1), on 'Committal to custody' for an offender receiving a 'youth sentence', states that 'a youth justice court shall not commit a young person to custody' except under specifically allowed circumstances, including that 'the young person has committed a violent offence' and that the young person has [previously] failed to comply with non-custodial sentences', while Section 39(2), on 'Alternatives to custody', orders that 'a youth justice court shall not impose a custodial sentence under section 42 (youth sentences) unless the court has considered all alternatives to custody raised at the sentencing hearing that are reasonable in the circumstances, and determined that there is not a reasonable alternative, or combination of alternatives, that is in accordance with the purpose and principles [of sentencing] set out in section 38'. Advocates of the YCJA may well contend that sections such as these pose a major challenge to 'get tough' notions about sentencing, and that the legislation can have a long-term significant impact on the reduction of custody sentences and the increased use of more restorative community-based options.

Although it is far too early to tell what the effect of these new pretentiously more-restorative provisions will be over the long-term, there is already anecdotal and some statistical evidence that they are having at least a short-term effect in reducing court use and custody sentences for first time and less-serious young offenders. According to the latest figures from Statistics Canada, the country's youth incarceration rate in 2002–3 hit its lowest point in eight years. Manitoba, which is usually only next to Saskatchewan for having the highest youth incarceration rate in the country, recorded a 30% decrease in youth custodial sentences, along with a substantial reported increase in the use of police discretion in cautioning youths without charging them (Canada, Statistics Canada, 2004; Owen, 2004). It has also been reported that crown cautions are now routinely being used in Manitoba to deal with less serious property offences such as shoplifting, with a claimed 90% 'success' rate (Rabson, 2005). Similar reports of substantial short-term reductions in the use of incarceration of young offenders as a result of the YCJA have been published in various provinces, and youth justice court judges have noted anecdotally and in recent reported case law decisions, the effect of the YCJA in this regard (Bala and Anand, 2004; Elliot, 2005; Harris et al., 2004).

However, there are a number of factors that may potentially undermine the restorative pretensions of the YCJA, and perhaps, in turn, contribute to bringing about a return to higher youth incarceration rates in the future. One of these is the real possibility that volunteer youth justice committees and other community groups that are recruited to carry out 'conferences' and impose 'extrajudicial' sanctions will become overwhelmed by large caseloads, and hindered by inadequate funding and training (Hillian et al., 2004). Another problem derives from the YCJA delegating the power to create guidelines for 'non-judicial conferences' to provincial and territorial governments (Sections 19(3) and (4); Harris et al., 2004: 381). This makes it inevitable that there will be significant inter-provincial and even local community-by-community variation in the manner in which conferences are carried out, which is similar to what happened with the implementation of 'alternative measures' provisions in the YOA (Hillian et al., 2004). Another related possibility is that, despite the best intentions of youth justice court judges to employ more restorative non-custodial sentencing options and make use of referrals to child welfare and other community agencies (through applying Section 35), the resources may simply not be in place at the local level to support these alternatives, which will lead to more young offenders coming back to court; possibly for the failure to comply with previous non-custodial sentences, or to face more serious charges. Ultimately, if these scenarios play themselves out in the typical Canadian fashion, what we will most likely see is that under-resourced and over-burdened 'communities', such as many of Canada's remote Aboriginal communities, will eventually be seen to have failed at developing adequate community-based 'restorative' measures for dealing with 'their' youth. This in turn may well perpetuate the tragic-damaging cycle of individual and institutional racism and recurrent law- and-order 'moral panics' that have been directed historically at Aboriginal youth, as well as at other most often urban, and more frequently poor, visible minority youth in Canada. Despite these and other features of the YCJA, which show that opportunities for perpetuating race and class discrimination are clearly enabled through the legislation, these issues are largely overlooked in the dominant academic and governmental (state) discourse around 'restorative' justice and youth conferencing in Canada (cf. Calhoun and Borch, 2002; Chatterjee and Elliott, 2003; Elliott, 2005; Green and Healy, 2003).

Hope for the future? The YCJA and the UN Convention on the Rights of the Child

A final issue that needs to be addressed is the extent to which Canadian youth justice legislation complies with the UN Convention on the Rights of the Child, and whether this raises any hope for better treatment of young offenders in Canada in the years to come. As noted earlier in the chapter, a second legislative agenda reflected in the content of the YCJA was a very explicitly-stated concern for meeting Canada's commitment to respecting the UN Convention on the Rights of the Child. Thus, it is important to highlight parts of the YCJA that were enacted in order to make Canadian youth justice legislation more compliant with the UN Convention, and at least briefly review arguments that have been advanced regarding the likely effects of this greater compliance on the treatment of young offenders.

The preamble to the YCJA boldly states that 'Canada is a party to the United Nations Convention on the Rights of the Child and recognizes that young persons have rights and freedoms, including those stated in the Canadian Charter of Rights and Freedoms and the Canadian Bill of Rights, and have special guarantees of their rights and freedoms'. These rights are expanded upon at different points in the YCJA, and most relevantly with regard to the UN Convention, under sentencing principles which state that the sentence imposed on a young offender 'must not result in a punishment that is greater than the punishment that would be appropriate for an adult who has been convicted of the same offence committed in similar circumstances' (Section 38(2)(a)) and that 'all available sanctions other than custody that are reasonable in the circumstances should be considered for all young persons' (Section 38(2)(d)). Also, Section 39(5) even more explicitly states that 'a youth justice court shall not use custody as a substitute for appropriate child protection, mental health or other social measures', while Section 35 (which deals with 'Referral to Child Welfare Agency') adds that 'a youth justice court may, at any stage of proceedings against a young person, refer the young person to a child welfare agency for assessment to determine whether the young person is in need of child welfare services'.

What do we make of these provisions? First, it is clear that the YCJA does attempt to comply with many aspects of the UN Convention including the principle of non-discrimination, the guarantee of specific legal rights, and the principle of the 'minimum use of custody' (Bala, 2003; Denov, 2004; Muncie, 2005: 45). However, some academic commentators, like Doob and Sprott (2004), and even Federal government Department of Justice officials (Canada, Department of Justice, 2003), suggest that the YCJA actually goes beyond the UN Convention in the degree to which it places strict limits on the use of custody sentences, because of its strict adherence to a 'proportionality framework' which requires that the sentence 'must be proportionate to the seriousness of the offence and the degree of responsibility of the young person for that offence' (Canada, Department of Justice, 2003; YCJA, section 38(2)(c)). In other words, implicitly throughout the Act, and quite explicitly in Section 39(5), the YCJA purposefully discourages youth justice court judges from taking into account 'child welfare' concerns affecting the young offender that would presumably be dealt with better through a 'child-welfare' agency; which, collectively (perhaps not coincidentally), happen to be funded mainly from the coffers of provincial and territorial governments. As the Department of Justice authoritatively proclaims on its website, 'others believe it is necessary to incarcerate youth for longer periods than warranted by the seriousness of the offence in order to treat a youth's problems. Even though the child-welfare rooted Juvenile Delinquents Act of 1908 was replaced in 1984 with the more rights-oriented Young Offenders Act, some sectors still see the criminal law as a tool to paternalistic ends. Using coercive authorities, like the criminal law power, under the guise of "doing what is best to help the youth" can result in unquestioned breaches of protections that would normally shield an accused' (Canada, Department of Justice, 2003). While it seems likely that the narrowly-defined 'legal rights' of young persons will fare reasonably well under the YCJA, unfortunately there is already ample evidence that if the 'proportionality framework' becomes the one that is followed most closely in Canadian youth justice court proceedings in the years to come, the 'social welfare rights' of young persons granted by the UN Convention will not enjoy much protection. If this happens, there is room to question whether the YCJA is really any improvement over earlier legislative regimes for administering juvenile justice in Canada.

References

Anand, S. and Bala, N. (2003) 'The Québec Court of Appeal youth justice reference: striking down the toughest part of the new act', *Criminal Reports* (6th) 10: 397–418.

Bala, N. (1997) *Young Offenders Law*. Toronto: Irwin.

Bala, N. (2003) *Youth Criminal Justice Law*. Toronto: Irwin.

Bala, N. and Anand, S. (2004) 'The first months under the Youth Criminal Justice Act: A survey and analysis of case law', *Canadian Journal of Criminology and Criminal Justice* 46(3): 251–71.

Bala, N., Hornick, J., Snyder, H. and Paetsch, J. (eds) (2002) *Juvenile Justice Systems: An International Comparison of Problems and Solutions*. Toronto: Thompson Educational Publishing.

Barnhorst, R. (2004) 'The Youth Criminal Justice Act: New directions and implementation issues', *Canadian Journal of Criminology and Criminal Justice,* 46(3): 231–50.

Benzie, R. (2003) 'Youths will get away with murder: Ottawa's failure to appeal court ruling endangering lives, Cauchon warned', *National Post*, 9 May.

Bertrand, L., Paetsch, J. and Bala, N. (2002) 'Juvenile crime and justice in Canada', in N. Bala et al. (eds), *Juvenile Justice Systems: An International Comparison of Problems and Solutions*. Toronto: Thompson Educational Publishing. pp. 19–42.

Calhoun, A.J., and Borch, D. (2002) 'Justice in relationships: Calgary community conferencing as a demonstration project'. *Contemporary Justice Review,* 5(3): 249–60.

Canada (2000) House of Commons, *Debates (Hansard)*, 25 and 26 September.

Canada (2002) Youth Criminal Justice Act, assented to 19 February. Available at: http://laws. justice.gc.ca/en/y-1.5/106975.html.

Canada, Department of Justice (2003) 'Rights for young accused and limits of the criminal law power in responding to delinquency in Canada'. Available at: http://canada.justice.gc.ca/ en/ps/yj/repository/4refrenc/4000301a.html.

Canada, Statistics Canada (2000) *Juristat: Alternative Measures in Canada, 1998/99*, 20(6).

Canada, Statistics Canada (2003a) *2001 Census. Analysis Series. Aboriginal Peoples of Canada: A Demographic Profile*. Ottawa, Canada: Minister of Industry.

Canada, Statistics Canada (2003b) *2001 Census. Analysis Series. Canada's Ethnocultural Portrait: The Changing Mosaic*. Ottawa, Canada: Minister of Industry.

Canada, Statistics Canada (2004) *Juristat: Youth Custody and Community Services in Canada, 2002/03*, 24(9).

Chatterjee, J. and Elliott, L. (2003) 'Restorative policing in Canada: The Royal Canadian Mounted Police, community justice forums, and the YCJA', *Police Practice and Research*, 4(4): 347–59.

Cohen, S. (2001) 'Youth deviance and moral panics', in R. Smandych (ed.) *Youth Justice: History, Legislation, and Reform*. Toronto: Harcourt Canada. pp. 69–83.

Daly, K. (2002) 'Restorative justice: The real story', *Punishment and Society*, 4(1): 55–79.

Denov, M. (2004) 'Children's rights or rhetoric? Assessing Canada's Youth Criminal Justice Act and its compliance with the UN Convention on the Rights of the Child', *International Journal of Children's Rights*, 12: 1–20.

Doob, A. and Sprott, J. (2004) 'Changing models of youth justice in Canada', in M. Tonry and A. Doob (eds) *Youth Crime and Youth Justice: Comparative and Cross-National Perspectives*. Chicago: University of Chicago Press. pp. 185–242.

Elliott, L. (2005) 'Restorative justice in Canadian approaches to youth crime: Origins, practices, and retributive frameworks', in K. Campbell (ed.), *Understanding Youth Justice in Canada*. Toronto: Pearson. pp. 242–62.

Gillis, C., Benzie, R. and Curry, B. (2003a) 'Ontario, Alberta "outraged" by plan to soften youth laws: Runciman says Ottawa is giving in to Québec's lenient approach to crime', *National Post*, 3 May: 3.

Gillis, C., Benzie, R. and Seskus, T. (2003b) 'Ontario fights youth-crime changes: Ottawa to soften new act', *National Post*, 6 May.

Green, R. and Healy, K. (2003) *Tough on Kids: Rethinking Approaches to Youth Justice*. Saskatoon: Purich Publishing.

Hannah-Moffat, K. (2005) 'Criminogenic needs and the transformative risk subject: Hybridizations of risk/need in penality', *Punishment and Society*, 7(1): 29–51.

Harris, P., Weagant, B., Cole, D. and Weinper, F. (2004) 'Working "in the trenches" with the YCJA', *Canadian Journal of Criminology and Criminal Justice*, 46(3): 367–89.

Hillian, D., Reitsma-Street, M. and Hackler, J. (2004) 'Conferencing in the Youth Criminal Justice Act of Canada: policy developments in British Columbia', *Canadian Journal of Criminology and Criminal Justice*, 46(3): 343–66.

Hogeveen, B. (2005) '"If we are tough on crime, if we punish crime, then people get the message": Constructing and governing the punishable young offender in Canada during the late 1990s', *Punishment and Society*, 7(1): 73–89.

Hogeveen, B., and Smandych, R. (2001) 'Origins of the newly proposed Canadian *Youth Criminal Justice Act*: Political discourse and the perceived crisis in youth crime in the 1990s', in R. Smandych (ed.) *Youth Justice: History, Legislation, and Reform*. Toronto: Harcourt Canada. pp. 144–68.

Muncie, J. (2005) 'The globalization of crime control – the case of youth and juvenile justice: Neo-liberalism, policy convergence and international conventions', *Theoretical Criminology*, 9(1): 35–64.

Owen, B. (2004) 'Youth incarceration rate shows signs of dropping', *Winnipeg Free Press*, 14 October.

Québec, Court of Appeal (2003) *Reference Re Bill C-7* [Québec (Department of Justice) c. Canada (Department of Justice)], *Criminal Reports* (6th) 10: 281–396.

Rabson, M. (2003) 'Manitoba calls new youth justice act "rat's nest"', *Winnipeg Free Press*, 1 April.

Rabson, M. (2005) 'Crack down on teen shoplifters, Tory argues: Warning letters to parents rapped', *Winnipeg Free Press*, 3 February.

Roberts, J. (2003) 'Sentencing juvenile offenders in Canada: an analysis of recent reform legislation', *Journal of Contemporary Criminal Justice,* 19(4): 413–34.

Sanders, T. (2000) 'Sentencing of young offenders in Canada, 1998/99', *Juristat*, 20(7).

Schissel, B. (1997) *Blaming Children: Youth Crime, Moral Panics and the Politics of Hate*. Halifax: Fernwood.

Smandych, R. (2001) 'Accounting for changes in Canadian youth justice: from the invention to the disappearance of childhood', in R. Smandych (ed.) *Youth Justice: History, Legislation and Reform*. Toronto: Harcourt Canada. pp. 4–23.

Tonry, M. and Doob, A. (eds) (2004) *Youth Crime and Youth Justice: Comparative and Cross-National Perspectives*. Chicago: University of Chicago Press.

Trépanier, J. (2004) 'What did Québec not want? Opposition to the adoption of the Youth Criminal Justice Act in Québec', *Canadian Journal of Criminology and Criminal Justice,* 46(3): 273–99.

Winterdyck, J. (1997) 'Juvenile justice and young offenders: An overview of Canada', in J. Winterdyck (ed.) *Juvenile Justice Systems: International Perspectives*. Toronto: Canadian Scholars' Press. pp. 139–75.

England and Wales: The New Correctionalism

3

John Muncie and Barry Goldson

Introduction

The pace of youth justice reform in England and Wales over the past decade has been unprecedented. Since as early as 1993 when the New Labour motif of 'tough on crime, tough on the causes of crime' was first formulated, youth justice has been centre stage of the 'modernising' agenda. An increasing tendency to responsibilise children, their families and working-class communities, and a reliance on an expanding control apparatus to 'manage' poverty and disadvantage, have led to a relentless stream of 'crackdowns', initiatives, targets, policy proposals, pilot schemes, action plans and legislative enactments. Not only has it become an arduous task to simply keep abreast of the content of this reforming zeal, it is also difficult to identify any consistent rationale and/or philosophical core. The purpose of youth justice has become obscured as each new wave of reform has been accreted on the previous. This chapter focuses on arguably two of the most significant developments in England and Wales: namely the targeting of the non-criminal as well as the criminal within formal systems of justice; and the persistent punitive incarceration of children despite a 'new' rhetoric of youth crime prevention, restoration and social inclusion.

Welfare, justice and risk prediction

In common with most Western jurisdictions, the values of penal welfarism characterised juvenile justice in England and Wales for much of the 20th century. The prevailing argument was that age and family circumstances should be taken into account when adjudicating on juveniles. The 1908 Children Act created a separate and distinct system of justice based on the juvenile court; the 1933 Children and Young Persons Act formally required the court to take account of welfare considerations in all cases involving child 'offenders'; and the 1969 Children and Young Persons Act advocated the phasing out of criminal, in favour of civil, proceedings. By the 1960s both penal and welfare based institutions were also being criticised as stigmatising, dehumanising, and criminogenic rather than as 'rehabilitative' and 'therapeutic' agencies capable of preventing further offending. In their place a range of community based 'intermediate treatment' initiatives were advocated.

Welfarism though has never been universally accepted as the most propitious means of responding to youth crime. A strong law and order lobby in England and Wales ensured that a range of punitive custodial options – borstals, 'short, sharp shock' detention centres, youth custody centres, secure training centres – remained a key feature of 20th century juvenile justice. Consequently, welfarism never replaced the punitive but rather acted to expand the range of interventions and disposals available to the court. At best welfare discourse may have allowed for an acknowledgement of the reduced culpability of children, but this in turn has been (and continues to be) used to justify early intervention against those considered to be 'at risk'. Rarely, if ever, has it meant that children are dealt with more leniently (King and Piper, 1995). Moreover, by the 1980s liberal lawyers, civil libertarians and radical social workers were also becoming increasingly critical of 'welfare-based' procedures and sentencing. The welfare principle of 'meeting needs' acted as a spurious justification for placing excessive restrictions on individual liberty, particularly for girls and young women, which were out of proportion either to the seriousness of the offence or to the realities of being in 'need of care and protection'. Welfarism not only preserved explanations of individual pathology, but also drew children and young people into the judicial process at an ever-earlier age, from which there was rarely any 'escape'. In the wake of these criticisms, justice based models of corrections emerged (not only in England and Wales but in numerous Western jurisdictions) based on the principles of: proportionality of punishment to crime; determinacy of sentencing; an end to judicial, professional and administrative discretion; protection of rights through due process and the diversionary principle of 'minimum necessary intervention'. These notions of the normality of much youth offending and of punishing the crime, not the person, did appear to be successful initially. Between 1981 and 1992, the recorded number of young offenders in England and Wales reduced quite dramatically, as did the number of those sent to custody. Diversion from prosecution was achieved through informal police cautioning (rather than prosecution) and diversion from penal institutions was secured by the development of intensive community-based alternatives to custody schemes (Rutherford, 1989).

This 'progressive' moment was, however, short-lived. By the early 1990s the language of 'justice and rights' was appropriated by the law and order lobby as one of 'individual responsibility and obligation'. Renewed fears of persistent young offenders, and in particular the political fallout from the murder of a two year old child, James Bulger, by two 10 year olds in 1993, ensured that the youth justice system took a decisively retributive turn. Custody was once more promoted as the key means to prevent re-offending through the Conservative ministerial slogans of 'prison works' and 'condemn more, understand less' (Haydon and Scraton, 2000). A legal discourse of guilt, responsibility and punishment re-surfaced as the dominant position in the definition and adjudication of youth offending. Fionda (1998), for example, noted how a series of legislative changes and reformulations of policy at this time, constructed a system that institutionalised 'an almost stubborn blindness' to welfare principles and the mitigating circumstances of age. Since the election of the first New Labour government in 1997 this punitive intolerance, rather than being curtailed as some may have hoped, has percolated through all aspects of youth justice (Muncie, 1999).

The pivotal New Labour legislation was the Crime and Disorder Act 1998. This abolished the principle of *doli incapax* meaning that 10–13 year olds had legal safeguards removed and could be adjudged as culpable as any adult 'offender' (Bandalli, 2000). Under a general rubric of crime prevention, a wide range of legislative initiatives were targeted at 'disorderly' as well as criminal behaviour. Children below the age of criminal responsibility (which currently stands at 10 in England and Wales) were also drawn into formal networks of social control for 'their own good'. Much of this early and pre-emptive intervention (as distinct from diversion) became (and remains) justified through notions of 'child protection' or 'nipping crime in the bud' (Goldson, 2000). The prevailing contention is that crime runs in certain families and that 'anti-social behaviour' in childhood is a predictor of later criminality. Thus the need is to build the system of youth justice around assessments of those who might present a future 'risk'. What may previously have been an indicator of the need for family welfare support is now read as a possible precursor to criminality. 'Risk' is increasingly associated with pathological constructions of wilful irresponsibility and family/individual failure (Goldson and Jamieson, 2002). To gain access to welfare services, or perhaps more accurately to be 'targeted' by an 'intervention', children and families must be seen to have 'failed' or be 'failing', to be 'posing risk', to be 'threatening' (either actually or potentially). Prior notions of universality and welfare for *all* children 'in need', have retreated into a context of classification, control and correction where interventions are targeted at the 'criminal', the 'near criminal', the 'possibly criminal', the 'sub-criminal', the 'anti-social', the 'disorderly', the 'disrespectful' or the 'potentially problematic' in some way or another.

Low level disorder and incivilities have always been a major New Labour target. One of the most radical initiatives of its reforming agenda has been the introduction of new *civil* orders and powers that can be made other than as a sentence for a criminal offence. This 'civilianisation of law' allows New Labour to claim some welfarist credentials but is also highly moralising in tone. Child safety orders, Local child curfews and Anti-social behaviour orders (all included in the Crime and Disorder Act 1998) do not necessarily require either the prosecution or indeed the commission of a criminal offence. As a result the Crime and Disorder Act was the first piece of criminal justice legislation in England and Wales (at least since the Vagrancy Statutes of the early 19th century) to explicitly target legal *and* moral/social transgressions. *Child safety orders* can be made by a family proceedings court on a child below the age of criminal responsibility if that child is considered 'at risk'. Justified as a 'protective' measure it places the child under the supervision of a social worker or a member of a youth offending team for a period of up to 12 months. The court can specify certain requirements such as attending specified programmes or avoiding particular places and people. Breach may result in the substitution of a care order under the provisions of the Children Act 1989. In addition local authorities can, after consultation with the police and local community, introduce a *local child curfew* to apply to *all* children under the age of 10 in a specific area. This places a ban on unsupervised children being in a specified area between 9pm and 6am. The reach of such curfews was extended to 15 year olds in 2001. In a similar vein Youth Inclusion and Support Panels (YISPs) were introduced in 2004 to 'identify' the 'most *at risk* 7–13 year olds' in 92 local authority areas of England and Wales and engage them in 'programmes' (Home Office, 2004: 41, emphasis added).

An *anti-social behaviour order* (ASBO) is a civil order which can be imposed by the police/local authority on anyone over the age of 10 whose behaviour is *thought likely* to cause alarm, distress or harassment. Breach is punishable by up to five years imprisonment. It has been subject to a barrage of criticism such as its merging of civil and criminal law, its ignoring of due process, the eligibility of hearsay 'evidence', its criminalisation of incivility and its exclusionary effects (Ashworth et al., 1998; Stone, 2004). Though initially justified as a means to control 'nuisance neighbours', there is increasing evidence that ASBOs are primarily targeted at youthful 'rowdy and unruly' behaviour. Their use exemplifies a certain 'justice by geography' with by far the greatest number of ASBOs being issued in Greater Manchester. Between July and September 2000, 21 ASBOs were imposed nationally on young people, rising to 153 between October and December 2003 (Burney, 2004). In Campbell's (2002) review 74% were made on under 21s. The 'anti-social' is often synonymous with police perceptions of problems with young people (Bland and Read, 2000). Moreover the breach of an ASBO can lead directly to a prison sentence even when the original 'offence' was non-imprisonable. Around 42% of ASBOs made against juveniles are breached and 46% of those breaches receive a custodial sentence. Some 50 children a month are being incarcerated under anti-social behaviour legislation (www.statewatch.org/asbo. Accessed June 2005). In September 2003 the first national census of anti-social behaviour was launched with numerous agencies from police to street cleaners required to record any 'undesirable' behaviour. Within 13 broad headings the 'anti-social' included a diverse array of behaviours from prostitution and vandalism to littering, noise, swearing, begging and street drinking. The Anti-Social Behaviour Act 2003 extended police and local authority powers to confiscate stereos, to criminalise begging, to give fixed penalty fines for 'disorderly' 16 and 17 year olds and to ban the sale of spray paints and fireworks to those under 18. Significantly it granted groups other than the police, including private security guards, the power to issue fixed penalty fines. Among an extended menu of punitive measures that focus upon the young, the police are granted further powers to remove under 16 year olds from public places if they 'believe' that a member of the public 'might be' 'intimidated, harassed, alarmed or distressed', and if two or more young people, together in a public place, fail to disperse under the instruction of a police officer they commit a criminal offence and face the prospect of custodial detention (Walsh, 2003; Burney, 2005). This Act also made the parents of children regarded as 'disorderly', 'anti-social' or 'criminally inclined', eligible targets for formal statutory orders. In addition, the Serious Organised Crime and Police Act 2005 removed legal safeguards protecting the anonymity of children who breach the terms of their ASBO. They can now be publicly 'named and shamed'. This appears to directly contravene article 40 of the United Nations Convention on the Rights of the Child (UNCRC) which guarantees privacy at all stages of criminal proceedings.

In May 2005 the Prime Minister also launched his respect agenda which culminated in the publication of the Respect Action Plan at the beginning of 2006. This promised extra powers for community support officers to conduct truancy sweeps, extra requirements for 'problem families' to undertake compulsory parental training or else lose housing benefit and/or face eviction and the establishment of a national parenting academy (Respect Task Force, 2006).

All of these measures might be described as 'defining deviance up', but with the paradoxical result that public tolerance to incivility is progressively lowered (Young and Matthews, 2003). Intensified modes of intervention, premised and legitimised by reference to 'prevention', seem to have no boundaries and make the system insatiable. But in response to the UN Committee on the Rights of the Child in 1999, Labour has claimed that early intervention is an 'entitlement' and that such pre-emptive policies contribute to 'the *right* of children to develop responsibility for themselves'(UK Government, 1999). In these ways a discourse of rights is appropriated to justify degrees of authoritarianism that are far removed from UN intentions. Anti-social behaviour legislation remains particularly controversial because of its ill-defined nature and lack of firm theoretical grounding. If anything, it draws upon Wilson and Kelling's (1982) influential 'broken windows' thesis which claims a causal, repetitious and vicious circle of anti-social behaviour – crime – neighbourhood decline. Yet numerous researchers reverse this causal logic and contend that the best way to deal with disorder is through regenerating neighbourhoods rather than further demonising the children of the poor and disadvantaged (Matthews, 2003). The establishment of curfew and dispersal zones from which under 16 year olds can be removed irrespective of committal, or even suspicion, of 'bad behaviour' has also been subject to legal challenge. In 2005 the High Court ruled this particular police power to be in breach of the international obligation to 'treat each child as an autonomous human being'.

Risk assessment and pre-emptive intervention

New Labour's obsession with identifying and targeting those considered at 'risk' is in no small part derived from multi-variate correlational analyses, which have identified the quality of parent–child relationships as a key 'risk factor' in the onset of offending (Graham and Bowling, 1995; Utting, 1996). A major influence is the empirical longitudinal study of 'delinquent families' that has been conducted by the Cambridge Institute of Criminology since the 1960s (Farrington, 1996). Six variables have been consistently promoted as predictors of future criminality: socio-economic deprivation (low family income/poor housing); poor parenting and family conflict; criminal and anti-social families; low intelligence and school failure; hyperactivity, impulsivity, attention deficiency; anti-social behaviour (heavy drinking, drug taking, promiscuous sex). Farrington's analysis of the interrelations between working-class families, 'dysfunctionality' and criminality has become the credo of New Labour's youth governance:

> ... children from poorer families are likely to offend because they are less able to achieve their goals legally and because they value some goals (e.g. excitement) especially highly. Children with low intelligence are more likely to offend because they tend to fail in school. Impulsive children ... are more likely to offend because they do not give sufficient consideration and weight to the possible consequences. Children who are exposed to poor child rearing behaviour, disharmony or separation on the part of their parents are likely to offend because they do not build up internal controls over socially disapproved behaviour, while children from criminal families and those with delinquent friends tend to build up anti-authority attitudes and the belief that offending is justifiable. The whole process is self-perpetuating ... '. (Farrington, 1994: 558–9)

On this basis a wide range of pre-emptive interventions has been introduced targeting those below the age of criminal responsibility as well as those over the age of 10. Much of this is clouded in a rhetoric of care within a reconstituted welfarism: 'Children under ten need *help* to change their bad behaviour just as much as older children' (Home Office, 1997: 18, emphasis added). Farrington (1996) suggested that the 'most hopeful' methods to tackle crime and anti-social behaviour (derived from experimental research in the USA and Canada) included home visiting by health professionals to give advice on infant development and to reduce parental child abuse; pre-school programmes to stimulate thinking and reasoning skills in young children; and parenting education programmes. Such conclusions are now uncritically accepted by most official agencies (see, for example, Sutton et al., 2004; Audit Commission, 1996; Utting, 1996; and the Home Office's (Goldblatt and Lewis, 1998) assessments of 'what works').

These projects of course tell us that if we grant the necessary educational and economic resources to socially deprived families their children are likely to benefit. However, when attached to a preoccupation with law and order they are read as the need to discipline 'failing families' (Pitts, 2001: 97). As a result, concerns over irresponsibility and lack of parental discipline characterised key provisions of the Crime and Disorder Act. For example, New Labour introduced the parenting order requiring the parents of convicted young people to attend counselling and guidance classes and to comply with specified requirements, such as ensuring regular school attendance. In 2001 a new offence of 'aggravated truancy' was created carrying a fine or 3 month prison sentence for parents who seemed to condone truancy and £90 million was given to schools to develop the electronic tracking of pupils. In May 2002 a mother in Oxfordshire was imprisoned for failing to ensure her daughters attended school; in July of the same year parents in London were fined £4,000. In December 2002 plans were announced to give head teachers the power to issue fixed penalty fines for 'failing' parents. In August 2004 plans were announced to track and monitor all children who have a parent in prison. In December 2004 fixed penalty fines were extended from 16 year olds to 10 year olds, with powers to imprison parents if the fine is not met.

In such ways the targets of early intervention are invariably the symptoms, rather than the causes of young people's disaffection and dislocation. The social contexts of offending are bypassed. The disadvantages faced by young people are obscured by a narrow focus on 'risk' and troublesome behaviour (Muncie: 2004a). Throughout this remoralisation strategy lies the objective of compelling parents to take 'proper' care and control of their children, while by the age of 10 children will be held fully responsible themselves (Goldson, 1999). The 'weak family' is viewed as the key driver of crime. 'Weak families' are those with poor parenting skills, teenage pregnancies, single parenting and 'broken homes'. New Labour promulgates a discourse of individual and family responsibility and formulates interventions based on developmental psychology which relegate and marginalise structural explanations and material contexts. Further, *guilt* is no longer the founding principle of youth justice. Intervention can be triggered without an 'offence' being committed, premised instead upon a 'condition', a 'character' or a 'mode of life' that is adjudged to be 'failing' or posing 'risk'. This comprises a major departure from the fundamental principles of justice. The conventional applications of youth justice require first, publicly specified offences, and second, proven guilt and responsibility; proven that is according to strict and transparent codes of evidence, fact and law. They involve an open trial in a court of law, clearly defined safeguards in the form of defence and professional representation/advocacy, and the availability of review and appeal procedures. In contrast, the new modes of risk classification and early intervention are unencumbered by such legal principles. Instead, intervention is triggered by assessment, discretion and the spurious logic of prediction and actuarialism. Children face judgement, and are exposed to intervention, not only on the basis of what they *have done*, but what they *might do*, who *they are* or who they are *thought to be*. Above all it reveals a growing tendency to use authoritarian youth (criminal) justice agencies to tackle issues of family support and failures in welfare services (Goldson and Jamiesen, 2002).

The appeal of this risk factor paradigm of prevention lies not in its ostensible scientific rigour but in its fit with prevailing ideological imperatives and its pragmatic orientation for both identifying the inter-related risk factors behind anti-social behaviour and 'curing' or managing the problem by means of specific targeted prevention techniques. At its core is the claim that the approach is 'evidence-based' and predicated upon the credo of 'what works'. A burgeoning industry in psychological risk profiling is indicative of much contemporary theory and practice in youth crime prevention which combines the techniques of risk calculation with a continuing 'rehabilitative' commitment to 'changing people'. But the primary outcome of this interventionism is a relative decline in such 'lenient' disposals as final warnings and fines and a substantial up-tariffing effect towards intensive community sentences and ultimately dramatic rises in custody. Identification of those 'at risk' has simply contributed to the criminalisation of younger and relatively minor offenders (Smith 2003: 137). Pitts (2001) condemns the 'what works' industry as the subordination of science to governance. Research is used selectively and only when it seems to confirm pre-determined governmental policies. This view seems to be reinforced in the way that New Labour has often 'rolled out' pilot programmes before any evaluation has been able to report (Wilcox, 2003). Either way, actuarial assessments tend to simply focus on that which can be measured easily (such as the time interval between arrest and court appearance), while that which eludes simple quantification (such as histories of multiple disadvantage) is ignored. Practice becomes geared to meeting (and manipulating) internal targets rather than responding to the needs and circumstances of offenders. Formulaic service delivery negates professional autonomy and traps decision-making within an inflexible 'technocratic framework of routinized operations' (Webb, 2001: 71). Further, the clamour for the pragmatic 'quick fix' precludes not only critical research but also policy proposals which might look to the long term and the more fundamentally transformative (Muncie, 2002).

Restoration and responsibilisation

Much has been made of the principles of restorative justice – and its potential for restitution, reparation and reconciliation – that ostensibly underpin some of

New Labour's legislative initiatives. Within restorative justice the talk is less of formal crime control and more of informal offender/victim mediation and harm minimisation. The Crime and Disorder Act 1998 replaced the previous practice of police cautioning with a system of reprimands and final warnings. In 1994 guidelines had already been issued to discourage the use of second cautions even though they had been successful in diverting many young people out of the system altogether (Goldson, 2000). Now on a second offence a final warning usually involves some community-based intervention whereby the offender is referred to a youth offending team for assessment and allocation to a programme designed to address the causes of offending, even though no formal prosecution has taken place. Non-compliance with a programme may be reported in court on the committal of future offences. A further grounding of elements of restoration in English/Welsh youth justice has been made possible through the introduction of reparation and action plan orders in the Crime and Disorder Act 1998 and the introduction of referral orders and youth offender panels following the Youth Justice and Criminal Evidence Act 1999.

Referral orders are essentially a *mandatory*, standard sentence imposed on nearly all offenders, no matter how relatively minor the offence, as long as they are under 18 years old, have no previous convictions, and plead guilty. The major exceptions are those sent directly to custody or made subject of a Hospital Order. Following pilots in 11 areas, referral orders went national in 2002. Offenders are referred to a youth offender panel (made up of local volunteers) to agree a programme of behaviour to address their offending. There is no provision for legal representation. It is not a formal community sentence but does require a contract to be agreed to last from a minimum of 3 months to a maximum of 12. The programme may include victim reparation, victim mediation, curfew, school attendance, staying away from specified places and persons, participation in specified activities, as well as a general compliance with the terms of the contract for supervision and monitoring purposes. Through such measures it has been claimed that youth justice is in the midst of a potentially radical shift from being exclusionary and punitive to becoming inclusionary and restorative (Crawford and Newburn, 2003).

Critical perspectives on restorative justice have, however, begun to emerge from a number of different avenues. Evaluations of the referral orders, for example, have lauded the more positive lines of communication that have been opened up between offenders, parents, victims and communities, but have lamented its coercive nature, problems of low victim participation, blurred lines of accountability and a general failure to provide offenders with the socioeconomic resources necessary for them to develop a 'stake-hold' in community life (Crawford and Newburn, 2003; Gray, 2003). Gelsthorpe and Morris (2002) contend that restorative principles are additions to, rather than core defining components of, a system that remains built around, and continues to act upon, notions of just deserts, punishment and retribution. Restorative processes simply deal with low-level offenders who, through a combination of New Labour's other measures in crime prevention and pre-emptive early intervention, are being drawn into the youth justice system (and thereby criminalised) at an increasingly earlier age. Neither does restorative justice offer any challenge to risk management strategies. Rather it may serve an integral role in sorting the 'high risk' from the 'low' (Cunneen, 2003). A danger also remains that any form of compulsory restoration may degenerate into a ceremony of public shaming and degradation, particularly when it operates within a system of justice that is also driven by retributive and punitive intent. Within restorative programmes the burden tends to remain on individuals to atone or change their behaviour, rather than on the state to recognise that it also has a responsibility (within international conventions and rules) to its citizens (Haines, 2000). For example, Article 6 of the Human Rights Act provides for the right to a fair trial with legal representation and a right to appeal. The introduction nationwide of referral orders with lay youth offender panels deliberating on 'programmes of behaviour' with no legal representation would appear to deny such rights. Article 8 confers the right to respect for private and family life and protects families from arbitrary interference. Parenting orders, child curfews and anti-social behaviour orders, in particular, would again appear to be in contempt (Freeman, 2002). More seriously, many of the principles of restorative justice which rely on informality, flexibility and discretion sit uneasily against legal requirements for due process and a fair and just trial.

Notions of individual responsibility rather than those of community empowerment, social inclusion and 'restorative *social* justice' tend to proliferate (White, 2003).

Authoritarianism and repenalisation

The mood of youth justice in England and Wales in the early 21st century is arguably best captured in Prime Minister Tony Blair's edict that we should not be surprised if 'the penalties are tougher when we have been given the opportunities but don't take them'. If the opportunities and requirements for restoration and reintegration are ignored or failed, then punitive incarceration awaits. According to Offender Management Caseload statistics released in December 2004, the number of 15 to 17 year olds held in prison establishments rose from 769 in 1993 to 2089 in 2002 (National Offender Management Service (NOMS), 2004). By November 2004 there were 3211 under 18 year olds in custody (242 in secure homes, 223 in secure training centres and 2746 in prisons). This represented an increase of some 24% since New Labour came to power in 1997 (Howard League, 2005: 22). In addition the average length of sentence for 15–17 year old boys convicted of indictable offences, rose from 9.2 months in 1992 to 10.8 months in 2001 (National Association for the Care and Resettlement of Offenders (Nacro), 2003). Legislative reform, most notably the Criminal Justice and Public Order Act 1994 and the Crime and Disorder Act 1998, has provided for the detention of younger children. In 1992 approximately 100 children under the age of 15 years were sentenced to custody. In 2001 however, 800 children under 15 years were similarly sentenced, an increase of 800%. More girls are also being locked up, and the rate of growth is proportionately higher than that which relates to boys. Although the baseline comprises relatively small numbers, the use of custody in relation to girls over the last decade has increased by 400% (Nacro, 2003). This is set against data that indicates that girls have not become more criminally inclined (Worrall, 1999). Similarly, the substantial over-representation of black children and young people continues to prevail at every discrete stage of the youth justice system from pre-arrest to post-sentence (Goldson and Chigwada-Bailey, 1999), and this is particularly evident in relation to penal detention (Wilson, 2004). Meanwhile, research suggests that there are no significant differences in the self-reported patterns of offending between white and black children and young people (Graham and Bowling, 1995; Goldson and Chigwada-Bailey, 1999).

These national statistics do, however, mask some significant regional differences. This is reflected in the wide disparities between courts in the custodial sentencing of young people. These range in England and Wales from 1 custodial sentence for every 10 community sentences in the South West to 1 in 5 in the West Midlands and the NorthWest (Bateman and Stanley, 2002). Localism is also reflected in the haphazard implementation of national legislation and youth justice standards in different areas (Holdaway et al., 2001). Indeed Cross et al. (2003) detect divergences between policy and practice in Wales and in England. Significantly the Welsh Assembly government decided to locate youth justice services in the portfolio of Health and Social Services rather than Crime Prevention, thus potentially prioritising a 'children first' rather than an 'offender first' philosophy (as in England) (Welsh Assembly/Youth Justice Board, 2004).

Nevertheless England and Wales now lock up more young people than any other country in Europe: four times that in France, 12 times that in the Netherlands and 160 times that in Norway, Sweden and Finland (Muncie, 2004a); and often in conditions condemned by the Chief Inspector of Prisons as 'utterly unsuitable' and as 'unworthy of any country that claims to be called civilised' (Children's Rights Alliance, 2002). With reconviction rates of ex-prisoners as high as 88% and increasing evidence of inappropriate and brutalising regimes characterised by bullying, self-harm and suicide, it is clear that child incarceration is an expensive failure (Goldson, 2002; Goldson and Peters, 2000).

The UN Convention on the Rights of the Child stipulates that children should be protected from custody whenever possible and when deprived of liberty should be treated with humanity and respect. The Convention states at article 37 that imprisonment of a child 'shall be used only as a measure of last resort and for the shortest appropriate period of time'. In England age reductions in the detention of young people coupled with increases in sentence length appear directly at odds with such provisions. Moreover, as there are limited young offender institutions for girls, they are held in adult prisons often sharing the same facilities as adults. Again this appears in contravention of the UNCRC that states that 'every child deprived of liberty shall be separated from adults unless it is considered in the child's best interests not to do so' (Howard League, 1999). The UN's 2002 observations on the UK's implementation of the UNCRC repeated the concerns first made a decade earlier about the extremely low age of criminal responsibility, the failure to ban corporal punishment, the increasing numbers of children in custody, at earlier ages for lesser offences and for longer periods, and the persistence of custodial conditions that do not adequately protect children from violence, bullying and self-harm. In November 2004 Jaap Doek, chair of the UN Committee on the Rights of the Child, called for urgent action to stop abuses, recalling the death of two children in custody that year and asking why England and Wales continued to tolerate the unnecessary jailing of juveniles (The *Guardian*, 29 November 2004).

England and Wales' adherence to principles of children's rights clearly does not preclude the pursuit of policies which exacerbate structural inequalities and punitive institutional regimes.

References

Audit Commission (1996) *Misspent Youth*. London: Audit Commission.

Bandalli, S. (2000) 'Children, responsibility and the New Youth Justice', in B. Goldson (ed.) *The New Youth Justice*. Lyme Regis: Russell House.

Bateman, T. and Stanley, C. (2002) *Patterns of Sentencing*. London: NACRO/Youth Justice Board.

Bland, N. and Read, T. (2000) *Policing Anti-social Behaviour*, Police Research Series No. 123. London: Home Office.

Burney, E. (2004) 'Nuisance or crime? The changing uses of anti-social behaviour control' *Criminal Justice Matters*, 57: 4–5.

Burney, E. (2005) *Making People Behave: Anti-social behaviour, politics and policy*. Cullompton: Willan.

Campbell. S. (2002) *A Review of Anti-social Behaviour Orders*, Home Office Research Study no. 236. London: Home Office.

Children's Rights Alliance (2002) *Rethinking Child Imprisonment*. London: Children's Rights Alliance.

Crawford, A. and Newburn, T. (2003) *Youth Offending and Restorative Justice*. Cullompton: Willan.

Cross, N., Evans, P. and Minkes, J. (2003) 'Still children first? Developments in youth justice in Wales' *Youth Justice,* 2(3): 151–162.

Cunneen, C. (2003) 'Thinking critically about restorative justice' in E. McLaughlin, R. Fergusson, G. Hughes and L. Westmarland (eds) *Restorative Justice: Critical Issues*. London: Sage.

Farrington, D. (1994) 'Human development and criminal careers', in M. Maguire, R. Morgan and R. Reiner (eds) *The Oxford Handbook of Criminology*. Oxford: Clarendon.

Farrington, D. (1996) *Understanding and Preventing Youth Crime*, Social Policy Research Findings, no. 93. York: Joseph Rowntree Foundation.

Fionda, J. (1998) 'The age of innocence? – the concept of childhood in the punishment of young offenders' *Child and Family Law Quarterly*, 10(1): 77–87.

Freeman, M. (2002) 'Children's rights ten years after ratification', in B. Franklin (ed.) *The New Handbook of Children's Rights*. London: Routledge.

Gelsthorpe, L and Morris A. (2002) 'Restorative justice: the last vestiges of welfare?', in J. Muncie, G. Hughes and E. McLaughlin (eds) *Youth Justice: Critical Readings*. London: Sage.

Goldblatt, P. and Lewis, C. (eds) (1998) *Reducing Offending*, Home Office Research Study, no. 187. London: HMSO.

Goldson, B. (1999) 'Youth (in)justice: Contemporary developments in policy and practice', in B. Goldson (ed.) *Youth Justice: Contemporary Policy and Practice*. Aldershot: Ashgate.

Goldson, B. (2000) 'Wither diversion? Interventionism and the new youth justice', in B. Goldson (ed.) *The New Youth Justice*. Lyme Regis: Russell House Publishing.

Goldson, B. (2002) 'New punitiveness: The politics of child incarceration', in J. Muncie, G. Hughes and E. McLaughlin (eds) *Youth Justice: Critical Readings*, London, Sage.

Goldson, B. and Chigwada-Bailey, R. (1999) '(What) justice for black children and young people?', in B. Goldson (ed.) *Youth Justice: Contemporary Policy and Practice*. Aldershot: Ashgate, pp. 51–74.

Goldson, B. and Jamieson, J. (2002) 'Youth crime, the "parenting deficit" and state intervention: A contextual critique', *Youth Justice*, 2(2): 82–99.

Goldson, B. and Peters, E. (2000) *Tough Justice*. London: The Children's Society.

Graham, J. (1998) 'What Works in Preventing Criminality', in P. Goldblatt and C. Lewis (eds) *Reducing Offending*, Home Office Research Study no. 187. London: Home Office.

Graham, J. and Bowling, B. (1995) *Young People and Crime*, Research Study 145. London: Home Office.

Gray, P. (2003) *An Evaluation of the Plymouth Restorative Justice Programme*, University of Plymouth, Department of Social Policy and Social Work.

Haines, K. (2000) 'Referral orders and youth offender panels: Restorative approaches and the new youth justice', in B. Goldson (ed.) *The New Youth Justice*. Dorset: Russell House Publishing, pp. 58–80.

Haydon, D. and Scraton, P. (2000) 'Condemn a Little More, Understand a Little Less? The Political Context and Rights Implications of the Domestic and European Rulings in the Venables-Thompson Case', *Journal of Law and Society*, 27(3): 416–448.

Holdaway, S. Davidson, N., Dignan, J., Hammersley, R., Hine, J. and Marsh, P. (2001) *New Strategies to Address Youth Offending: The National Evaluation of the Pilot Youth Offending Teams,* Research Directorate Occasional paper no. 69. London: Home Office.

Home Office (1997) *No More Excuses: A New Approach to Tackling Youth Crime in England and Wales*, cm 3809. London: HMSO.

Home Office (2003) *Respect and Responsibility: Taking a Stand Against Anti-social Behaviour,* cm 5778. London: HMSO.

Home Office (2004) *Confident Communities in a Secure Britain: The Home Office Strategic Plan 2004–08*. London: The Stationery Office.

House of Lords/House of Commons Joint Committee on Human Rights (2003) *Tenth Report of Session 2002–03: The UN Convention on the Rights of the Child*. London: The Stationery Office.

Howard League (1999) *Protecting the Rights of Children*. London: The Howard League for Penal Reform.

Howard League (2005) *Children in Custody: Promoting the Legal and Human Rights of Children*. London: The Howard League for Penal Reform.

King, M. and Piper, C. (1995) *How the Law Thinks About Children*. Aldershot: Ashgate.

Matthews, R. (2003) 'Enforcing respect and reducing responsibility: a response to the White Paper on anti-social behaviour' *Community Safety Journal*, 2(4): 5–8.

Muncie, J. (1999) 'Institutionalised intolerance: Youth justice and the 1998 Crime and Disorder Act', *Critical Social Policy*, 19(2): 147–175.

Muncie, J. (2002) 'A new deal for youth?: early intervention and correctionalism' in G. Hughes, E. McLaughlin and J. Muncie (eds) *Crime Prevention and Community Safety: New Directions*. London: Sage.

Muncie, J. (2004a) *Youth and Crime*. London: Sage.

Muncie, J. (2004b) 'Youth justice: globalisation and multi-modal governance', in T. Newburn and R. Sparks (eds) *Criminal Justice and Political Cultures*. Cullompton: Willan.

Muncie, J. and Hughes, G. (2002) 'Modes of youth governance: political rationalities, criminalisation and resistance' in J. Muncie, G. Hughes and E. McLaughlin (eds) *Youth Justice: Critical Readings*. London: Sage.

Nacro (2003) *A Failure of Justice*. London: Nacro.

NOMS (2004) *Offender Management Caseload Statistics, 2003*. London: National Statistics.

Pitts, J. (2001) *The New Politics of Youth Crime: Discipline or Solidarity?* Basingstoke: Palgrave.

Respect Task Force (2006) *Respect Action Plan*. London: Home Office.

Rutherford, A. (1989) 'The mood and temper of penal policy: curious happenings in England during the 1980s', *Youth and Policy*, 27: 27–31.

Smith, R. (2003) *Youth Justice: Ideas, Policy, Practice*. Collumpton: Willan.

Stone, N. (2004) 'Orders in respect of anti-social behaviour: Recent judicial developments', *Youth Justice*, 4(1): 46–54.

Sutton, C., Utting, D. and Farrington, D. (2004) *Support from the Start: Working with Young Children and their Families to Reduce the Risks of Crime and Anti-Social Behaviour*, Research Brief 524, March. London: Department for Education and Skills.

UK Government (1999) *Convention on the Rights of the Child: Second Report to the UN Committee on the Rights of the Child by the United Kingdom*. London: HMSO.

United Nations Committee on the Rights of the Child (2002) *Concluding Observations of the Committee on the Rights of the Child: United Kingdom of Great Britain and Northern Ireland*. Geneva: United Nations.

Utting, D. (1996) *Reducing Criminality Among Young People: A Sample of Relevant Programmes in the UK*, Home Office Research Study, no. 161. London: HMSO.

Walsh, C. (2002) 'Curfews: No more hanging around', *Youth Justice*, 2(2): 70–81.

Walsh, C. (2003) 'Dispersal of rights: A critical comment on specified provisions of the anti-social behaviour bill', *Youth Justice*, 3(2): 104–111.

Webb, S. (2001) 'Some considerations on the validity of evidence based practice in social work', *British Journal of Social Work*, 31(1): 57–79.

Welsh Assembly/Youth Justice Board (2004) *All Wales Youth Offending Strategy*. London: YJB.

Wilcox, A. (2003) 'Evidence-based youth justice?' *Youth Justice*, 3(1): 19–33.

Wilson, D. (2004) "Keeping quiet' or 'Going nuts': Strategies used by young, black, men in custody', *The Howard Journal of Criminal Justice*, 43(3): 317–330.

Wilson, J. Q. and Kelling, G. (1982) 'Broken windows', *Atlantic Monthly*, March, pp. 29–38.

Worrall, A. (1999) 'Troubled or troublesome? Justice for girls and young women', in B. Goldson (ed.) *Youth Justice: Contemporary Policy and Practice*. Aldershot: Ashgate, pp. 28–50.

Young, J. and Matthews, R. (2003) 'New Labour, crime control and social exclusion' in R. Matthews and J. Young (eds) *The New Politics of Crime and Punishment*. Cullompton: Willan.

France: The Politicization of Youth Justice

Sophie Gendrot

Introduction

Youth delinquency is what society decides it to be and the concept of the 'dangerous other' is often applied arbitrarily (Body-Gendrot, 2002). There is little difference in the way these categories were constructed formerly and the way socially marginalized youth are stigmatized today. Old processes continue to operate; the past may be transformed, but it is not obliterated. Definitions of 'problem youth' represent stakes within the fragmented state apparatus and they change according to economic cycles and electoral priorities. For example, in France in the 1980s punitive populism was softened by preventive measures, but since the 1990s policies of social crime prevention have been increasingly challenged by more rigorous orientations on crime control.

A feature distinguishes France, however: the Ministry of Justice is relatively insulated from political interest and public opinion. For example, the framework of juvenile justice based on the progressive edict of 1945 was able to resist the conservatives' will of dismantlement. Its main ideas are that sentencing should be alleviated for youth and that juvenile court judges retain their capacity to impose education as a priority, and to take mitigating circumstances into account and resist the pressures of prosecutors, at least to some extent. It has been observed that countries with a history of *noblesse oblige* display a *de haut en bas* mercy (Whitman, 2003: 205) – this may be the case in France. In 1990 the government wished to discard this edict, but the bill never reached Parliament. While the edict has been amended 16 times, its main ideas persist. The number of incarcerated 13–18 year olds in France stands at between 500 and 1000 at any one time, that is some 1–1.5% of the total number of inmates (ENAP, 2002). This places France in an average position in Europe between the UK on one hand and Scandinavian countries on the other. On average the length of detention is between five and seven weeks. While 63% of French approve of transferring juvenile delinquents to adult courts (*Libération*, 28 October 2001), so far France respects article 37 of the UN Convention on Children's Rights, requiring specific treatment for juveniles and their isolation from detained adults. Although this Convention is not publicly well known and a culture of rights certainly does not characterize a French society committed to a 'monarchical republicanism', the consolidation of the European community influences the penal norms adopted by member countries of the Council of Europe. In particular an important lobby in France remains the protection of children's and families' rights. This chapter examines major historical developments experienced by France in the last quarter of the 20th century, in particular the shift from social crime prevention to an over-riding concern with security. The first part of this chapter addresses the historical evolution of youth justice and the politicization of the issue. The second part examines different sources of data relative to juvenile delinquents' profiles and types of sentencing. The third part examines the changing status of ethnicity as related to youth justice.

The historical evolution of youth justice in France

The idea that juvenile delinquents should be the object of a specific justice treatment is relatively recent in France. As in most European countries, the phenomenon emerged at the beginning of the 20th century. Until then, youth were perceived as adults-to-be. Gradually, not only did nuclear families grant more importance to the fewer children they had, but society needing children in good physical and mental health (in part to supply labour and military demands), gave them more attention.

The evolution of the treatment of delinquency is marked by the progressive elimination of closed institutions. The criminal code of 1791 required that a minor under 16 who had committed a serious crime be locked up and educated until he seemed fit for social reintegration. In 1836, the first educational facility of La Petite Roquette was established in Paris and aimed at vagrant children. In 1839 the first agricultural colony for juveniles, north of Tours, sheltered as many as 700 youth under a strict disciplinary regime. Several penitentiary colonies (or correctional facilities as they were later called) were created in subsequent years

(*Le Monde*, 23 March 2002: 11).[1] The law of 1912 created juvenile courts (in large cities), thereby formally recognizing the phenomenon of *juvenile* delinquency. Yet empirically, the only key difference from other courts was that their proceedings were no longer held in public. The real legislative turn took place after World War II, with the edict of 2 February 1945.

The 1945 edict

Before 1945, the notion of discernement led judges to lean towards either correction or detention. The first priority of the 1945 edict was to establish education over repression. The post-war context explains why France came to develop such a consensus: the nation was in need of reconstruction, many families had disappeared and the state was compelled to invest itself in juvenile delinquents' reintegration particularly through work training. The interventionist role of the state as 'instituting society' is a typically French conception.

According to the edict, juvenile courts and jurors must provide 'measures of protection, support, surveillance or education' (article 2). A new branch within the Ministry of Justice was created, called 'education under surveillance'. An absence of links with the Penitentiary Administration marked the lawmakers' will to avoid punitive sentencing except for the most serious crimes. The specialized juvenile judge was required to lead a lengthy investigation with the appropriate services in order to fully understand youth's physical, psychological, behavioural characteristics as well as their family and social environments. Only then, it was thought, would the judge and the minor be able to negotiate the best possible decision. It was a form of justice by consent, but from which victims and the community were excluded.

After the revision of the edict in 1958, another conception appeared: 'youth at risk', (perceived as both being in risk or as a risk to others). The judge could choose to send him/her to one of the numerous and diversified types of institutions appearing at that time, from private boarding facilities to specialized educative establishments. In practice, 15 years elapsed before the administrative judicial protection agency was created to unify four previous subdivisions: delinquent youth; youth at risk; problematic youth between 18–21; and the control of welfare to families. This delay may be explained by the tension between two ideological trends; one liberal and private with specialized educators in favour of minimal state intervention and the other, public, requiring the state to be committed and involved as a major actor in charge of youth's problems. This is reflected in social services autonomously developing prevention on the demand of territorial départements in charge of youth at risk (but taking more

---

1. In the 1930s, after youth rebellions erupted, these negatively perceived facilities gradually disappeared.

and more supervision of juvenile delinquents) or by those enforcing juvenile court judges' decisions.[2]

In 1972, the first facilities (SES – Specialized Education under Surveillance) opened, approved by the local bureaus of health and social action (DDASS) in each département. Later, these were superseded by homes (foyers) for educative action.

Two dimensions were central to the institutionalization of this preventive strategy. The first contextualized interventions within geographic sectors marked by high levels of delinquency, while the second indicated that the target population was young, delinquent or potentially delinquent. The second turned the job of specialized educator into an occupation certified by a State diploma, and imposed a de facto administration via authorization procedures and supervision.

The educators' intervention, working within a paradigm of *disability* – a term close to maladjustment and marginalization – justified an individualized approach thus ignoring that juvenile offenders are frequently socialized by their peers and act collectively. M. Autès (1977) emphasized the importance of 'psychologism' in the training and work of these educators: it functioned as an ideological discourse for social work, protecting the sector autonomy from both local government and central administration. It also prevented partnership and 'team work' (Duprez, 1987).

These particular circumstances explain why mayors were deprived of any initiative in the prevention of youth offending up to the turn of the 1980s and why specialized education was not related to the sphere of judicial intervention.

The evolution of social crime prevention policies

When the Left were returned to power at the beginning of the 1980s, a third period started. The new prevention policy implemented in the early 1980s was largely a reaction to the shortcomings of specialized prevention and of social work in general.[3] But it was also an emergency development following the 'events' in the Minguettes neighbourhood in the summer of 1981, which initiated a cycle of collective disorders, described by the police as 'hot' or 'riot'[4]

---

2. According to the 1945 edict, the education-related decisions taken by judges are implemented by educators working for Education under Surveillance, the department in charge of education for juvenile delinquents, now called the Judicial Protection of Youth (PJJ). They are civil servants, employed by the Ministry of Justice, recruited after their high school graduation via a competitive examination and trained in a specialized school. There is a possibility of in-house recruiting for agents in the Ministry of Justice however, in which case the baccalauréat is not required. In a study done in the mid-1980s, differences in trajectory and ideology appeared between PJJ educators and specialized educators (Duprez, 1987).

3. This part owes much to the work Dominique Duprez and I conducted thanks to a GERN seminar in 1990 (see Body-Gendrot and Duprez, 2002).

4. The term 'riot' used by the media and public authorities is excessive and should be understood as urban disorders.

summers (Body-Gendrot, 2000). What distinguished these collective disorders from those in other post-industrialized countries was that their targets were frequently public sector or street-level employees. Attacks against policemen, bus drivers, firemen and teachers as well as arson and vandalism revealed a collective distrust of society and of its norms.

As early as 1983, Gilbert Bonnemaison, a Member of Parliament and the mayor of a locality in the Parisian Region, succeeded in gathering elected officials from various political parties within a new structure named the Conseil National de Prévention de la Délinquance (CNPD) – National Council for Preventing Offending – which headed the decentralized local committees (CCPD). It endorsed a three-faceted policy of prevention, repression[5] and solidarity. Repression was inserted on purpose in the middle. The police were deliberately omitted from these partnerships; they were perceived as 'a necessary evil, dark and frightening' (Monjardet, 1996). If repression there must be, it should be aimed not so much at young people who commit petty and moderately serious offenses and are taken care of by prevention measures, as at 'true criminals and hardened recidivists', who should receive 'appropriate punishment' (Dourlens and Vidal-Naquet, 1994: 15–16). Thus, the treatment of juvenile delinquency was submerged within a much broader policy designed to combat social exclusion and to improve space, mass education, labour wages, and so on.

The first preventive scheme was the 'anti-hot summer' scheme: a 'coup' thinking set up in 1982 in an attempt to avoid the repetition of the violent incidents that had occurred in the suburbs east of Lyons and to prevent their propagation to other cities. Media exposure was a turning point. The new youth-oriented public policies were implemented in a context that facilitated attempts to turn potential 'young neighbourhood leaders' into professionals who could replace social workers, who were considered to be too socially and ethnically different from those they were supposed to be supporting. While the idea of leaders or 'older brothers' controlling neighbourhood youth turned out to be a myth, it appealed to upwardly mobile immigrant youngsters from the sensitive neighborhoods who thus became 'go-betweens' between institutions and their communities.

At that time, France was often being cited by other countries as a model in implementing original public policies aimed at preventing juvenile delinquency and at dealing with the 'roots of crime'. Social crime prevention was widely perceived as a radical alternative to the dominant forms of situational crime prevention as developed in the UK and the USA.

Police statistics on youth offending were, however, constantly on the rise throughout the 1980s: the police 'under obligation to be silent', were so exclusively focused on order-maintenance and fighting serious crime that it gave the impression they cared little about the security of local communities. As for social educators, they

---

5. In 1982, 'a whole series of words gradually became taboo, almost shocking ... The outcome was (to reinforce) the negativity of terms such as punishment, prison, violence, offending ... but also testimony and civic education' (G. Bonnemaison quoted in Dourlens and Vidal-Naquet, 1994: 13).

were experiencing an institutional crisis, due to an overload of young delinquents, and to the length of time taken from judicial decision to implementation (sometimes a year and a half) resulting in more delinquency in the meanwhile.

The link between justice and this *politique de la ville* evolved in four stages: a strict formal presence in the local councils of crime prevention at the beginning of the 1980s; after 1988, the development of mediating processes in targeted areas; the extension of decentralized Houses of Justice and of the development of restorative measures; and after 1994, a zero tolerance and punitive approach to 'hard core' juveniles. In 1990, the decentralized Houses of Justice in 'problematic areas' reinforced the goal of a justice system more closely reflecting people's concerns with incivilities. Petty delinquency and neighbourhood conflict was targeted. Some cases were put on a fast track to ensure an immediate appearance in court and rapid intervention (mediation, restitution or warning, for instance) (Body-Gendrot, 2000). Short-term incarceration (a long weekend) was also used sometimes for those considered 'hard core' delinquents. But there remains a consensus among the Justice authorities that penitentiaries for young offenders should remain an exception because of their criminogenic qualities. Current re-offending rates stand at some 40% (des Désert, 1999: 74).

It is easy retrospectively to criticize the political option of the Left: the avoidance of repression and an idealized vision of social work efficiency. In practice, it cannot be denied that the measures lacked coherence. Some were redundant because experimentations which should have remained limited to problem-ridden areas were soon generalized under pressures from local mayors who were the natural constituents of the Left. In practice, these forms of 'territorial affirmative action policies' had little visibility for the most concerned populations. Nevertheless they probably regulated social tensions and avoided clashes and violence of all sorts at a time of high unemployment for multicultural populations trapped in stigmatized places. This was a considerable achievement. There is every reason to believe that these policies were instrumental in limiting disenfranchisement and the consequences of an underground economy based on drugs and trafficking. Yet the expansion of the National Front linking immigration, youth, violence and housing projects in sensitive neighborhoods convinced the elites in government that policy should be revised. The Far Right denounced the softness of public policies, the inaction of the police and the laxity of judges. It diffused the idea of 'ethnic danger'. Elected officials on the Left, for their part, had more to gain in addressing a major concern of the electorate – fear of crime – than in trying to defend the benefits of a policy of social crime prevention which had never been evaluated and whose success could only be measured in the long term.

From prevention to crime control

The shift from social prevention policies to security-oriented policies marks a fourth stage in the recent history of French juvenile justice. It cannot be grasped without an analysis of changes in attitudes towards and perceptions of *urban insecurity*.

During the 1980s and the 1990s, *banlieues* in France came to epitomize the anxiety elicited by deep political, economic and social/spatial transformations. As both geographic and social entities, *banlieues* focalized debates revolving around 'insecurity'. Some countries construct 'dangerous others' out of asylum seekers, racial minorities, nationalists, hooligans. France constructed a 'peril' out of the 'urban male youngsters' – particularly the poor Muslim male, born from North-African parents. For politicians, insecurity emanating from 'them' became the most visible, most easily identified and most familiar way of coming to terms with politically unmanageable issues such as demands for less unemployment or upward mobility for future generations. Many elected officials chose the easy way of targeting young delinquents living in marginalized parts of the city (that were not as dangerous as they seemed), in order to distract attention from more pressing issues that they were unable to address.

Pressured by the impact of crime statistics, electoral considerations and European orientations, the Left took a tougher stance when it was returned to power in the spring of 1998. Prevention policy did continue with urban restructuring, economic revitalization and social programs (though much of this was characterized by rhetoric, symbolic gestures and small budgets) but the priority was now on the repression of trouble-makers.

In October 1997, a conference entitled *Safe Cities for Free Citizens*, at Villepinte near Paris, solemnly asserted the right of every individual to security. The Minister of the Interior interpreted security as a left-wing concept and security contracts were launched involving mayors, Préfets, public prosecutors and other local actors, requiring them to audit the nature and extent of delinquency in their community. Hundreds of local security contracts were signed. The presence of citizens through the 'Houses of Justice', the call for parents to co-operate with schools, and a repositioning of local crime prevention and security councils were all measures that symbolized a new local, territorialized approach.

Youth judges, for their part, were more and more confronted with a *delinquency of exclusion* (Salas, 1998). This was characterized by the notion that specific areas generated delinquency through territorialization, ethnicization and marginalization. Crime was viewed as 'normal' within specific forms of socialization and subculture. Youth growing up in such areas were considered as in a normative blur (due to the absence of adults), and with identity disorders (due to their dual backgrounds as French and as immigrants' children).

In the late 1990s, new crime laws and edicts were passed, lengthening and increasing sentences for anti-social behaviours and assaults. Youth judges were now urged to take into account the concerns of victims, to prevent social 'risks' and to opt for immediate court appearances and measures of restoration. As more partners were involved and as prosecutors leaning to a zero tolerance approach gained ground, judges were gradually losing their face-to-face monopoly with young offenders. The French justice system was more than ever 'subterranean, horizontal, with ramifications, linkages and partnerships here, and individual punctual actions, initiatives and extensions there' (Dourlens and

Vidal-Naquet, 1994: 93). Few people know – because of a lack of dissemination of criminal statistics – that between 1994 and 1996, the number of juveniles sent to court increased by 46% (from 18,100 to 26,500). Out of 144,000 procedures related to juveniles, 54,000 received warnings or were closed (Body-Gendrot, 2000: 91). In 1996, 17 units of reinforced education (later called CPI – Immediate Placement Centers) opened, a measure supported a year later by the Left (Mucchielli, 2005: 17–18).

At the same time, French institutions so far have remained singularly resistant to punitive populism and to an excessive obsession with security. That juveniles be tried as adults, be sent to boot camps, be submitted to public shaming (as in America) is little less than shocking for most French Europeans. It is indeed alarming that 'public clamour' would require a prosecutor from Michigan to try a 6 year old as an adult (he refused); that the family of a 14 year old sentenced to 28 years without possibility of parole (could) be heard describing his punishment as 'just'; that 'the extension of criminal liability to minors is, in its way, an expression of authentic American ideals' (Whitman, 2003: 3; 45–47). In France, an ideal of *solidarity* and consideration of life inequalities still prevail over punitiveness. A commitment to youth re-socialization endures despite doubts about the efficacy of rehabilitation programs. Politicians remain receptive to professional advice. In 1997 the *Conseil d'État* (the highest administrative court) denied mayors the right to introduce curfews (a controversial, inappropriately war-like term) and ruled against introducing legislation to control aggressive begging unless the duration of sanctions was limited and applied only to specific places. The possibility of suspending child benefits for parents of delinquents remains highly controversial.

Electoral stakes in 2002

As the Presidential campaign of Spring 2002 was getting closer, political parties chose fear of crime as a major theme of their campaigns. Already in the polls of 1998, 82% of the French thought that acts of violence in cities and suburbs had reached a dramatic, unprecedented level. Of those under 25, 70% agreed. Only one-third of the French thought that the Left could do better on this issue (Body-Gendrot, 2000: 93). The media frenzily covered isolated incidents as if the country was under siege. Boarding correctional facilities for hard-core offenders were presented as the solution by most political parties. Not surprisingly, the Far Right candidate playing on a punitive populism and stigmatizing immigrants came second in the first round of the Presidential election.

After the Conservatives were back in power, Parliament passed a new comprehensive law, defining priorities for Justice. A controversy arose about the reform of an article of the 1945 edict, stipulating that no minor under 16 could be sent to prison. With the new law, hard-core offenders disrespecting the rules of the youth detention centres could be sent temporarily to prison as young as 13. After which, the juvenile court judges would find the appropriate measures for the concerned youth.

Ten detention centres, each holding eight to ten persistent offenders, are currently managed by judicial protection educators. The length of detention is usually six months. Other privately managed structures exist. The lawmakers' central idea here is to keep young hard-core offenders away from their usual environment and from their home in particular and, hopefully, to submit them to job training. Opponents to the centres have denounced the militarization of bodies and minds required to conform to middle-class norms (Mucchielli, 2005).

The key question remains: Are these reforms and new institutions only explained rationally by a hardening of young offenders' behaviours which increasingly threaten mainstream society?

How objective is the threat of violent urban youth in French cities?

As in all European countries, official data concerning young offenders is ambiguous and controversial. Detailed statistics about juvenile offenders have been available since 1974. Once released to the media, all the constructed discourses are overloaded with political and professional stakes. The statistics from the police called 'the statistics of delinquency' generally have the highest public visibility; but these are beset by the usual problems of being reflections of particular recording practices and policing priorities. As stated by Philippe Robert, the intensity of the crime debate is inversely proportional to the scarcity and reliability of data sources (Robert et al., 1994). Statistics are dispersed, hard to find and decipher. Factual errors and the recategorization or decategorization of types of offence create continuous problems.

Over the past two decades these statistics have reinforced the same message: delinquents are becoming younger and younger and more and more violent (see Table 4.1).

According to Ministry of the Interior data, the number of juvenile delinquents (petrial) has rocketed from 75,846 in 1974 to 180,382 in 2000, an increase of 137% (see Figure 4.1). Juveniles are thought to be responsible for 21% of all crimes, particularly street crime, burglaries and thefts.

However, such statistics refer to cases which were cleared. When types of crime are examined, they reveal a different picture. The transgression of anti-drug laws or of immigration laws, the rebellion and outrage towards law-enforcers are, for instance, well recorded by the police. By contrast, only 9% of burglaries, 7% of car or motorcycle thefts and 3% of other thefts are cleared (Mucchielli, 2004). This means that the higher proportion of juvenile delinquents coincides on the one hand with crimes which are the most easily detected by the police because they are the most visible and on the other, that are the most frequently transmitted to prosecutors, following legal changes already mentioned. For example, the number of youth consuming narcotics and arrested increased by 155% from 1993 to 1995 and those expressing rebellion and outrage towards law enforcers increased by 76% (Aubusson de Cavarlay et al., 2002).

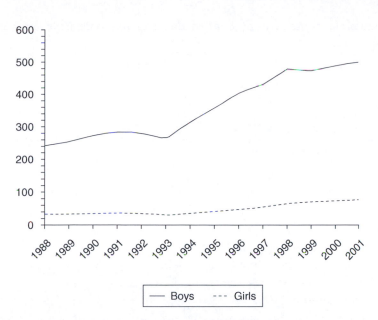

Figure 4.1 Number of 10–17 year old minors placed under suspicion by the police in France from 1988–2001 (per 10,000 residents)

Source: Ministry of the Interior, Mucchielli, 2004: 103

The question of desistance from delinquency is important and is related to age. The demographic cohort of youth under 25 decreased by 17% after 1980 in France but less so in marginalized areas sheltering large immigrant families (Mucchielli, 2004: 107). Many criminologists think that ageing fulfils an important function in putting an end to rites of passages (Farrington, 1986). To evaluate crimes committed by juvenile delinquents, self-reported delinquency, judicial sources and regional victimization surveys are helpful, compensating for the lack of data at the national level (Roché et al., 2000: 13–14; Pottier et al., 2002).

The self-reported delinquency survey[6] reveals that violence is far less prevalent than fare-dodging (76%), the purchase of stolen goods (32%), thefts in large stores (24%), and different types of vandalism (13–18%). The judicial sources, due to legal reforms, are difficult to decipher. But they show that for the whole youth group, convictions for thefts are less numerous between 1980–2000 because the police cannot clear the cases. The youngest cohort (under 13) does not use firearms and tends to steal less than his/her predecessor. The 13–15 year

---

6. In the two metropolitan areas of Grenoble and in St. Etienne, 2,300 young people aged 13–19 were surveyed in their schools. It provides information on the 15% of youth who committed a serious offence (assault with physical harm, throwing stones at people or cars, theft with violence), 9% of those who, after a minor offence, were caught by the police and on 2% of those who were referred to a judge.

Table 4.1 Collective acts of violence reported in the press in the Paris region in the 1990s (%)

Violence committed by	1992–96	1996–99
Groups of youths fighting one another	28	52
Youths and the police	32	25
Youths and other institutions (firemen bus drivers, city hall employees, etc.)	40	23

Source: Lagrange, 2001: 43

olds represent 8% of all the convictions for theft (that 20 youngsters or so in the whole cohort used firearms for bank robbery started a moral panic, although the phenomenon remains marginal). The core of the convicted group is the 16–25 year olds who steal to gain the symbols of a consumption society (cellular phones, scooters, cars, and so on) (Mucchielli, 2004: 109–111).

As for interpersonal violence involving youth, according to police and justice statistics, it increased by 5.2% between 1993 and 2001. It is noteworthy to point out a recent evolution: the more public employees in marginalized neighborhoods have resorted to situational crime prevention and learned to better protect themselves with surveillance systems and cameras, the more violence has occurred between young males from various housing projects (see Table 4.1).

Interpersonal violence involves on average one victim out of 20. But in a recent survey of school violence among 17,000 students aged 12–18 by INSERM, one boy out of four and one girl out of eight declared they had received blows, the proportion increasing in vocational high schools (Laronche, 2005: 6). One should, however, be cautious of such data since even acts without physical damage can be categorized as blows and injuries due to aggravating circumstances. Mucchielli (2004: 114–116) points out that assaults were experienced by the whole youth group; yet, between 1984–2000, the assault rate was multiplied by 4.5 for juveniles under 13 and by 6.5 for 13–15 year olds. Delinquents under 13 convicted for interpersonal violence represented 0.4% of the whole sample in 2000 (no increase from 1984) while the number of 18–25 year olds grew by 240%.

The three week disturbances which occurred in several regions of France in November 2005 give an impression of 'déjà vu'. Rather pessimistically, an American journalist wrote that: 'The rioting in France's ghetto suburbs is a phenomenon of futility – but a revelation nonetheless. It has no ideology and no purpose other than to make a statement of distress and anger. It is beyond politics. It broke out spontaneously and spread in the same way, communicated by televised example, ratified by the huge attention it won from the press and television and the politicians, none of whom had any idea what to do. It has been an immensely pathetic spectacle, whose primary meaning has been that it happened' (Pfaff, 2005: 88). Although the term ghetto could be contested in the case of France, it is accurate to observe that acting out more than the instrumentalization of violence, was what motivated the 10% or so of participants, a large part being high school students eager to be seen on television. Paris was not burning and the burnt cars which attracted the television crews were frequently limited to two streets in any 'banlieue' where disturbances occurred. Besides the two deaths from the accidental electrocutions of the boys who thought the police were after them (this point is not clear at the time of writing), two other deaths occurred, one which seems to have been motivated by a murderer's personal revenge rather than by a youth participating in the disorders. The mayors' reluctance to resort to curfews and the restraint with which most of them, as well as educators and other social actors, acted after an emergency law was passed is a proof in point. There were indeed numerous motivations in the burning of 10,000 vehicles, 255 schools, 233 public buildings, and 51 post offices and 140 public-transport vehicles stoned. On 14 November, around 2,800 people had been placed in custody. 375 were sent to prison. Among the 498 juveniles sent to a juvenile court judge, 108 were locked up (Arteta, 2005: 100). Most high school students previously unknown in terms of delinquency were set free by the judges after their arrest.

Is there anything new then? The length of the riots, their relative contagion reveal the depth of the social revolt of these areas' residents who since the beginning of the 1980s have felt that no governmental policy would improve their social and economic mobility, would give them more efficient institutions, would deal with the contempt, discrimination and racism that they experience, or would solicit their participation. They may be right to think that despite the new emergency measures which have been decided by the Villepin government, nothing much will change for them. Politicians are likely to make symbolic, short-term and populist decisions to calm an alarmed public, mostly because the presidential elections of 2007 are already looming with the far right set to make the most of these disorders. Only long-term, substantial and largely invisible reforms – including a reform of the French 'monarchical' state – could have a chance of improving the tension-ridden social question in France.

Ethnic identity and youth violence in France

The taboo regarding the ethnicity of the youth participating in the recent disorders has been even more controversial and more politicized than it has ever been since the first disturbances of 1981.[7] Are young French Muslims more stopped and searched by the police in the *banlieues*? How many are imprisoned?

---

7. Due to lack of space gender will not be treated here. Official figures on juvenile delinquency reveal that less than 12% of offenders are girls, their major offence being that of fraud (see the Senate Report by Schosteck and Carle, 2001: 37: 127).

One should remember that in France, the term 'ethnic minorities' is not statistically categorized, despite the fact that in the last 20 years or so, the 'ethnicization' of social relations has constantly increased in daily practices and that racism is multilateral. The conceptual obscurity of the concept of ethnicity cannot be denied. It is located between *race* (but the country is supposed to be race-blind) and *culture* (but the Republican model of integration does not take into account communities in the public space). Social scientists agree that the core of ethnicity lies in a sense of group belonging, that its dynamics are rooted in social interaction, in boundaries of identification and differentiation among collective and individual actors.

The role of ethnic origin is probably real but modest in the emergence of delinquency.[8] An important variable may come from unemployment disproportionately affecting young males of immigrant origin living in France (in the 751 problematic zones as defined by the French administration, 38% of the 15–24 year old males are unemployed vs. 15% in other urban zones in 2003. Those without the French nationality can be hit 15–17% more in certain areas, (DIV, 2004: 4)). Some analysts argue that youths resort to theft when they are least able to afford consumption goods. A recent investigation, led by Luc Bronner, on 'hard-core offenders' from a suburban locality in the Parisian region who attacked high school students demonstrating against a governmental educational reform, revealed that ethnicity distinguished the victims (white) from the offenders (black) whose major motivations were to steal cellular phones, take social revenge and experience the pleasure of physical intimidation (*Le Monde*, 15 March 2005 and 28 March 2005). But this is an isolated testimony which should be taken cautiously.

In a self-reported delinquency survey, 22% of male offenders of North African origin said that they had at least three friends who had been arrested by the police for theft (vs. 7% of the French of French origin), 15% had had their brother or sister arrested. Of those under justice supervision 43% had parents who were born abroad (Choquet, 2000). Khosrokhavar estimates that in the 18–24 year old cohort, those with a North African father are 9.27 times more likely to be prosecuted than those whose father was born in France; a rate similar for the 25–29 year old cohort (2004: 280). That justice would convict them more often (due to lack of residential stability, family rupture, unemployment and lack of guarantees) would not be surprising. Xenophobia cannot be ruled either out or in (Tournier, 1997: 548). Ethnicity doesn't exist in isolation and the importance of socio-economic disparities in the production of social and political inequalities of treatment must be kept in mind. National data on self-reported delinquency show, however, that 50% of offences are caused by French of French origin, 20% of mixed origin, 32% of foreign origin (both parents are born abroad). A quarter of these are of North African origin. For

---

8. A monograph reconstructs entries into delinquency and the representation of young offenders in prison according to their ethnicity. See Zanna and Lacombe, 2005.

serious offences, the profile is more or less the same, except that those whose parents are born abroad form 46% of the cohort (Roché, 2000).

Finally, are the relationships of these youth with the police so tense that it accelerates their route to court? Do they display a stronger antagonism than others? Do they resent the abuse of force and a lack of respect from law enforcers more forcefully than others?

No one can deny that the local dimension of the problem is of paramount importance: the lack of respect of insufficiently trained young policemen for those that they consider as their natural antagonists; the perception of the police as another rival gang by the youth; the lack of legitimacy granted to institutions and the constitution of counter-worlds are part of the explanation. As observed by criminologist W. de Haan, 'the police would do well to take away the distrust of the youth and gain their confidence by offering them something which they need – namely protection in violent surroundings. A first step in that direction would be to take the perspective of young people more seriously. The police do not have to accept or tolerate violence committed by youth. However, in order to respond to violence adequately, it is important to realize that lacking other means and possibilities, violence is sometimes the only means to ensure safety and autonomy. As long as the police lack insight into the motivation among youth to use violence as a form of self-help, even the most well intended attempts to diminish and prevent youth violence will likely overshoot the mark' (de Haan, 2005). In the words of all the French of African and North African origin that we met, the unfairness of the justice system is even more unbearable than the police's behaviour (Body-Gendrot, 2004).

It is unusual for judges to side with vulnerable categories against policemen. In 1995, only 21 out of 253 complaints led to the conviction of police officers and in 1996, it was 12 out of 166 (Jobard, 2002). Judges have most difficulties in obtaining complete files and cases are frequently closed for lack of evidence. Police status grants them impunity. In recent years, as violent incidents have increased, complaints of 'rebellion and outrage' by the police have also increased. Those youth who consider themselves as victims of racist behaviours by the police are condemned to pay damages to those who physically hurt them. Between the words of the police and the words of their victims, the relation is asymmetrical.

There is then something of a crisis in traditional French representative democracy. As remarked by P. Robert, 'the government centre ... is unable to get the *suburbs* to enter the political scene, probably because it doesn't really try to, and above all, it has nothing to offer those fringes that would be worth their while' (2000).

Conclusion

A deep evolution has marked youth justice in France in the last quarter of the 20th century. The violent collective disturbances which accompanied the return of the

Left to power at the beginning of the 1980s initiated an original initiative of providing education, mediation and vocational opportunities for male youths who otherwise had little prospect in the post-industrial economy. Entrepreneurial politicians, mobilized by an ideal for social justice, were eager to be 'tough with the causes of crime' and with the socio-economic conditions producing youth marginalization. But the major mutations experienced by French society in the 1990s increased a general feeling of insecurity and a loss of confidence, exploited by far-right ideologues. For electoral stakes, laws became tougher for young offenders, the police were required to proceed to more arrests and restore law and order while fast-track processing was introduced into the justice system.

Research of urban violence has become more complex over the past 25 years. Grand narratives with binary interpretations have been discarded in favour of approaches more attuned to the complexity of processes and to the hybridity of their subjects. While compassion is expressed for the structural victims of society's indifference and double standards and hope maintained for a greater fairness in the institutional treatment of offenders, it cannot be denied that young offenders are also violent, usually in their own neighbourhoods as demonstrated recently and that their victims are entitled to demand retribution and protection. It becomes more and more difficult to perpetuate a simplistic view of 'us' and 'them' on issues of law and order. Research on the treatment of young delinquents should abandon its ideological stance and take into account complexity, fragmentation, hesitations, the questioning of former norms, and the emergence of the 'new'. It should examine more closely the new profile of actors, the circumstances of their acts, and the varied responses provided by local institutions. Even in a centralized country like France, place matters. It cannot be repeated enough. Understanding the overlapping of structures from one level to the other, the blurring of boundaries and the complex games of actors formulating national policies on youth delinquency is difficult in a state characterized by its lack of transparency. What is clear though is that the purpose of this lack of clarity is not innocent.

References

Arteta, S. (2005) 'Pluie de condamnations', *Le Nouvel Observateur*, November 17–23: 100.

Bailleau, F. (2002) 'La justice pénale des mineurs en France ou l'émergence d'un nouveau modèle de gestion des illégalismes', *Déviance et société*, 26(3): 403–421.

Body-Gendrot, S. (2005) 'Deconstructing youth violence', *European Journal on Crime, Criminal law and Criminal justice*, forthcoming.

Body-Gendrot, S. (2004) 'Police relations in England and in France – Policy and practices', in G. Mesko and B. Dobovsek (eds) *Dilemmas of Contemporary Criminal Justice*, Faculty of Criminal Justice, University of Maribor, Slovenia, pp. 134–145.

Body-Gendrot, S. (2002) 'The dangerous others: Changing views on urban risks and violence in France', in J. Eade and C. Mele, (eds) *Understanding the City: Contemporary and Future Perspectives*, Oxford: Blackwell. pp. 82–106.

Body-Gendrot, S. and Duprez, D. (2002) 'The politics of prevention and security in France' in D. Duprez and P. Hebberecht (eds) *The Politics of Prevention and Security in Europe*. Bruxelles: UCV University Press, pp. 95–132.

Body-Gendrot, S. (2000) *The Social Control of Cities? A Comparative Perspective*. Oxford: Blackwell.

Bonnemaison, G. (1982) Face à la délinquance: prévention, répression, solidarité, *Commission des maires sur la sécurité*, Rapport au Premier ministre, La Documentation Française.

Choquet, M. (2000) La violence des jeunes: données épidémiologiques. In C. Rey (ed.), *Les Adolescents face à la violence*, Paris, Syros, pp. 61–74.

de Cavarlay, A., Lalam, B., Padieu, N., and Zamora, P. (2002) 'Les statistiques de la délinquance' in *France, portrait social*. Paris: INSEE, pp. 141–157.

de Cavarlay, A., Lalam, B., Padieu, N., and Zamora, P. (2002) Les statistiques de la délinquance, *Portrait social 2002–2003*. Paris: INSEE, pp. 151–158.

de Haan, W. and Nijboer, J. (2005) 'Youth, police and self-help', *European Journal on Crime, Criminal law and Criminal Justice* (forthcoming).

Délégation interministérielle á la ville (2004) *Zones urbaines sensibles: un enjeu territorial de la cohésion sociale*, September, 1–8.

des Déserts, S. (1999) 'Délinquance juvénile en hausse', *Le Nouvel Observateur*, 21 January: 74.

Dourlens, C. and Vidal-Naquet, P. (1994) *L'autorité comme prestation*. Paris: CERPE.

Duprez, D. (1987) Prévention de la délinquance et protection judiciaire de la jeunesse, Rapport de recherche pour le Conseil de la recherche du ministère de la Justice, mimeo, Lille, CLERSE.

ENAP (2002) Le débat sur la justice des mineurs: quelle politique pénitentiaire? Quelles perspectives?, *Synthèse d'actualité* (8), September.

Farrington, D. (1986) 'Age and Crime', in M. Tonry and N. Morris (eds), *Crime and Justice: An Annual Review of Research*. Chicago: University of Chicago Press, (7), 189–250.

Hobsbawn, E. (1959) *Primitive Rebels*, Manchester: Manchester University Press.

Jobard, F. (2002)'Compter les violences policières, faits bruts et mises en récit' *Questions pénales*, XV, 3 June.

Khosrokhavar, F. (2004) *L'islam dans les prisons*. Paris: Balland.

Lagrange, H. (2001) *De l'affrontement à l'esquive*: Paris: Syros.

Laronche, M. (2005) 'La violence dans les ZEP ne serait pas plus importante qu'ailleurs', *Le Monde*, March 28: 6.

Le Toqueux, J. L. and Moreau, J. (2002) 'Les Zones urbaines sensibles', *Insee Première* (835).

Monjardet, D. (1996) *Ce que fait la police, sociologie de la force publique*. Paris: La Découverte.

Mucchielli, L. (2004) 'L'évolution de la délinquance', *Sociétés Contemporaines* 53: 101–134.

Mucchielli, L. (2005) 'Les "centres éducatifs fermés": rupture ou continuité dans le traitement des mineurs délinquants?', *Le temps de l'histoire*, June.

Pfaff, W. (2005) 'The French riots: Will they change anything?', *The New York Review of Books*, December 15, 88–89.

Pottier, M.-L., Robert, P., Zauberman, R. (2002) *Victimation et insécurité en Ile de France*, *Final Report*. Paris: IAURIF-CESDIP.

Robert, P. (2000) 'Les territoires du contrôle social, quels changements?', *Déviance et Société* (24)3, 215–236.

Robert, P., Aubusson de Cavarlay, B., Pottier, M.-L., Tournier, P. (1994) *Les comptes du crime. Les délinquances en France et leurs mesures*. Paris: L'Harmattan.

Roché S. (2000) *La délinquance des jeunes. Les jeunes de 13–19 and racontent leurs délits*. Paris: Le Seuil.

Salas, D. (1998) 'La délinquance des mineurs', *Problèmes politiques et sociaux*. Paris: La documentation française (812) November.

Schosteck, and Carle *Délinquance des mineurs, la République en quête de respect*, 340: 2001–2002.

Tournier, P. (1997) 'Nationality, crime and criminal justice in France' in M. Tonry (ed.) *Ethnicity, Crime, and Immigration*. Chicago: University of Chicago Press.

Whitman, J. Q. (2003), *Harsh Justice*. New York: Oxford University Press.

Zanna, O. and Lacombe, P. (2005) 'L'entrée en délinquance de mineurs incarcérés. Analyse comparative entre des jeunes "d'origine française" et des jeunes "d'origine maghrébine"', *Déviance et société* (29)1: 55–74.

The Netherlands: Penal-welfarism and Risk Management

5

**Jolande uit Beijerse and
René van Swaaningen**

Introduction

Today there seems to be little left of the once famous 'Dutch tolerance' in law enforcement. The development of the prison system from a system led by rehabilitation and prisoners' rights to an actuarial model of incapacitation probably best exemplifies this shift (Downes and van Swaaningen, forthcoming). Because Dutch youth justice, more than any other part of the criminal justice system, is a hybrid of punitive and welfare rationales, it is particularly pertinent to analyse whether a shift from 'penal-welfarism' to a 'culture of control' (Garland, 2001) has taken place in this area as well.

In doing so, we will first deal with some legal questions. The legal debate is dominated by the question of at what age young persons can be held fully responsible for their actions. The answer to this question determines whether juveniles are placed under civil law surveillance, and whether they will be judged according to juvenile or adult criminal law. Second, we consider recent policy developments. The key issue here is the increasing use of risk assessments as a basis for preventative measures. Next, we describe the steep increase of diversion projects and community sanctions for juveniles. These stand in some contrast to a parallel contemporary trend in which the old idea that prison can be used as a means to (re-)educate juveniles seems to have been rediscovered.

The law: education, punishment and the age of responsibility

In the Netherlands, the notion that juvenile offenders were primarily in need of care first surfaced between 1833 and 1886. Before then juvenile offenders received a 'normal' adult prison sentence, but gradually more and more educational elements were introduced. By 1886, most children were placed in special coercive educational institutions (*rijksopvoedingsgestichten*). Changing ideas about the capacity of children to judge right from wrong, and the acknowledgement that parents were often more to blame than the delinquent child itself, were the main factors behind this development. Historian Chris Leonards (1995) has characterised this period as 'the discovery of the innocent criminal child'.

It took, however, until 1905 before a special juvenile criminal law was introduced. One element in the mixed package of Children Acts of that year was the introduction of specific procedures and sanctions for the juvenile delinquent. Despite important changes in 1921 and 1965, the principles of youth justice remained the protection and education of juvenile offenders. These leading principles were only abandoned in 1995, when 'protecting society' became the leading rationale. Since then youth justice has increasingly come to resemble adult criminal justice (Bartels, 2003; de Jonge and van der Linden, 2004).

In 1905 the 'improvement' of the individual was seen to be the main aim of punishment. Sanctions for juvenile delinquents were all directed towards (re-)education with a minimum of retributive elements. A reprimand or informing the parents without further punishment were in most cases thought sufficient. For more serious delinquency two new penalties were introduced: 1) placement in a borstal-like institution (*tuchtschool*), where the juvenile was supposed to learn order and discipline during a period of up to six months; and 2) 'compulsory education' (*dwangopvoeding*), that lasted until the juvenile reached the age of 23. In 1965 a penalty of 'short arrest' (*korte arreststraf*) was introduced, together with a special hospital order for juveniles with mental disturbance: the so-called 'placement in an institution for special care' (*pibb*). The latter penal-psychiatric hybrid had already existed for adults since 1928, under the name of *terbeschikkingstelling* (detention during Her Majesty's pleasure). In 1905, parliament decided that the juvenile criminal law was applicable to everybody below the age of 18. Because some MPs wanted to set the limit at 16, a special regulation for 16 and 17 year olds was introduced that enabled the judge to apply, in exceptional cases, adult criminal law. This could only be justified by both the seriousness of the offence and the personality of the offender. The law of 1905 did not mention any lower age limit, and left it to the judge to decide whether an offender had acted with full knowledge of their wrongdoing. In 1965 an explicit lower limit of 12 years was introduced.

In 1921, a special youth judge (*kinderrechter*) was given the power to hear both civil and criminal cases – normally these fields are separated. The youth judge should possess educational as well as legal skills. Inquiry into the social and family situation of the minor could be called for. The youth judge can also remand children in custody. In adult law, this is done by a special magistrate of inquiry (*rechtercommissaris*).

The democratisation movement of the 1960s began to criticise the omnipotent and discretionary role of the youth judge and argued for more rights for juveniles. It would, however, take until 1989 before any such reform was enacted. By then, the political and penal climate had already changed towards a more punitive approach towards juvenile offenders. A revised version of the 1989 law, finally passed in 1995, not only curtailed the power of youth judges and improved litigation possibilities for juvenile offenders, but also sharpened the youth justice system in the direction of adult criminal law. Two already existing measures, coercive education and the treatment of mentally disturbed juvenile offenders, were fused into one measure of 'placement in an institution for juveniles' (PIJ). The term borstal (*tuchtschool*) was replaced by youth detention, and the maximum length of sentence was increased from 6 to 12 months for children up to 15 years old and to 24 months for 16 and 17 year olds. For this latter group, the potential of being judged according to adult criminal law has also increased.

Because of the special rules for 16 and 17 year olds, the Netherlands made a reservation to the requirement of separate detention of adults and juveniles when it ratified the UN Convention on the Rights of the Child. The UN Committee on children's rights has often pressed the Dutch government to withdraw this restriction. It has also been heavily criticised by Dutch experts on juvenile criminal law (de Jonge, 1998; Mijnarends, 2001).

The Murat D. case, called after the 17 year old who in 2004 killed his teacher at a school in The Hague, is a good illustration of the fact that this provision is now mainly used to judge a minor according to adult criminal law if the 'protection of society' so requires. In this case, both during first hearing and appeal, adult criminal law was applied. By the end of the 1990s the minimum age at which juvenile criminal law could be applied was also contested. Politicians increasingly identified 'criminals' under 12 years old who remained unpunished. The legal minimum age of 12 remained intact, but in 1999 the preventative, educational STOP measure was introduced for offenders *under* that age. It is modelled on the HALT programme (see below) and deals mainly with cases of vandalism, rowdiness and graffiti, but also with minor thefts, incidents with fireworks and assault (Slump et al., 2000). In more serious cases, civil measures can be applied for offenders under 12 years old.

As a result, the age limits of juvenile criminal law are being 'defined up': 16 and 17 year olds are increasingly being judged according to adult criminal law, and attempts are being made to bring children under 12 within the reach of youth justice. This 'adulteration' is reflected in a major shift in the rationale for youth justice from education and the protection of juveniles towards incapacitation and the protection of society.

Policy: risk groups and problematic neighbourhoods

Since the early 1990s, juvenile delinquency has been a major governmental concern. Fears of 'moral decay' and research arguing that juvenile delinquency was mainly concentrated among ethnic minority groups and that juveniles were becoming more violent at an earlier age, were the main drivers of increased policy attention. In 1994 the Van Montfrans committee produced the report *Facing the Facts (Met de neus op de feiten)*. Its motto was 'early, swift and consistent intervention'. *Facing the Facts* led to a series of organisational reforms: the police were given more powers, the prosecution service devoted more time to juvenile delinquency, a special youth probation service was established, capacity in juvenile detention centres was expanded, a monitoring system for youth with a high risk profile (*cliëntvolgsysteem*) was established and attempts were made to reduce the waiting lists in juvenile courts. New platforms for juvenile delinquency, established at the level of court districts, were designed to improve collaboration between the various 'partners' in youth justice – police, the judicial Child Protection Board (*Raad voor de Kinderbescherming*), prosecution service, judiciary, probation, prison service. These are to work in partnership with preventative networks at a community level with respect to schools, youth work, sport clubs, mosques, and so on.

This development has been accompanied by new policy instruments, such as *Communities that Care*, neighbourhood justice centres (*Justitie in de Buurt* or *JiB*), intensive social skills programmes for risk groups (*Individuele Traject Begeleiding* or *ITB*), new forms of treatment, experiments with night detention and the STOP programme mentioned earlier. Furthermore, parenting support schemes (*Opvoedingsondersteuning en Ontwikkelingsstimulering*) have been developed and an action programme, based on 'best practices' with respect to preventing children dropping out of school was established.

In 2002, two different policy plans on youth justice appeared: one by the then ruling Left-liberal government, and one by its Right-wing successor. The first 2002 plan – 'Persistent and Effective' (*Vasthoudend en effectief*) – was very much in line with the recommendations of the Van Montfrans Committee of 1994. Juvenile delinquents were to be targeted at an early stage through a balance of preventative and repressive measures. The effectiveness of different measures was to be monitored carefully: the beginning of an ever increasing popularity of a 'what works?' approach.

With the new populist Right-wing cabinet, juvenile delinquency remained firmly on the political agenda, but with different emphases. These included an increased focus on the swiftness of the reaction (fast-tracking), and on the re-education of serious juvenile delinquents. The general principles of the 2002 White Paper Towards a Safer Society (*Naar een veiliger samenleving*) were elaborated on in a special action programme on juvenile delinquency for the period 2003–6 entitled *Jeugd Terecht* (an untranslatable pun that means both 'youth recovered' and indicates that juveniles are to be brought to justice). In accordance with the ever-present managerial discourse, the slogan of this policy paper was 'fast, efficient and cut to size'. The similarities with 'Persistent and Effective' are quite evident, but the term 'cut to size' indicates a special focus on specific categories of offenders: (1) first offenders, (2) moderately delinquent juveniles, and (3) structural and serious juvenile offenders. With respect to the first group, parents are to be mobilised, the psycho-social background of the problems charted out, and parenting assistance or social work provided. In these cases, general social work, provided by the municipal bureaus of youth care, are thought to be more helpful than fines or penalties. With respect to the second group, an analysis is made of psycho-social risk-factors and a specific 'trajectory' is set out accordingly. The main aim with respect to the third group is to get them off the street, while their detention as such is aimed at re-education and rehabilitation.

The action programme argues that police intervention is to be concentrated on those places and hours that are known for high crime and in locations where juveniles create nuisance. This information is based on, and will further feed the development of, a national crime map which maps out structural offenders, delinquent youth groups, the ethnic background of juvenile offenders and 'hot spots'. Knowledge of the offenders' ethnic background is legitimised through the development of ethnically specific training schemes. The relatively small group of structural offenders is specifically monitored. When the police signal that a particular youngster is slipping into more serious delinquency, they are to intervene immediately and report it to the judicial Child Protection Board, which prepares the social inquiry reports for the youth judge. If they find shortcomings in the juvenile's educational or family situation, then that juvenile is transferred to social workers of the bureaus for youth care.

Another aim of the action programme is that immediately after the first police contact a coherent reaction is developed in consultation between the police, prosecution service and Child Protection Board. If parents are unwilling to collaborate voluntarily, a more coercive approach will follow that can imply regular house visits and financial penalties. Parenting assistance can also be enforced by a supervision order (ondertoezichtstelling) under civil law. If it concerns children under 12 years old, a shorter period of parenting assistance can also be part of the above-mentioned STOP programme. If a young child is suspected of a serious offence, it is always reported to the bureau for youth care. The child is assessed and parenting assistance is ordered according to a so-called 'persuasion and coercion' (drang en dwang) measure.

A third element of the action programme concerns the effectiveness of penalties. A 'tit for tat' approach, such as the confiscation of popular consumer goods, scooters, mobile phones, MP3 players, game-boys, and so on is thought to be particularly effective; as is the use of remand to temporarily remove someone from the street. A faster resort to youth detention is proposed if community sanctions are not (fully) fulfilled. Night detention, educational programmes and social skills training in closed settings are also advocated as means to improve the possibilities for rehabilitation and re-education. The final part of the action programme involves obligatory aftercare and the application of a uniform instrument of future risk assessment. These measures are yet to be evaluated.

Prevention: targeting the young and minority communities

There is a rich tradition of research into juvenile delinquency in Dutch criminology, and it is interesting to observe how it follows academic fashions. Over the last 25 years the main focus has shifted from studies of strain, subculture and attachment to studies in the tradition of developmental criminology – mainly in the style of Farrington and Moffitt, but also in that of Sampson and Laub's life course perspective (Weerman, forthcoming). 'Culture' – both in the societal sense and as ethnicity – has also become an increasingly important issue.

After a consistently steep increase since the early 1960s, the extent of juvenile delinquency seems to have stabilised since 1997. The main concern now lies, however, in its perceived increased seriousness. A similar concern was voiced about adult crime, when from 1984 onwards property offences stabilised, while violent offences rose. Nonetheless, property offences still make up the vast majority of juvenile delinquency – though vandalism and violence against people are increasing the most. Since the 1980s, reported violence against people increased nearly fourfold. Also the police figures on juveniles committing a sexual offence show an increase, as does the number of juvenile delinquents with severe personality disorders. It is clear here that there is a relation between changing police priorities and the revival of (bio-)psychological research into juvenile delinquency over this very same period of time.

Police reports indicate a shift from 'verbal fights' to physical fights and an increasing number of juveniles possess and use weapons – particularly knives. According to police statistics, the number of girls assaulting other people shows a nearly fourfold increase from 1985 to 2000. Whereas in the 1980s, the average age of juvenile offenders was around 16, large numbers of serious offences are now recorded for 14 and 15 year olds. Younger children, between 8 and 12 years old, also seem to regularly get into trouble with the police. It is such statistics and prediction studies that have been turned to legitimise intensive early intervention (e.g. Dorelijers and Domburg, 2004).

The remark in the policy plan that focusing on the ethnic background of offenders would have long been a taboo-issue in the Netherlands is particularly interesting in the context of the recent Right-wing populist revolution (van Swaaningen, 2005). First, there is the question whether this statement is true, and second there is the question whether it makes sense to focus so strongly on the ethnic background of offenders. Particularly in the 1970s and 1980s, the relation between crime and ethnicity was studied mainly to reveal discriminatory practices within the criminal justice system. Researchers were often hesitant to blame the over-representation of various ethnic minority groups in police figures on these groups themselves. Since 1990, this has generally been seen as just a reflection of reality. Thus, to argue in a policy plan of 2002 that this would be taboo had not been true for some time. Rather the tendency has been to move to the other extreme and blame ethnic minorities for virtually everything that goes wrong in the Netherlands. In 1997, an influential policy plan on Crime in Relation to the Integration of Ethnic Minorities (CRIEM) emerged, in which the over-representation of ethnic minorities in crime was basically blamed on their failure to integrate into Dutch society – an idea that has been contested by experts on migration issues (de Haan and Bovenkerk, 1995). Despite all this attention, the vast majority of the aetiological criminological research on juvenile offenders remains primarily oriented at white youth.

The second question – What sense does it make to focus so strongly on the ethnic background of offenders? – is possibly even harder to answer. Recognition of, and claims to, ethnic background is a central feature of Dutch society. Whereas an American from, let us say, Afghan descent is first of all addressed as an American, even a third generation immigrant in the Netherlands will still be referred to as a Turk, Surinamese, and so on. They are what is called (with a strange neologism), 'allochtonous': not originating here. This official policy term results in a large, hybrid category of people who do have Dutch nationality, but who are not fully seen as Dutch citizens. Second, the old argument that most ethnic minority groups are younger and poorer than the white Dutch, live nearly exclusively in the larger cities, and are discriminated against on the labour market and socially, and that higher crime rates should therefore not surprise us, is still valid. And third, registration is incoherent: in some statistics people are registered on the basis of their nationality, in others on their country of birth, and again in others on the country of birth of one of their parents.

Police, court and prison figures point to a significant over-representation of ethnic minorities. More than half (53.7%) of the population of youth detention centres are foreign born – the number of juvenile prisoners whose parents are foreign born would thus be even higher. In absolute terms, children born in the Netherlands still make up the largest number of police contacts, followed by Moroccans and Antilleans. Expressed as a percentage of the number of their own ethnic group, Antilleans show by far the highest over-representation in police contacts, followed by Africans (Moroccans excluded), children from former Yugoslavia, Moroccans and Eastern Europeans. For girls, the ethnic composition is different. Antilleans, Surinamese and Yugoslavian girls show the largest over-representation, whereas Moroccan or Turkish girls hardly appear to get into trouble with the police.

Most criminological research is on the Antilleans, Moroccans, Surinamese and Turks. Of other ethnic groups of juvenile offenders, we still know very little. A recent study speaks of the 'shadowy worlds' and of a rising number of juveniles that get into trouble with the police from – in this ranking order – Russia, Congo, Sierra Leone, Angola, Somalia, Sudan, former Yugoslavia, Ethiopia and Eritrea, Iran and Iraq (Kromhout and van San, 2003). Specific attention is given to the fact that many of these children come from a situation of war and lawlessness, and have very unclear future expectations, partly due to the often long and uncertain asylum procedure. Though the study argues that specific measures have to be developed for these groups, the recommendations are not the strongest part of the research: it is all by and large in line with general policy plans on both juvenile delinquency and on immigration – or should we say expulsion?

'Persistent and Effective' includes a rather wide variety of preventative measures, mostly oriented at the domains of 1) family and upbringing, 2) social work and youth care, 3) health care, 4) school, and 5) sport. With respect to the latter two, specific attention is given to relations with friends and group-formation. There are also initiatives in the style of restorative justice and family conferencing. With respect to ethnic minorities, we can recognise most of the notions from the 1997 CRIEM-plan. Starting from the – questionable – hypothesis that their high crime rates are (partly) caused by failing to integrate into Dutch society, a far stronger focus is put on family and upbringing, on teaching minorities how to speak and write correct Dutch, and on social skills (basically less machismo and so-called 'defence of honour' and more talking).

The tone of the action programme *Jeugd Terecht* is rather different; less welfare-oriented and more driven by crime control. It argues that the discussion on causes of crime has made way for a discussion on risk factors. But it remains unclear how, first, such risk factors can actually be developed without aetiological studies, and second, whether all causes can be translated into risk factors. Let us just mention some concerns that are widely reported in the media – and on which there is some, albeit limited, research – that are hardly reflected in the policy plans on juvenile delinquency. First, there is the tendency of a dangerous radicalisation of some youth groups. Some young Muslims in the major Dutch cities have sought refuge in religious fanaticism – and terrorism – and some groups of white Dutch youth from the countryside have turned to neo-Nazism. Second, there is the subtle everyday racism and social exclusion non-whites are confronted with, and their (partly) related discrimination on the labour market. And third, youth culture appears marked by a new culture of narcissism, with swollen but unstable egos and very low frustration-tolerance levels (e.g. van den Brink, 2001). There is still little research on these issues and subsequently very few policy responses.

With respect to repression, the two 2002 policy plans devote a lot of attention to screening and risk assessment based mainly on the social inquiry reports of the Child Protection Board and the youth probation service. Again, ethnic minorities receive specific attention, as do structural and serious offenders. For both groups, special, intensive and coercive trajectories with a rehabilitative focus are developed – called respectively *ITB-CRIEM* and *ITB-Harde Kern* (Bosker and van der Klei, 2002).

Community sanctions: diversion, education and work

In the Netherlands, prosecutors can waive further prosecution if they feel this is in the public interest. Conditions can also be attached (*voorwaardelijk beleidssepot*). This form of diversion developed in a context in which, since the 1970s, community sanctions have been widely introduced in the Netherlands (van Swaaningen and uit Beijerse, 1993). Diversion in youth justice started much earlier and went much further than in adult criminal law. It is explicitly meant to protect the child against the stigma of court procedure and punishment. In cases of juvenile delinquency, the police are also given the discretion to dismiss a case conditionally.

This is also how, in 1981, HALT (a pun that indicates stopping offending, but is actually an abbreviation of 'the alternative') emerged. The idea of HALT first evolved from the Rotterdam public transport company that suffered from vandalism. Their idea was to put the perpetrators to work and let them clean and repair the bus-stops and trams they had vandalised. It gradually developed as a project of crime prevention. Soon after, HALT was adopted in other cities. From 11 HALT bureaus in 1987 it grew to 64 in the early 1990s. Though the number of HALT bureaus then stabilised, its use as a sanction increased from 1200 in 1987 to 11,000 in the early 1990s and to 21,000 in 1996. This expansion is partly due to the fact that a diversion to HALT has been made possible for a wider range of offences than just vandalism and graffiti. In the mid 1980s, it was also used in cases of arson and playing with fireworks, and since 1995 it has even been used for (petty) thefts. In 2003, only one-third of the diversions to HALT still concerned vandalism and graffiti, another third was for shoplifting and theft, and the rest concerned the use of fireworks, truancy and fights. HALT is only possible when the juvenile pleads guilty. It is often argued that this works to the disadvantage of those ethnic minorities in whose culture it would be 'not done' to admit that you have done anything wrong, but research shows this is merely a myth that is strategically used by some boys. In reality there is a large disparity in the effectiveness of HALT with respect to different groups, accountable mainly by the willingness of parents to collaborate. Surinamese mothers collaborate actively, whereas Moroccan mothers tend not to, favouring a more punitive approach. Politically HALT *must* be called a success, but the evaluation research is too superficial to prove that claim (Korf, 2003).

With the massive increase of diversions, HALT has also changed character. Initially it was intended to 'mirror' the infraction, repairing the damage created, but with such large numbers that is no longer possible. HALT can now also involve a 20 hour sanction that consists of either restoring the damage, or of paying for the damage that is done (only for offenders over 13) or of a measure with an educational purpose. The juvenile has to sign an agreement, and for 12 to 15 year olds their parents should too. If the agreement is not signed or if the juvenile has not fulfilled the task, the case is sent to the prosecutor, who then *must* prosecute.

At the prosecutorial level there are even wider possibilities to divert a case than at the level of the police. The prosecutor can, for example, caution a juvenile offender and add an agreement, in which the offender promises to do certain tasks. As with HALT, it depends on a guilty plea. The conditions the prosecutor can impose are wider than in HALT cases. They can include a six months period of supervision by the bureau for youth care, a youth probation order, or a community sanction consisting of work or education to a maximum of 40 hours. As well as the juvenile and their parents, the Child Protection Board is also present at the prosecutor's hearing. And, if it concerns a community sanction of more than 20 hours or a 'prosecutorial fine' (*transactie*) of more than 150 Euro, a defence lawyer is also present.

The prosecution service also takes the lead in the local multi-agency consultations on juvenile delinquency (*Justitieel Casusoverleg Jeugdcriminaliteit*) introduced in 2002. These consultations often take place in neighbourhood justice centres (*Justitie in de Buurt*). Neighbourhood justice centres were established in 1997 as an antenna of the prosecutor's office in 'problematic neighbourhoods', where security problems can be reported and (later) be addressed by multi-agency staff, with representatives of the Child Protection Board and victim support. There are 25 such offices now, all of them with a different style and goal. Yet it can be safely argued that in most cases little time is spent on discussing safety problems with community representatives, and neighbourhood justice is merely used as an efficiency measure to prevent an overload of court cases. Neighbourhood justice is yet another example of something that has been pushed through for political reasons, before any serious evaluation could be made. Without knowledge of practical implications and effects, it is also difficult to arrive at sensible policy recommendations.

The Child Protection Board needs to find a suitable community sanction for a juvenile offender and ensure that it is carried out. Community sanctions were developed in the early 1980s as an alternative to youth detention. The increased use of community sanctions is very high: in 1983 there were 300 community sanctions imposed, in 1990 there were 2,700. After the Van Montfrans report of 1994 its growth was even more rapid: from 4,400 community sanctions in 1995 to 12,000 in 2000 and 17,000 in 2003. Of all community sanctions 72% consist of work assignments, 21% educational measures and 7% a combination of the two. It is, however, doubtful whether the massive increase in diversions to HALT bureaus or to community sanctions also resulted in less children in court and in prison.

The expansion of juvenile detention

Whereas under adult criminal law, remand, prison sentences and hospital orders (*TBS*) are executed in different institutions, in youth justice all three take place in the same detention centre. Moreover, juveniles with a civil child protection measure are also placed in these same institutions. The number of places in youth detention centres has more than tripled over the last decade: from 700 in 1990 to 2,400 in 2003. Half of the population are offenders. Of these offenders, nearly half are there for psychiatric or psychological treatment (*PIJ*). The *PIJ* order takes at least two years and can be extended up to six years, even if the child has by then reached the age of majority. Of the remaining juvenile offenders, no less than 82% are on remand and only 18% are serving an actual prison sentence. The percentage of juveniles remanded in custody is far higher than in adult prisons. The explanation is that prison sentences in youth justice are still relatively short, so most time that is actually served is on remand, even if with hindsight it was actually the first part of a prison sentence. Because of this, new means to suspend remand under certain conditions are being developed.

The earlier mentioned intensive social skills trajectories for risk groups (ITB) is one of the most applied conditions. ITB involves supervision by the youth probation service for a period of between three to six months, in which parents are also obliged to participate. Based on the individual psycho-social problematic or 'risk factors', a scheme is drawn up in collaboration with the child and his parents, and a contract is signed in which the juvenile agrees to observe conditions like going to school, no disorderly behaviour, agreements on a curfew and restrictions of movement, and so on.

Because the imposition of youth detention exceeds the cell capacity, two dubious new Acts were passed in 2002 that affect the quality of youth justice. A new law on police cells makes it possible to prolong the period that can be spent at a police station by another 10 days – the law on youth detention centres only makes an exception for juveniles between 12 and 15 years old. Though it has not been widely applied, it is legally possible for 16 or 17 year olds to spend 16 days and 15 hours at a police station, in a cell which is little more than a 'cage' without any facilities. It was not so long ago that such a place was considered an unsuitable place for a juvenile for *any* period of time.

The second dubious act is the 2002 emergency law on drug traffickers, which is also applicable to 16 and 17 year olds. This law was the result of political turmoil about drug capsule-swallowers who were, for a lack of capacity, not remanded in custody, but simply deported after the confiscation of their drugs. This was felt to be unjustifiable by a political majority, and special detention centres, without any facilities or qualified staff, were established (Downes and van Swaaningen, 2006). In these drug detention centres, juveniles *are* incarcerated together with adults, and are deprived of their right to education.

The placement of 16 and 17 year olds together with adults is also possible for those juveniles who are tried according to adult criminal law. In 2004, 97 cells in adult prisons were occupied by juveniles – that is slightly more than the number of cells available in youth detention centres for those sentenced! Recently, capacity problems and budget cuts have led to some more radical changes in penal policy. First, two prisoners are placed in one cell – whereas one to a cell has always been the leading principle – and second, the time that can be spent outside of the cell has been reduced. These changes also affect youth detention centres. Yet, there is also some 'good news' with respect to rehabilitation. First, night detention has been introduced, which enables juveniles to go to school during daytime while serving their time, and second it has become possible to follow educational programmes and social skills training schemes *during* the last phase of one's sentence.

As we have seen above, the 2002 action programme *Jeugd Terecht* is a strong advocate of the incapacitation of structural offenders. The use of remand has been expanded. A new measure, modelled after the British Anti-Social Behaviour Orders, that is to be applied as a condition for suspension of the remand is still under discussion.

Though the main aim is clearly incapacitation, the detention of structural offenders should, according to policy rhetoric, also be for their re-education and rehabilitation. Two boarding-school-like institutions with rather unorthodox disciplinary techniques have received a lot of appraisal in this respect. The first of these – the Glen Mills School – was established in 1999 after an American model. It claims to appeal to the juveniles' own ideas of social status, group-hierarchy and group-norms. It is a private institution, where the Ministry of Justice 'buys' 100 places a year. Glen Mills claims high success rates, but the empirical data to support that claim are as yet not available (van der Laan, 2004). The second institution of this kind, called Den Engh, is a state institution, but uses different educational socio-group-strategies. By addressing the inmates as a group with mutual responsibilities, the boys learn to collaborate in a constructive way. As far as 'success' is concerned it is comparable with Glen Mills: high expectations, but as yet little evidence.

Conclusion

Despite many developments that support the argument, the thesis of a shift from penal welfarism to a culture of control cannot be wholly sustained with respect to youth justice in the Netherlands. It remains strongly inflected with social work values, and its core rationale remains that of rehabilitation and re-education. However, whereas some 25 years ago these aims were to be reached by diversion from prison, now rehabilitation and re-education are assumed to be deliverable in a closed setting. Moreover, at least two important elements have been added: 1) a strongly actuarial orientation at early intervention, based on (mainly psychological) risk factors, and 2) a strongly moralistic orientation towards norms, order and discipline. In some respects, this returns youth justice in the Netherlands to the original principles of youth detention of 1905.

Over the last 25 years, the population that the youth justice system has to deal with has undoubtedly become more diverse and more difficult. To some extent these changes in the population are reflected in changes in the system. But, there still are very few serious empirical studies into important recent social developments – such as the treatment of different migrant groups. Moreover, existing research into some (social) causes of juvenile delinquency is barely used in policy, because it cannot be translated into actuarial terms. Leaving aside the question as to whether inventories of 'best practice' will bring universal happiness, it is interesting to note that 'what works' criteria can hardly be applied in the Netherlands, because the quality of most of the (effect) evaluation research is simply not good enough for that. Moreover the managerial mission to keep costs as low as possible is likely to further cut into the basic care available for juveniles – and that may be the biggest threat for youth justice in the Netherlands; the danger that a dubious mixture of 'planning and control' chatter and moralistic parlance about discipline leave no room for creativity, commitment, care and children's rights.

References

Bartels, J. A. C. (2003) *Jeugdstrafrecht*. Deventer: Kluwer.

Bosker, J. and van der Klei, M. (2002) 'ITB harde kern, theorie en werkelijkheid, *Proces*', 81(1): 3–7.

Brink, G. van den (2001) *Geweld als uitdaging; de betekenis van agressief gedrag bij jongeren.* Utrecht: NIZW.

Downes, D. and van Swaaningen, R. (2006) 'The road to dystopia; changes in the penal climate in the Netherlands', in Michael Tonry and Catrien Bijleveld (eds) *Crime and Justice in the Netherlands.* Chicago: Chicago University Press.

Dorelijers, Th. A. H., van Domburg, L. et al. (2004) *Zeer jeugdige 'delinquenten' in Nederland; een zorgwekkende ontwikkeling? Pilotstudie naar de sociaal-demografische, ontwikkelingspsycho-(patho)logische en delictgerelateerde kenmerken van door de politie geregistreerde twaalf-minners.* Amsterdam: VU Medical Centre.

Garland, D. (2001) *The Culture of Control: Crime and Social Order in Contemporary Society.* Oxford: Oxford University Press.

Haan, W. de and Bovenkerk, F. (1995) 'Sociale integratie en criminaliteit', in: Gofried Engbersen en René Gabriëls (eds), *Sferen van integratie. Naar een gedifferentieerd allochtonenbeleid.* Meppel: Boom: pp. 223–248.

Jonge, G. de (1998) Het Nederlandse jeugdstraf(proces)recht en het IVRK: 't kan nog beter', *FJR* 20(1): 11–14.

Jonge, G. de and Van der Linden, A. P. (2004) *Jeugd and Strafrecht.* Deventer: Kluwer.

Korf, D. J. (2003) 'Hoe succesvol is Halt? Een beschouwing over recidive', in *Tijdschrift voor Criminologie,* 45(1): 17–34.

Kromhout, M. and van San, M. (2003) *Schimmige werelden; nieuwe etnische groepen en jeugd-criminaliteit.* Den Haag: BoomJu.

Laan, P. van der, Spaans, E. and Verhagen, J. (2004) De Glen Mills School onderzocht ... Over goede bedoelingen, hoge verwachtingen en een twijfelachtig rapport, *Delikt & Delinkwent,* 34(8): 809–825.

Leonards, C. (1995) *De ontdekking van het onschuldige criminele kind; bestraffing en opvoeding van criminele kinderen in jeugdgevangenis en opvoedingsgesticht 1833–1886.* Hilversum: Verloren.

Mijnarends, I. (2001) 'De betekenis van het Internationaal Verdrag inzake de Rechten van het Kind voor het Nederlandse jeugdstrafrecht', *FJR* 23(11): 302–307.

Slump, G.-J., Van Dijk, E., Klooster, E. and Rietveld, M. (2000) *Stop-reactie. Bereik, ervaringen en effecten tijdens het experimentele jaar*. The Hague: Ministerie van Justitie-Sdu.

Swaaningen, R. van and uit Beijerse, J. (1993) 'From punishment to diversion and back again: the debate on non-custodial sanctions and penal reform in the Netherlands', *The Howard Journal of Criminal Justice,* 32(2): 136–156.

Swaaningen, R. van (2005) 'Public safety and the management of fear', *Theoretical Criminology,* (3): 289–305.

Weerman, F. M. (2006) 'Dutch research on juvenile offending', in M. Tonry and C. Bijleveld (eds) *Crime and Justice in the Netherlands*. Chicago: Chicago University Press.

Consulted websites

http://www.dji.nl

http://www.halt.nl

http://www.justitie.nl/Images/nota_jeugdcriminaliteit_tcm74–39775.pdf

http://www.justitie.nl/Images/20021213_5201211b%20Actieprogramma%20aanpak%20jeugd
criminaliteit_tcm74–39772.pdf

http://www.raadvoordekinderbescherming.nl

http://www.wodc.nl

Demythologising Youth Justice in Aotearoa/New Zealand

6

Trevor Bradley, Juan Tauri*
and Reece Walters

Introduction

Youth justice in New Zealand represents a clear and practical example of the maxim 'what you see depends on where you stand'. Here, two broad coalitions of competing interests present contradictory claims about youth crime in pursuit of divergent but equally self-serving agendas. On the one hand, a loose conservative coalition of leading opposition politicians and citizen-based lobby groups paint a disturbing picture of 'youth crime out of control' and the 'youth justice system as a failure'. On the other hand, in stark contrast, a liberal coalition including youth court practitioners, juvenile justice researchers and policy analysts paint a more optimistic picture. Election campaigns typically provide a graphic illustration of these two divergent depictions of youth crime and their respective solutions. In 2005 an added dynamic was the competition between parliamentary members of the conservative coalition made up of the National, ACT,[1] New Zealand First and United Future parties, to provide the 'toughest' response to the 'spiralling problem of youth crime' (ACT, 2005). The National

---

* The views of the author are his own.
1. ACT is an abbreviation for Association of Consumers and Taxpayers.

Party, the main parliamentary opposition, proposed to reduce the age of criminal responsibility from 14 to 12, to reduce the use of diversion, to fast-track cases involving children over 12 to the Youth Court, and to introduce a 'yellow card system' where children who offend on two or more occasions would be automatically referred to court. Moreover, the proposal sought to follow Britain's example by 'holding parents accountable for the actions of their offspring' (see Brash, 2005; cf Espiner, 2005). For their part, ACT pledged to 'restore non-association orders as a routine consequence' for offenders, 'punish bad parents' and 'restore shame' as a key feature of the country's response to youth offending (ACT, 2005).

Such a law and order 'auction' among the conservative coalition reflects a growing ascendancy, particularly since the late 1990s, of a populist and authoritarian ideology. In the 1999 national referendum on law and order, over 92% of the voting public 'supported greater emphasis on the needs of victims ... imposing minimum sentences and hard labour for all serious, violent offences' (Karp and Aimer, 2002: 146–147). During the general election of 2002, according to pre-election 'issue' surveys, law and order and particularly violent crime were consistently placed as the number two 'substantive issue' of the campaign.[2] The Government, despite its history of support for more liberal approaches to 'law and order', has been at pains to demonstrate that it does and has, in fact, taken such demands very seriously. The incumbent Minister of Justice, for example, issued a press release in January 2005 in which he stated 'the government is delivering on its promise to take a tougher approach to crime ... offenders are getting longer jail terms and serving more of that sentence behind bars' (Goff, 2005: 1). The associated increase in prison sentences has necessitated a Government commitment to build at least four new prisons by 2007 (Goff, 2005: 2).

More specifically related to youth justice, the Government has not ruled out the National Party's suggestion of lowering the age of criminal responsibility from 14 to 12 (Espiner, 2005). There is a growing 'crisis' involving the use of police cells to detain young people in custody. Statistics released in late 2004 revealed that the number of young people being held in police custody, some for up to 12 nights, had increased from 447 in 2003 to 574 in 2004 (Bell, 2004: 4). This situation has been described by the Principal Youth Court Judge as 'intolerable in a civilised society' (Bell, 2004: 4). In response the Government announced plans to expand the detention capacity of the youth justice system with the construction of at least two new youth justice 'residences' in 2005 (Awhi Mai, 2005: 6).

Youth Court data also suggests a less tolerant and more punitive attitude on the part of New Zealand Police. Maxwell and Popplewell (2003: 15), for example, provide data which indicates a clear trend towards increased referrals to the Youth Court by Police for offences of moderate seriousness. In confirmation,

---

2. Law and order were placed ahead of education, tax policy, superannuation and the Treaty of Waitangi (see James, 2003: 51).

Spier and Lash (2004: 157) note that 2003 saw 4,315 prosecuted cases involving young offenders, 'the highest number recorded in a decade'. Statistics on conviction and sentencing of young offenders also show that the proportion of proved cases resulting in Youth Court supervision orders, including 'supervision with residence', had increased from 32% in 1997 to almost 40% in 2003 (Spiers and Lash, 2004: 158).

A significant outcome of this sustained politicisation has been that New Zealand, a country renowned for its progressive youth justice system because of the leading role it played in developing restorative justice through family group conferencing (see Braithwaite and Mugford, 1994; O'Connor, 1997), now confronts a growing political challenge to its previously dominant 'liberalism'.[3] The liberal coalition, particularly those members with a 'hands on' involvement in youth justice, has been forced to issue a constant stream of denials and defences. It has made regular appeals to the empirical 'evidence' provided by research on the effectiveness of the 'system' (see Becroft, 2004; Kingi and Robertson, 2003; Kingi et al., 2003; Maxwell, 2004). Judge Becroft, the incumbent Principal Youth Court Judge, for example, has resorted to the use of media releases and a Youth Court publication – 'Court in the Act'[4] – to present 'the real picture' on youth crime (Becroft, 2004: 1). In contrast to the picture painted by opposition politicians and citizen based lobby groups such as the 'Sensible Sentencing Trust', youth crime has remained remarkably stable despite a sizeable increase in the population of 10 to 16 year olds. Between 1995 and 2003, while police apprehension increased by 5.3%, the total population in that age group increased by more than 14%. Becroft (2004: 10) further points out that youth offending has 'stabilised in the past five to eight years ... has increased no more than total offending and, for the last 14 years, has remained constantly at about 22% of overall offending'. It is, therefore, not possible to reconcile the claims that youth crime is 'rampant' or 'out of control' with the empirical evidence.

One of the most startling features of youth crime in New Zealand is the disproportionate representation of Maori. According to data presented by Statistics New Zealand (2004), of the 41,454 apprehensions of young people between the ages of 10 to 16 in 2004 almost 50% were Maori. This has been a consistent feature of youth crime since the early 1990s even though, according to the 2001 Population Census (Statistics New Zealand, 2002), only 21% of the population in this age group were Maori. In addition, in some locations such as Rotorua, young Maori and Pacific Islanders comprise a staggering 90% of all Youth Court appearances (see Becroft, 2004: 10).

---

3. At the time of writing (April 2005), figures from the Department of Corrections reveal that the New Zealand prison population has reached an all time high of 7,000 inmates.

4. 'Court in the Act' is an internal youth court publication originally designed for youth court judges. However, more recently it has been used to promote the activities of the juvenile justice system (see Becroft, 2004: 1).

Youth justice in New Zealand

The operations of the youth justice system in New Zealand are governed by the Children, Young Persons and their Families Act 1989. However, before its enactment child and young offenders were dealt with under the provision of the Children and Young Persons Act 1974. Due largely to its founding principle – 'the interests of the child or young person as the first and paramount consideration' – the 1974 Act, according to a Ministerial Review Team (1992: 8) represented the 'apotheosis' of the welfare approach to youth justice. The 1974 legislation introduced three key innovations: it legally distinguished children (0 to 14) and young persons or juveniles (14 to 17); it formalised diversion for child offenders through the establishment of Children's Boards;[5] and took steps to reform the Children's Court (Watt, 2003: 10–11).

Moreover, it prescribed different approaches for child and juvenile offenders. Defining the legal age of criminal responsibility as 10, it stated that no child (under 14) would be subject to criminal prosecution unless for charges of murder or manslaughter. Such offenders would appear in the Children and Young Person's Court (which replaced the Children's Court) only through proceedings brought against their parents on the grounds that the child was in need of 'care and protection'. The Act aimed to divert child offenders from court appearances whenever possible.

The enthusiasm accompanying the passing of the 1974 Act, which signalled the end of the 50 year Child Welfare Act 1925, was soon displaced by criticisms of its welfare-based, open-ended sanctions and the number of inappropriate, stigmatising arrests of young people. At the same time it was also recognised that many young offenders were not the victims of particular social or family problems or other 'pathologies'. A significant consequence of this recognition was a perceived lack of 'accountability' for young offenders. As a result, holding all offenders 'accountable' subsequently formed a major objective of the 1989 Act and has since become a mantra of criminal justice in New Zealand. With the above criticisms exacerbated by an apparent inability to reduce aggregate rates of juvenile offending, and a perceived failure to deal effectively with persistent offenders, New Zealand experienced a loss of faith in the 'welfare model' (Department of Social Welfare, 1984; Ministerial Review Team, 1992).

Beyond these criticisms, Watt (2003: 12–15) has identified three other major sources of concern, each of which was specifically addressed by the successor 1989 Act. The first included police reluctance to utilise diversion. As Morris and Young (1987: 124) noted, police had no 'confidence in the diversionary systems' preferring instead to arrest and prosecute, thus subverting the principle of the 'court as last resort'. A further criticism, and one that has also been levelled in relation to the 1989 Act, was that diversionary procedures introduced a 'net-widening'

---

5. Children's Boards were 'informal community hearings' that attempted to avoid court appearances for young offenders (see Watt, 2003: 11).

effect, which formalised a previously informal mode of processing petty offenders. Related to the 'undue-reliance on court procedures' (Watt, 2003: 14), and the police preference to side-step the Children's Boards, the second major source of concern was the failure to involve offenders and victims. The third, and perhaps the most intractable problem, included dissatisfaction with the mono-cultural nature of the 1974 Act. Examples of this were the contradictions between its adversarialism and Maori practices of justice, and the virtual exclusion of whanua, hapu and iwi[6] from the consultation process. Moreover, a 1987 review of the Children and Young Person's Bill (1987: 9) recognised that the governing principle of the 1974 Act – 'the interests of the child or young person shall be first and paramount consideration' – ignored the vital role played by whanau, hapu and iwi[7] in the life of the child/young person. More generally, and measured by the disproportionate rate of Maori arrest and conviction, it was clearly apparent that young Maori were alienated and discriminated against in the justice system. According to a 1986 report to the Minister of Justice, 'the present system is ... completely ignoring the cultural systems of the Maori and breaking down completely that system, completely alienating the Maori ... leaving them at the whim of the system' (cited in Watt, 2003: 15). Despite the introduction of the 1989 Act, this issue continues to be of significant concern.

The 1974 Act not only failed to meet the needs of Maori, and other ethnic minorities such as Pacific Island Peoples, but was also seen to be perpetuating systemic bias and reducing practitioner confidence. Coinciding with more general calls by Maori for tino rangatiratanga (sovereignty, sovereign power and status) or arikitanga (Chieftanship) demands were made for an autonomous form of Maori justice. In spite of such demands, and a later Department of Justice commissioned report that strongly recommended a 'separate' system of justice for Maori (Jackson, 1988); the best that was delivered to Maori, in our view, was an 'indigenised' European system (see Tauri, 1998, and later discussion in this chapter).

A new paradigm of justice: the Children, Young Person's and their Families Act 1989

The Children, Young Person's and their Families Act 1989 took four years from review to inception, and indicating the level and strength of opposition to various aspects of it, the preceding Bill went through two Government working parties and was the subject of over 900 submissions (Wittman, 1995). The passing of the Act, according to an early process-based evaluation, introduced 'a new

---

6. The closest English translation of these Maori words are family, sub-tribe or clan and tribe, although it is important to note that 'these words carry additional meaning relating to the way Maori society functions and the role these basic kinships play in social organisation' (see Kingi and Robertson, 2003: 3).

7. For example, Lovell and Norris (1992) found that young Maori were six times more likely to come to official police attention than non-Maori.

paradigm of youth justice' (Morris and Maxwell, 1993: 1). In introducing an approach 'unprecedented in the English speaking world' (Kingi and Robertson, 2003: 3) the 1989 Act 'revolutionised' youth justice proceedings in New Zealand (Shipley, 1993). The Act laid out statutory principles and for the first time separated cases of youth justice from care and protection.

Referring equally to both youth justice and care and protection, Kingi and Robertson (2003: 3) note that the Act provided a series of general principles that emphasise the need to:

- involve family, whanua, hapu and iwi in decision-making processes;
- strengthen and maintain child/family relationships;
- consider the wishes of the child or young person;
- obtain the support of the child or young person.

Specific youth justice principles were set out in section 208 of the Act including:

- Criminal proceedings should not be used if there are alternative means.
- Criminal proceedings should not be used for welfare purposes.
- Young people should be kept in the community as far as possible.
- Measures to deal with young offenders ought to strengthen the family, whanua, hapu, iwi and other family groups and foster their own skills to deal with offending by their young people.
- Sanctions should be the least restrictive as possible and promote juvenile development.
- Due regard should be given to the interests of the victim (see also Kingi and Robertson, 2003: 4; Maxwell, 2004: 5–7; Watt, 2003: 26–27).

It was generally hoped that the 1989 Act would not only introduce a more 'culturally appropriate' law, but would also act to *de-emphasise, de-dramatise* and ultimately *de-politicise* the issue of 'youth crime'.

Pathways through the new paradigm

Maxwell and Morris (1993: 8) argue that the intention of the 1989 Act is to encourage the police to adopt low key responses to juvenile offending and emphasise diversion from courts and custody. Minor offenders, particular first time offenders, are therefore expected to be 'diverted' from the system and only the most serious offenders are to be charged and appear in the Youth Court or, in extremely serious cases, made to appear in the District Court. The following section (and Figure 6.1 on page 87) provides a thorough description of the 'pathways through the system'.

Informal and formal warnings

In the New Zealand system the police are empowered to deal unilaterally with the offender and to take no action other than issuing an informal verbal warning. The precise number of young people dealt with by means of an informal, 'on the spot', verbal warning administered by police officers is not recorded and as such is unknown. If the offending is more serious, the young person can be referred to a specialist 'Youth Aid' section of police. Youth Aid officers then decide whether to issue a 'formal' written warning (or verbal warning in presence of parents) or arrange to 'formally' divert the young person away from the system which often involves making an apology to the victim, making a 'donation' to charity, or carrying out some work in the community. 44% of all cases of youth offending referred to police youth aid are dealt with by issuing a formal written warning. Once a formal warning has been issued, the young person is 'released' and exits the system. This practice is in keeping with a major principle of the 1989 Act that young offenders should be diverted from the formal justice system wherever possible. It also reflects the fact that the great majority of youth offending is relatively minor and does not warrant any further response.

Diversion

If a warning is thought to be insufficient, then, under section 208(a) of the Act, police are obliged to consider some form of diversionary programme. Approximately 32% of all offences are dealt with by diversion (or 'alternative action' as it is sometimes referred to). Administered by the Youth Aid section of the New Zealand Police, diversion is locally based and often involves some interaction with or work for the community (see Maxwell et al., 2002: 60–73). Police enjoy considerable discretion and autonomy when formulating such 'diversionary plans' or 'alternative action', although there is an expectation that in developing the plan, police will consult with both the offender and his/her family, and sometimes the victim (see Maxwell, 2004: 6). There are, however, certain objectives that diversionary plans are meant to achieve or at least contribute to. These include responses that satisfy victims, prevent re-offending and re-integrate young people into their communities (see Maxwell et al., 2002).

Research conducted on the practice of Police Youth Aid diversion by Maxwell et al. (2002: 60–73) studied 560 cases and revealed that the 'diversionary plan' consists of the following:

- Apologies to the victim (n = 335; 65%)
- Reparation (n = 108; 21%)
- Work in the Community (n = 171; 33%)
- Attending a programme (n = 98; 19%)
- Curfew (or other restriction) (n = 55; 11%)
- Donations (n = 20; 4%)
- Other (n = 75; 15%)

Clearly, the most prevalent component of Police youth diversionary plans was an apology to the victim, with written apologies rather than apologies in person being the most common (Maxwell et al., 2002: 60). It is interesting to note that despite the Act insisting on the 'least restrictive' measure, over 10% of the sample in the above study had curfews imposed. These included a night time curfew for over half, a 'family grounding' for another one in ten, while one in five involved non-associations with other specified young people. Included among the 'other' category, and which accounted for 15% of the sample cases, were essays, a tour of police cells, and good behaviour 'contracts'.

Pre-charge family group conferences

A more serious option for offenders that have not been arrested, but whom police intend to charge, is for youth aid officers, after consultation with 'youth justice co-ordinators'[8] and the victim(s), to refer the young person to a Family Group Conference (FGC). This is known as a 'pre-charge FGC' (Maxwell, 2004: 2) and is used as a mechanism to avoid prosecution. Approximately 8% of all 'serious' offenders coming to official notice (i.e. entering and being dealt within, as opposed to being diverted from the system) will be directly referred to an FGC by the police. Pre-charge FGCs account for almost half of all youth justice FGCs.

Typically, all those involved will formulate a 'plan' for the young person to complete. If it is satisfactorily completed this will usually be the end of the matter and the young person will exit the system. Alternatively, depending upon the seriousness of the offence and the offending history of the young person, the FGC may recommend that a charge be laid or, if the FGC plan is not completed, then a charge may be laid in the Youth Court.

Post-charge and 'court ordered' family group conferences

If the offending is regarded as serious enough, and after consultations with youth justice co-ordinators, charges are laid in the Youth Court. Those that are charged, and who do not 'deny' the charges, are referred to an FGC. This is known as a 'post-charge FGC' or a 'court-ordered FGC'. It is a mechanism used to determine how to deal with cases 'proved' in the Youth Court. Cases are 'proved', not via a trial process which can be stigmatising and thus counter-productive to the aims of the Act, but it simply refers to the fact that an offender does not 'deny' the charges. The 1989 Act insists that for each and every offender that appears before the Youth Court, and who does not deny the charges, the court must direct that an FGC be held. Once the FGC has been convened and a set of recommendations issued to the offender, the Youth Court then decides whether the implementation of the plan is a sufficient 'sanction'. Further sanctions

---

8. Youth justice co-ordinators are employed by the Department of Child, Youth and Family Services.

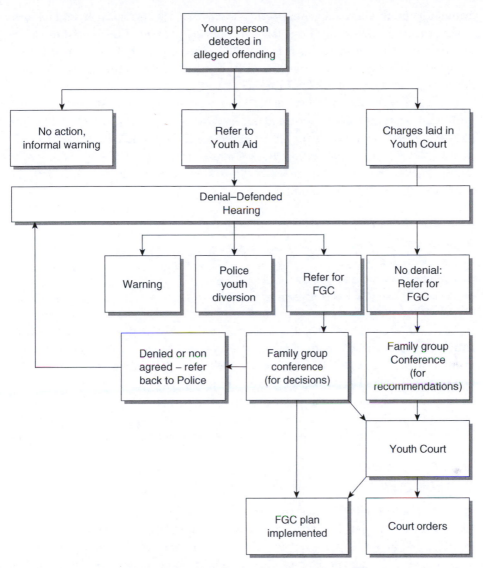

Figure 6.1 Pathways through the New Zealand Youth Justice system

Source: Kingi and Robertson 2003.

or 'court orders' are typically applied only when the FGC recommendations or 'plan' are not successfully completed (see Kingi and Robertson, 2003; Maxwell, 2004; cf Morris et al., 2003).

In 16% of cases, young offenders are referred directly to the Youth Court either as a result of an arrest, or following an 'unsuccessful' pre-charge FGC. If the charge is 'not denied' then an FGC must be convened. Around 98% of charges are 'not denied'. If the charge is 'admitted' at the FGC, then the conference will usually formulate a plan in which the young person is held 'accountable' for the offending. It should be formulated to prevent further offending and to allow the young person to develop in a 'socially beneficial way' without further offending. The plan will then be presented to the Youth Court, and in about 95% of the cases it is accepted. The case is then adjourned for the plan to be completed. Once satisfactorily completed the young person is often discharged under section 282 of the Act.

The number of 'youth justice' FGCs has remained relatively stable since 1995 with approximately 7,000 convened every year (Awhi Mai, 2005: 6). There has, however, been an increase in 'court directed' FGCs since 1998 (Ministry of Justice, 2002) which may reflect the increased referrals of young offenders to Youth Court by police. In common with 'diversionary plans', FGC 'plans' typically consist of the following elements:

- Apology to the Victim
- Reparation
- Community work
- Participation in a relevant programme
- Counselling (drug/alcohol or anger management)

If, however, a charge is denied, the matter is the subject of a defended hearing and is conducted in the normal adversarial manner as for adults, under the provisions of the Summary Proceedings Act 1957. If the charge is dismissed, the young person is free to go. If it is 'proved', then an FGC must be convened to consider sentencing options. The Youth Court will impose one of the orders set out in section 283 of the Act (see below) or, in some cases may grant an absolute discharge under section 282, whereby the charge is deemed never to have been laid.

The Youth Court

When young offenders appear before the Youth Court and have had the case against them 'proved', the Court can impose a number of 'orders'. In line with the desire to avoid stigmatising the offender, and thus inadvertently contribute to further offending, the language of 'guilty' or 'not guilty' and 'sentence' or 'punishment' is avoided. Instead, 'proved' or 'not proved' and 'court order' are the preferred terms.

Once a charge is proved, under section 283 of the Act, the Youth Court can impose a wide range of 'formal orders' on the offender. These include:

- Discharge (with a record of the charge remaining on the young person's history for use in future proceedings).
- Admonishment (carried out by the Judge in Court, and seldom used).
- An order for the offender to come up for further action if called on. In effect, this gives the Youth Court the power to recall a young person at any time in the 12 months following the making of the order if there is any further offending.

- Contribution to costs.
- Fine.
- Reparation.
- Restitution.
- Forfeiture of property.
- Disqualification from driving.
- Confiscation of a motor vehicle.
- Supervision (usually by Child, Youth and Family Services (CYFS).
- Community work.
- Supervision with activity.
- Supervision with residence (where the young person is detained for up to 3 months in a secure residence operated by CYFS, followed by a 6 month period of supervision).
- Conviction and transfer to the District Court for sentence (where a conviction is entered and the young person is transferred to the adult Courts where he or she may be subject to any sentence available in adult proceedings for the same offence.

A critical discussion of Youth Justice in New Zealand

Advocates of the 'new' paradigm of youth justice in New Zealand, particularly the FGC process, often display an almost religious-like faith in its 'healing' properties. For example, in what may be read by 'outsiders' as a sermon to parishioners, an editorial in a practitioners journal by the Principle Youth Court judge urged readers to 'hang onto *our* Act ...we must remember the "magic" of the Family Group Conference' (Becroft, 2002: 2, emphasis added). Relaying a conversation with FGC co-ordinators, he endorsed the suggestion that they 'view themselves as "kaitiaki" (guardians) of the FGC, and to ensure that the FGC and the [1989] Act are treated with respect' (Becroft, 2002: 2).

FGCs are indeed a formal and institutionalised aspect of the youth justice system in New Zealand and a routine component of both Youth Court and police youth aid procedures. For those offenders that do progress into the 'system' proper (i.e. beyond informal and formal warnings and diversion), the FGC process has become the 'lynchpin' of that system. Over 7,000 FGCs are convened each year. Regardless of whether an FGC is convened as a 'pre' or 'post' charge mechanism, they are a prescribed and mandatory component of the youth justice process.

A restorative process?

The core claim emanating from advocates of the new paradigm revolves around the 'restorative' properties of the FGC process and the Act in general. It is this 'restorative' aspect of youth justice in New Zealand which has attracted so much international acclaim and attention. It is interesting to note, then, that this particular feature was an addition to, rather than an original element of, the 1989 Act. That is, nowhere among the stated principles or aims and objectives of the 1989 Act are there any references to 'restorative justice' or restorative processes. FGCs have been belatedly identified as a restorative process. One of New Zealand's foremost youth justice researchers, and a strong and public advocate of restorative justice, has recently acknowledged this, stating: 'it is *now* recognised as the first formal adoption ... in any country of a system based on restorative principles and practice' Maxwell (2004: 1, emphasis added). Others have simply stated that the 1989 Act was the 'first legislated example of a restorative justice approach' (Kingi and Robertson, 2003: 4).

More substantial questions surround the extent to which FGCs have achieved restorative outcomes. The results of a large scale New Zealand study designed to identify factors associated with effective outcomes in the youth justice system, for example, have shown that a large number of victims never attend FGCs and that of those that do many felt uninvolved in the decision-making process. Thus Maxwell et al. (2004: 249) report that in their 'retrospective sample,'[9] in those cases where an identifiable victim was involved, just 48% of the victims or their representatives attended the FGC. In the smaller prospective study only 58% of victims or their representatives attended. The authors acknowledge that 'the figure for victims falls well short of what might be hoped for in a system designed to be inclusive of them'. It is interesting to note that the Maxwell et al. study found that the most frequently offered reason for non-attendance was that victims simply did not want to meet the offender (2004: 249).

Throwing further doubt on the extent to which the FGC achieved a restorative outcome for the victim was that of those victims that did attend FGCs only half reported that they felt involved in the decision-making, including the design of the FGC 'plan' (Maxwell et al., 2004: 249). Stenning has recently pointed out that the 'outcomes' of FGCs 'too frequently involve more or less passive acquiescence by participants in agreements that have actually been proposed by facilitators and police, rather than ... a product of genuine input of conference participants' (2004: 14). It is clear then that a great many victims were neither 'restored' nor 'empowered' by the FGC process. Stenning (2004: 14) also reminds that 'advocates of family group conferencing usually maintain that victims are the most significant beneficiaries' but that their lack of attendance and meaningful participation 'can hardly be considered very encouraging'. In spite of the 'restorative' aims of the system, the Maxwell et al. (2004: 249) study has meant that these authors, along with advocates more generally, now have to recognise that 'victims may not always be part of the process'.

---

9. The research comprised three main studies; a retrospective, a prospective and a Maori and Pacific Island study (see Maxwell et al., 2004: 22).

A culturally sensitive and empowering process?

Advocates of FGCs make a number of significant claims about its 'appropriateness' for dealing with offending and victimisation involving Maori youth and other ethnic groups, in particular Pacific Island peoples. One common claim is that the forum was created, in part, as a response to growing Maori criticisms of the criminal justice system (see Hassell, 1996). For example, Olsen et al. (1995) argue that the FGC process was a 'successful attempt by the state to culturally sensitise the youth justice system'. Similarly, Ormsby (1998: 20) argues that the significant influence Maori criticisms of the criminal justice system had on the development of the FGC forum, is reflected in the fact that it is designed to heal the damage caused by an offender's actions, encourage the participation of family, restore harmony between those affected by offending behaviour (Maxwell and Morris, 1993), empower the victim (LaPrairie, 1995) and positively 'reintegrate' participants back into the community (Stewart, 1996).

Thus far, the empirical record suggests otherwise. Evaluation of the FGC process in the 1990s (see Maxwell and Morris, 1993, and Olsen et al., 1995) reported that although more Maori than Pakeha FGCs were held at the offender's home; marae, or community-based equivalents were rarely used (in only 5% of cases). In contrast Social Welfare premises were used for 54% of Maori FGC's (Maxwell and Morris, 1993). Researchers attributed the choice of venue more to the convenience of the public service officials involved than to the wishes of the offender, the victim, their families or the community (see Ormsby, 1999).

Furthermore, the emphasis on the 'informal' aspects of the FGC process and features of the 1989 Act, tend to ignore the reality of who is in 'charge' of the principal mechanisms of the 'system', namely the Police, Youth Justice Co-ordinators, Social Workers, Advocates, and the like. In their large-scale study of youth justice 'outcomes' in New Zealand, for example, Maxwell et al. (2004: 298) found that 'conference decisions did not always reflect true consensus and questions were raised about the extent to which, at times, professionals dominated decision-making'. Maori expertise and approaches continue to be of secondary importance to the process (see also Tauri, 1999). The authors write that 'detail of particular (Maori) elders' involvement in facilitation were not usually available for the retrospective cases but that all the [FGC] co-ordinators who took part in this study reported that they did not normally delegate this role to anyone else although some reported asking elders to perform a mihi (greeting) or a karakia (prayer)' (Maxwell et al., 2004: 82). It would appear then, that the claims of FGC advocates, that the process empowers Maori participants, may be exaggerated. Instead, the empirical record shows that the process exhibits characteristics of a common justice sector response to Maori offending and to Maori concerns. That is, they reflect a tendency to 'utilise' specific features of Maori culture and practice, those required to fulfil the types of tasks (opening and closing prayers) that underline the 'cultural responsiveness' of the system, and that pose little threat to the states domination of the youth justice system (Tauri, in Walters and Bradley, 2005).

Maori concerns can be summarised as follows: an over-emphasis on the individual rather than the collective when attempting to identify the causes of criminal behaviour (Tauri, 1999); an over-reliance on punitive processes and sanctions that prohibits the restoration of individual self-worth and communal harmony (Webb, 2004); and the institutionally racist nature of the current system, reflected in its inability to acknowledge and appropriately support Maori conflict resolution practices (Jackson, 1988). Further, the Maori critique of the FGC process extends beyond the symbolic utilisation of their cultural practices. Maori commentators argue that while the use of specific features of Maori culture may signify the ability of the youth justice system to be 'cultural responsive', the potency of this response is diluted by the fact that Maori are provided little control over the way Maori youth offending is dealt with (Tauri, 2004). Instead, Maori commentators such as Webb (2004) and Tauri (1999, 2004) argue that the FGC process represents a continuation of the strategies of 'biculturalisation' and 'co-option' that have dominated the criminal justice system's response to Maori concerns over the past ten years.

The biculturalisation and co-option strategies involve the selective utilisation of elements of Maori culture designed to make the criminal justice system more culturally appropriate. However, divorced from processes that enable Maori to control the way their offenders and victims are dealt with, as some argue is their right under the Treaty of Waitangi, the co-optive strategy is designed more to appease Maori concerns by utilising 'acceptable' aspects of 'their' cultural system (Tauri, 1996; cf Sissons, 1990). In the process, co-option enables the 'biculturalisation' of criminal justice practice whereby Maori cultural traditions are rationalised, 'broken down and utilised in departmental practice to enable the state sector to signify its commitment to biculturalism and, therefore, to Maori' (Tauri, 1999: 4).

The use of biculturalisation and co-option in support of increasing the cultural responsiveness of government practice is pronounced in the criminal justice sector. These policies are distinguishable from so-called 'mainstream' programmes because elements of indigenous (Maori) cultural philosophy and practice are 'added-on', with a view of making them more responsive to indigenous offenders and their communities (Tauri, 1999). As with the greater majority of criminal justice policy, Western theoretical frameworks inform the design and delivery of the programmes (Webb, 2004). What the Maori critique highlights is that while forums such as the FGC may utilise elements of cultural practice, this does not automatically make them appropriate for or effective in dealing with indigenous offending. For example, some Maori commentators believe little will change until the criminal justice system allows Maori communities to take control of their own offenders and victims by integrating their own systems of justice (Nga Kaiwhakamarama I Nga Ture, 1999).

Conclusion

The growing 'moral clampdown' in New Zealand (epitomised by prison building, increases in the use of custody and a rise of surveillance) represents a growing challenge to previously dominant liberal approaches. The potential inherent in FGCs for a genuine 'empowerment' of all participants, 'culturally sensitive and appropriate' practice, restorative outcomes and increased informalism, are all jeopardised by the recent hyper-politicisation of youth crime. This has led leading penal commentators to now refer to New Zealand as the 'abusive society' (see Pratt, 2002).

The New Zealand FGC model has received international attention for its innovation and restorative principles. We endorse such innovations but suggest that its proposed 'successes' and 'failures' have been exaggerated and not adequately demonstrated by either side of the politicised debate. As Robertson (2005: 10) argues: 'In youth justice, New Zealand's Family Group Conferencing was, and still to a large extent is, unique. "Does it work – can it reduce offending?", to which we can only give a qualified answer. Can we assess "what works" in reducing offending in New Zealand? My answer would have to be – "with difficulty".'

In our view youth justice initiatives in New Zealand must facilitate the cultural empowerment of Maori and other ethnic minorities, in order to overcome the paternalistic demonstrations of co-option and indigenisation that characterise the system at present. Added to this, the system needs to enhance participants' ability to achieve the reparative and restorative outcomes supposedly inherent in the 1989 Act and the FGC process, before success can be claimed. To that extent, the New Zealand model has some way to go.

References

ACT New Zealand (2005) 'A Youth Justice Checklist from ACT', Press release, 21 March. Wellington: ACT New Zealand.

Awhi Mai (2005) 'Building Youth Justice South', Newsletter, Issue 3 – March. Wellington: Department of Child, Youth and Family Services.

Becroft, A. (2004) 'Youth Justice – The New Zealand Experience: Past lessons and future challenges', paper presented for the Australian Institute of Criminology Juvenile Justice Conference, 1–2 December 2003.

Bell, L. (2004) 'Police No Place for Youth – Judge', The Dominion Post, 7 December, p. 4.

Brash, D. (2005) 'Saving a Generation of Young People', National Party Leader, Youth Justice Policy Launch, 21 March.

Braithwaite, J. and Mugford, S. (1994) 'Conditions of Successful Reintegration Ceremonies', British Journal of Criminology (34): 139–171.

Department of Social Welfare (1984) 'Review of Children and Young Persons Legislation: Public Discussion Paper'. Wellington: Department of Social Welfare.

Espiner, C. (2005) 'MPs Take on Child Offenders', *The Press,* 22 March, p. 3.

Goff, P. (2005) 'Tougher Laws and Better Policing Pushing up Jail Numbers', Press Release, 23 January. Office of the Minister of Justice, Wellington: Ministry of Justice.

Hassell, I. (1996) 'Origin and Development of Family Group Conferences', in J. Hudson, A. Morris, G. Maxwell and B. Galaway (eds) *Family Group Conferences: Perspectives on Policy and Practice.* Leichardt: The Federation Press.

Jackson, M. (1988) *Maori and the Criminal Justice System: He Whaipaanga Hou: A New Perspective.* Wellington: Department of Justice.

James, C. (2003) 'Two Million Voters in Search of a Rationale', in J. Boston, S. Church, S. Levine, E. McLeay and N. Roberts (eds) *New Zealand Votes: The General Election of 2002.* Wellington: Victoria University Press.

Karp, J. and Aimer, J. (2002) 'Direct Democracy on Trial: Citizens-Initiated Referendums', in J. Vowles, P. Aimer, J. Karp, S. Banducci, R. Miller and A. Sullivan (eds) *Proportional Representation on Trial.* Auckland: Auckland University Press.

Kingi, V. and Robertson, J. (2003) 'Achieving Effective Outcomes in Youth Justice: a New Zealand Study', paper presented at the Australasian Evaluation Society Conference, 16–18 September.

Kingi, V., Morris, A., Maxwell, G., and Robertson, J. (2003) 'The Effectiveness of the New Zealand Youth Justice System: Diverting young people from courts and custody', unpublished paper presented at the Triennial District Court Judges Conference held on 1–4 April, Rotorua.

LaPraire, C. (1995) 'Altering Course: New Directions in Criminal Justice', *Australian and New Zealand Journal of Criminology* (special supplementary issue), 78–99.

Maxwell, G. (2004) 'Youth Justice: A Research Perspective', *Social Work Now,* 28, August, 4–10.

Maxwell, G. and Morris, A. (1993) *Families, Victims and Culture: Youth Justice in New Zealand.* Wellington: GP Print for Social Policy Agency Ropu Here Kaupapa and Institute of Criminology, Victoria University of Wellington.

Maxwell, G. and Poppelwell, E. (2003) *Youth Court Offending Rates: Final Report.* Wellington: Crime and Justice Research Centre, Victoria University.

Maxwell, G. Robertson, J. and Anderson, T. (2002) *Police Youth Diversion: Final Report.* Wellington: New Zealand Police/Ministry of Justice and Crime and Justice Research Centre Victoria University of Wellington.

Ministerial Review Team (1992) 'Report of the Ministerial Review Team', Minister of Social Welfare Hon. Jenny Shipley. Auckland.

Ministry of Justice (2002) *Youth Offending Strategy: Preventing and Reducing Offending and Re-offending by Children and Young People.* Wellington: Ministry of Justice/Ministry of Social Development.

Morris, A. and Maxwell, G. (1993) *Families, Victims and Culture: Youth Justice in New Zealand.* Wellington: Institute of Criminology and Social Policy Agency.

Morris, A. and Maxwell, G. (eds.) (1999) *Youth Justice in Focus – Conference Proceedings.* Wellington: Victoria University of Wellington.

Morris, A. and Young, W. (1987) 'Juvenile Justice in New Zealand: Policy and Practice', *Study Series 1,* Wellington: Institute of Criminology.

Nga Kaiwhakamarama I Nga Ture (ed.) (1999) 'Maori and the Criminal Justice System: Ten Years On'. Conference proceedings from the Maori and the Criminal Justice System Hui, July 1998, Wellington.

O'Connor, I. (1997) 'Models of Juvenile Justice', in A. Borowski and I. O'Connor (eds.) *Juvenile Crime Justice and Corrections.* South Melbourne: Addison Wesley Longman.

Olsen, T., Maxwell, G. and Morris, A. (1995) 'Maori and Youth Justice in New Zealand', in K. Hazelhurst (ed.) *Popular Justice and Community Regeneration*. London: Praeger. pp. 89–102.

Ormsby, M. (1998) 'Maori Tikanga and Criminal Justice: Modification of the New Zealand Criminal Justice System to Admit Maori Tikanga', unpublished paper.

Pratt, J. (2002) 'The Abusive Society: A Review Essay', *The Australian and New Zealand Journal of Criminology*, 35(3): 383–402.

Robertson, J. (2005) 'Evaluating offending outcomes for young offender programmes', unpublished paper.

Shipley, J. (1993) 'Foreword', in A. Morris and G. Maxwell (eds.) *Families, Victims and Culture: Youth Justice in New Zealand*. Wellington: Institute of Criminology and Social Policy Agency.

Sissons, J. (1990) 'The Future of Biculturalism in Aotearoa New Zealand', in J. Morss (ed.) *Social Science and the Future in New Zealand*. Dunedin: University of Otago Press. pp. 15–24.

Spier, P. and Lash, B. (2004) *Conviction and Sentencing of Offenders in New Zealand: 1994 to 2003*. Wellington: Ministry of Justice.

Statistics New Zealand (2004) 'New Zealand Recorded Crime Statistics: National Calendar year Apprehension Statistics'. http://www.stats.govt.nz/products-and-services/table-builder/crime-statistics/default.htm.

Stenning, P. (2004) 'Two Modes of Governance Is There a Viable Third Way?' Opening Plenary Address, delivered at the British Criminology Conference University of Portsmouth, UK 6 July.

Stewart, T. (1996) 'Family Group Conferences with Young Offenders in New Zealand', in Hudson, J., A., Morris, G. Maxwell and B. Galaway (eds) *Family Group Conferences: Perspectives on Policy and Practice*, Leichardt: The Federation press.

Tauri, J. (1996) 'Indigenous Justice or Popular Justice: Issues in the Development of a Maori Justice System', in P. Spoonley, D. Pearson, C. Macpherson (eds) *Nga Patai: Ethnic Relations and Racism in Aotearoa/New Zealand*. Palmerston North: Dunmore Press. pp. 202–216.

Tauri, J. (1998) 'Family Group Conferences: A Case Study of the Indigenisation of New Zealand's Justice System', *Current Issues in Youth Justice*, 10(2): 168–182.

Tauri, J. (1999) 'Empowering Maori or Biculturalising the State? Explaining Recent Innovations in New Zealand's Criminal Justice System', *The Australian, New Zealand Journal of Criminology*, Winter 32(2).

Tauri, J. (2004) 'Conferencing, Indigenisation and Orientalism: A Critique of Recent State Responses to Indigenous Offending', Paper presented at the conference of Qwi Quelstrom Gathering: Bringing Justice Back to the People, Mission B.C. 22–24 March.

Walters, R. and Bradley, T. (2005) *Introduction to Criminological Thought*. Albany: Longman.

Watkins, T. (2004) 'Hard Labour for Crimes, but no need for chains', *The Press*, 6 July, 2005, p. 3.

Watt, E. (2003) 'A History of Youth Justice in New Zealand', unpublished research commissioned by Principal Youth Court Judge, Wellington: Department for Courts.

Webb, R. (2004) 'Maori Crime: Possibilities and Limits of an Indigenous Criminology', unpublished PhD dissertation, Auckland University of Technology.

Wittman, M. R. (1995) 'Juvenile Justice Legislation in New Zealand 1974–1989: The Process of Lawmaking', unpublished LLM dissertation, Victoria University of Wellington: Wellington.

Australia: Control, Containment or Empowerment?

7

Chris Cunneen and Rob White

Introduction

An overview of juvenile justice in Australia highlights certain longer term continuities in approaches to young people, as well as a range of more recent changes which themselves often seem conflicting or contradictory. A fundamental continuity in juvenile justice has been the ongoing focus on working class, minority and Indigenous youth. However, there have also been changes in both the ideological underpinning of juvenile justice, as well as changes in policy and practice. The last decade has seen heightened public concern and moral panics about ethnic minority youth; the imposition of mandatory sentences on juvenile offenders; adoption of zero tolerance policing (especially in public spaces) and the significant extension of police powers; persistent over-representation of Indigenous young people within the juvenile justice system; and intensification of intervention in the lives of young offenders and non-offenders alike. Inequality and social polarisation have grown, accompanied by the racialisation of criminal justice and the criminalisation of the poor. Australia has also witnessed a widespread acceptance of risk prediction as an underlying principle of contemporary policy and practice.

On the positive side, much greater attention is now being given to the basic rights and well-being of young people. In particular, there has been a growth in the human rights perspective as a critical perspective by which to evaluate policing practices, the operation of courts and youth conferences, and the conditions under which young people are detained or sentenced to community work. Renewed emphasis in crime prevention has likewise been used to explicitly challenge coercive 'law and order' approaches. Meanwhile, the increasing popularity of 'restorative justice', with an emphasis on repairing social harm, holds some potential to serve as an important counterweight to traditional retributive methods. In fact, youth incarceration rates in Australia have generally remained steady in the past decade (and in some jurisdictions declined). The impact of punitive law and order policies has not been uniformly felt across the juvenile justice sector.

By way of introduction, it is important to provide some background to the operation of juvenile justice in Australia. The states of Australia developed different processes for dealing with young people during the nineteenth century. Separate institutions for incarcerating both 'neglected' and 'delinquent' young people were introduced in the mid-nineteenth century. Legislation was also introduced which allowed magistrates to apply specific procedures and penalties for young people convicted of certain property offences. Then, starting with South Australia in 1895, a system of children's courts was established across the country over the next decade. The focus of this system was the colonial working class. Aboriginal young people were dealt with under separate specific legislation and generally incarcerated in identified institutions separate from non-Aboriginal youth at least until the second half of the twentieth century (Cunneen and White, 2002). The massive over-representation of Aboriginal young people in the juvenile justice system is a phenomenon that begins at this time – currently Indigenous youth are approximately 2% of the total youth population, but make up 47% of all young people incarcerated in Australia.

Australia has a federal system where the eight states and territories generally exercise distinct responsibility for matters relating to criminal law, juvenile justice, child welfare and child protection. Thus, for example, there are eight children's court jurisdictions. While there are broad similarities across states and territories, there can also be important differences in law, policy and practice. For example, sentencing law varies, particularly where mandatory sentencing (or 'three strikes') laws have been introduced (such as in Western Australia and, previously, the Northern Territory). The differing rates of incarceration across the country most clearly illustrate some of these jurisdictional differences. The rate of incarceration for 10 to 17 year olds for Australia is 29.1 per 100,000. However, this varies from the lowest rate of 14.4 in Victoria to the highest rate of 92.1 in the Northern Territory (Charlton and McCall, 2004).

Public spaces and street policing

The public visibility and group behaviour of young people makes them more prone to arrest for certain types of activities than their adult counterparts (Cunneen and White, 2002). Simultaneously, non-criminal behaviour and less serious offending by young people are also subject to routine scrutiny by authority figures and other adults. Again, this is mainly due to the visibility of young people in public spaces. The very presence of young people, much less what they are actually doing, can be perceived as unsettling and problematic.

This phenomenon is by no means new. Certain types of behaviour, linked to certain social groups, have long been a site of public contention and contestation. For example, Queensland's Vagrant's Act has remained relatively unchanged since its enactment in 1931. Out-dated provisions, such as 'insufficient lawful means of support', are still used today to charge and convict people for eating out of garbage bins and sleeping in public places (Walsh, 2004). The use of vagrancy laws to police and harass marginalised public-space users, particularly homeless young people, recently prompted the formation of the 'Rights in Public Space Action Group'. Research and action taken by members of this group have highlighted how many of the homeless are treated differently from other public space users, whose behaviour is identical to theirs but nonetheless tolerated. Among the many criticisms of how the vagrancy laws are constructed and used, therefore, is the discriminatory operation of such laws – particularly against homeless people and indigenous people (see Walsh, 2004).

Perceptions of a 'problem' require some form of police 'solution'. In many cases, intervention is premised upon use of legislation that allows police to charge (usually young) people with offensive behaviour and/or offensive language. For example, the Summary Offences Act 1988 of New South Wales (as amended) has a separate provision for 'offensive language'. This is actively used by police in dealing with public order matters. The problem with reliance upon such legislation, however, is that such provisions are 'inevitably vague and open-ended, with the characterisation of the behaviour left to the discretion of the police in the first instance, and subsequently to the discretion of magistrates' (Brown et al., 2001). Case law in this area has been uneven, with decisions about what constitutes 'offensive language' varying greatly depending upon the predilections of the judge or magistrate, the specific circumstances, and the parties involved.

Public consternation and media attention given to street behaviour (usually focusing on anti-social activity, 'youth gangs', public drunkenness, drug use, visible minorities, and Indigenous people) have been reflected in discussions of 'zero tolerance' policing and new public order legislation (as in the Northern Territory) that expressly targets particular groups and particular types of social behaviour as being offensive. The use of offensive language and offensive behaviour offences is thus generally highly targeted, and socially patterned (White, 2002a). Data show that Indigenous people account for 15 times as many offensive language offences as would be expected by their population in the community (Cunneen, 2001).

While the legislative basis for action varies from state to state, the general trend around Australia has been for police services to be granted extensive new powers vis-à-vis young people (see for example, Blagg and Wilkie, 1995). These range from casual use of 'name-checks' (asking young people their names and addresses), 'move on' powers (the right to ask young people to move away from certain areas) and search powers for prohibited implements (such as knives or scissors), through to the enhanced ability to take fingerprints and bodily samples of alleged young offenders. A sample of the legislation introduced in one Australian jurisdiction (New South Wales) over a five year period signals the shift that has occurred in policing over recent years. The new laws affecting young people include the following:

- Children (Protection and Parental Responsibility) Act 1997
- Crimes Legislation Amendment (Police and Public Safety) Act 1998
- Police Powers (Vehicles) Act 1998
- Crimes (Forensic Procedures) Act 2000
- Child Protection (Offenders Registration) Act 2000
- Police Powers (Drug Premises) Act 2001
- Police Powers (Internally Concealed Drugs) Act 2001
- Justice Legislation (Non-Association and Places Restriction) Act 2001
- Police Powers (Vehicles) Amendment Act 2001
- Police Powers (Drug Detection Dogs) Act 2001
- Crimes Amendment (Aggravated Sexual Assault in Company) Act 2001
- Crimes Amendment (Gang and Vehicle Offences) Act 2001

Some of this legislation may be technically age-neutral, but in practice its implementation frequently has a disproportionate impact upon young people. For instance, the Crimes Legislation Amendment (Police and Public Safety) Act 1998 makes the carrying of a knife (and other 'implements' such as scissors, nail files, etc.) in a public place an offence. The same legislation gives police the power to search young people who they suspect of being in possession of prohibited implements. Possession of a prohibited implement is an offence, as is refusal to allow a search. Parents can also be found guilty of an offence if they knowingly allow their child to carry a prohibited implement. In the first 21 months after the legislation was introduced over 27,000 people were searched. Around one in five people were found to be carrying a prohibited implement (Fitzgerald, 2000: 2).

The legislation also enables police to give reasonable directions to persons to 'move on', where their behaviour or presence constitutes an obstruction, harassment, intimidation or causes fear in public places. According to the New South Wales Bureau of Crime Statistics and Research some 10,000 orders were issued in the first 12 months. Refusal to obey the order resulted in over 1,000 fines being issued (*Sydney Morning Herald*, 21 December 1999: 11). The NSW

Ombudsman found that those aged 15 to 19 years were much more likely to be stopped and searched for knives and prohibited implements than any other age group. While there were more knives found on 17 year olds than anyone else, the proportion of productive searches was relatively low for teenage suspects. In a similar vein, it was observed that 'a high number of teenagers were given directions by police to "move on" under the terms of the Act. Significantly, 48% of persons "moved on" were aged 17 years or younger, while 42% of persons searched were juveniles' (NSW Ombudsman, 1999: 37).

The removal of young people from public spaces has also been accomplished through specific youth-oriented legislative measures that are couched in a 'welfare' mode. For example, the Children (Protection and Parental Responsibility) Act allows the police to remove young people under 16 years of age from public places without charge if the police believe that the young people: are 'at risk' of committing an offence or of being affected by a crime; are not under the supervision or control of a responsible adult; or if it is believed the young person is in danger of being physically harmed or injured, or abused. This legislation does not automatically come into effect across the state; rather, local councils are required to apply to the Attorney-General to become operational areas. In the first six months of 1999, 145 young people were removed from public places in the four local government areas where the legislation was operational. Of these, 90% were Aboriginal children (Chan and Cunneen, 2000: 53). In fact, much of the legislation aimed at the use of public places by young people has been particularly heavily used in Aboriginal communities, with move on powers and search powers used at 10–15 times the rate found in the wider community (NSW Ombudsman, 1999).

Zero tolerance policing has also been accompanied by other measures which are designed to contain and manage people, especially in regard to their access to and use of public places. Youth curfews, for example, represent yet another way in which to clear the streets of young people, regardless of whether or not they have done anything wrong, much less illegal. The use of formal curfews is not standard practice in Australia. Arguably some police operational campaigns (as in Western Australia) and special legislation (as in New South Wales) do constitute de facto youth curfews. However, the latter tend to have an element of selectivity built into them, in the sense of being based on defined criteria (according to which certain categories of young people are deemed to be 'at risk'), and thus intervention is not supposed to be universal in application. Nevertheless, the idea of curfews has continued to strike a popular chord among state politicians and local city councillors. In places such as Exmouth in Western Australia and Port Augusta in South Australia, attempts have periodically been made to impose curfews, either unilaterally through local council directives or via agreements between the local council and the police. However, in such cases questions have been raised regarding the lack of legislative authority for police to enforce curfews of a general nature (rather than those tied to bail or community-service order conditions), and the ability of local councils to introduce curfews without prior legislation at the state government level which would extinguish common law rights relating to the right to move freely around the community (Simpson and Simpson, 1993).

If the presence of young people is not necessarily subject to formal regulation via curfews, the same cannot be said about their activities. There are examples across Australia where private companies and corporations are being granted extraordinary powers to police users of their privately owned but publicly accessible urban spaces. In 1994, for example, the Queensland Government introduced the Southbank Corporation Amendment By-Law (No.1) 1994, which provides power for security officers to stop people, ask for their name and address, and direct them to leave the site (Murray, 1995). The redevelopment of Southbank has turned the area into a major leisure, shopping and tourist destination in Brisbane. The relevant by-laws were amended in December 1995 to enable security officers to unilaterally ban people with written notice from returning to the site for up to 10 days if the person disobeys a direction, is drunk or disorderly, or even if they simply consider the ban is 'justified in the circumstances'. They can also apply to the court to ban them for up to one year. It is important to note that the law gives private police greater potential powers of exclusion than available to state police.

A particular area that has changed both police and court powers in relation to young people has been the development of more restrictive approaches to bail. The presumption in favour of bail has been removed for a very wide range of people, and release on bail is increasingly seen as a privilege for a restricted class. Exceptions to the presumption in favour of bail used to relate to situations where there was a grave concern that the person would not attend court or would commit serious offences if not detained. Through changes in legislation in some jurisdictions the presumption in favour of bail has been removed for a wide range of people: anyone on a bond or order who re-offends, anyone who has previously failed to appear in court, or has previously been convicted of an indictable offence. The potential group includes a large range of minor offenders who are also repeat offenders.

In addition there have been other changes that adversely affect young people in relation to bail and other court orders. The Non-Association and Place Restriction Act 2001 provides the power to prohibit or restrict a person from associating with other specified people (including communicating by *any* means), and to prohibit or restrict a person from frequenting or visiting a specified place or district. These orders can relate to bail conditions, parole conditions, conditions of leave, home detention and the sentencing for any offence punishable by a penalty of six months' imprisonment or more. The order is in addition to any other penalty that might be imposed. The orders can be used with children and adults.

The Non-Association and Place Restriction Act was introduced as an 'anti-gang' measure, but in reality does little or nothing to break-up criminal gangs. Instead, it is used mainly against young people who are alleged to have committed minor public order, property and drug offences. Ironically, most of the offences to which non-association and place restriction orders have been attached appeared not to have been committed in groups, let alone being gang-related.

The Shopfront Youth Legal Centre in Sydney is a free legal service for homeless and disadvantaged young people aged 25 and under. Many of its clients have mental health problems, intellectual disabilities, or limited literacy and numeracy. The Legal Service has found that the non-association and place restriction orders have been used in a way which restrict young people's access to legitimate and necessary services such as: health centres, drug and other counselling services, legal services and welfare services in areas such as Kings Cross, Redfern and Cabramatta.

Many of these reforms formally apply equally to both young people and adults. Yet this belies a growing tendency to disregard any consideration of the special needs of children and young people. It is increasingly commonplace to introduce legislation that impacts on young people without any consideration of the effects. Children and young people are being increasingly treated the same as adults and being held to the same levels of responsibility. This is likely to have serious long-term implications.

We also believe that there is a greater bifurcation in criminal justice responses to those who are classified as repeat offenders and those who are not. In the Australian context, such a bifurcation has specific discriminatory impacts on Aboriginal youth because they have a greater likelihood of a previous offending history, and a greater likelihood of failing to appear in court. The data suggests that over half non-Aboriginal young people appearing in court in Australia in any one year have no previous criminal record. By way of contrast 70% of Aboriginal young people have at least one prior proven court appearance (Cunneen, 2001). Any regime that treats repeat offenders more harshly will adversely impact on Aboriginal youth.

The rise of risk in juvenile justice

One of the most far-reaching changes in theory and practice in relation to juvenile justice has been an increased emphasis on the *prediction of risk*. The concepts of risk ('risk factors', 'risk assessment', 'risk prediction', 'risk management') permeate juvenile justice systems in Australia. Categorisations of 'risk' play an important role in determining process and outcomes. One's passage into, through and out of the juvenile justice system is determined by the classification of risk – that is, by the assumed probability of future behavioural patterns.

There are at least four different ways that the concept and measurement of 'risk' is used in juvenile justice:

- In the context of risk and protective factors associated with offending behaviour.
- As an assessment tool for access to programs for young people under supervision or serving a custodial sentence.

- As a classification tool for young people in custody to determine their security ratings.
- As a generic measure for activating legal intervention (for example, 'three-strikes' mandatory imprisonment).

The analysis of risk and protective factors associated with juvenile offending behaviour is an attempt to explain pathways into the juvenile justice systems by identifying factors associated with offending and non-offending behaviour. Recent Australian research follows the lead of Farrington (1996) and identifies a wide range of interacting and inter-related factors – pertaining to the individual, peer groups, family, school and community – as integral to any explanation of youth offending (see Developmental Crime Prevention Consortium, 1999). There are, however, serious limitations to this theoretical approach. For instance, the profiles of young offenders tend to look basically the same: young men, with low income, low educational achievement, no employment, a weak attachment to parents and who move frequently, are the most likely to wind up in juvenile detention centres. These characteristics basically describe the nature of the young offender; however, they do not explain young offending as such. Indeed, researchers may identify a multitude of 'risk factors' (such as drug abuse) and 'protective factors' (such as family cohesion) that influence whether or not an individual engages in criminal or anti-social behaviour (Catalano and Hawkins, 1996). In the end, however, it is the wider structural context of youth experience that fundamentally shapes overall life chances and life patterns (White and Wyn, 2004). Risk and protective factors are socially distributed.

To put it differently, rather than treating phenomenon such as 'socio-economic disadvantage' or 'unemployment' as specific causal factors, among many others, it is necessary to view such phenomena as *consequences* of wider structural features of a society. To address youth crime, therefore, requires that analysis shift from simple multi-factoral analyses, to consideration of the *generative* social processes that give rise to and exacerbate particular 'risk factors'. At an immediate concrete level, why certain young people commit certain crimes is answerable by consideration of their personal life history, their immediate life circumstances, and their position in the wider social structure. For example, the decision to commit vandalism, may incorporate elements of an abusive childhood, difficulties at school, unemployment and bad experiences with authority figures, or it could be as simple as 'having a good time'. But, in theoretical terms, these distinct individual biographies can be seen to be socially patterned. As a broad generalisation, they reflect deep structural inequalities and social divisions that predispose certain classes or groups of children and youth to live, and to behave, very differently than their more privileged peers.

Part of the problem with multi-factoral analysis is that it generally refrains from presenting a *hierarchy of causes*. The result of this is that immediate causes are cited (such as unemployment, racism, labelling, poor schooling), and reformist measures are advocated (such as training schemes, alternative schools), but rarely are substantial changes to the social structure as a whole demanded. Where multiple factors are at the foreground of analysis, the tendency is to respond to the phenomenon of youth crime through emphasis on developing specific projects and programmes. If all causal factors are treated the same (as often is implied in a descriptive 'list approach' to social problems), then obviously only those factors that lend themselves to immediate solutions will attract government attention and funding support. Poverty, for example, is usually put into the 'too hard' basket. Parent support (or blaming) is not.

It is for this reason that many governments, especially conservative ones, turn to multi-factor approaches. With a multitude of risk and protective factors to choose from, governments can appear to be doing something concrete, while not changing the status quo in a fundamental way. Moreover, this paradigm of action dovetails with the shift away from supporting public institutions (that have been subjected to cuts, privatisation, corporatisation, streamlining and so on) to constructing social policy around programs and projects (that are specific, contingent, sporadic, amenable to direct cost-benefit analysis and so on). The appearance of 'doing something' belies the real achievements taking place.

The theoretical model that informs much of the 'risk' and early intervention literature places a lot of onus on practitioners to intervene at the 'community' level and to do so with as many different parties as possible. Multiple causal factors have to be addressed, so the problem requires concerted efforts involving a constellation of projects, programmes and policies in each locality. However, there appears to be little analysis of the historical, political and economic context within which social life occurs. Much of the 'risk' literature is thereby mainly understood as individual and family failure. For example, we can ask, how can we consider such 'risk factors' as absent father, large family, long-term parental unemployment, etc. (Developmental Crime Prevention Consortium, 1999: 136), outside of specific state policies which are class and gender based? These include Federal family policies that provide tax incentives and financial support for two parent, mother-stay-at-home 'families' and the dearth of labour market policies that offer full employment opportunities. Surely a 'small family size' and 'more than two years between siblings' are protective factors (Developmental Crime Prevention Consortium, 1999: 138) only under particular economic and cultural conditions. In fact, many cultures would see an *extended* family as highly protective and economically sound.

The danger of the multi-factorial approaches found in the 'risk' literature is that too often we are left with an (apparently scientific) picture of children from a middle-class nuclear family of the dominant culture who own their own home as quintessentially law-abiding, and all those who do not fit this stereotype as potentially delinquent. Such images of normality and delinquency are profoundly ideological. Regardless of developmental intentions, such analyses lend themselves to greater punitive interventions rather than strategies for social support. This is particularly so under conservative and law-and-order governments that are hostile to providing the resources identified as necessary for community development.

The most fundamental difficulty with explanatory predictors or factors associated with juvenile offending is whether they can be divorced from the operation and processes of criminalisation. Are young people who have trouble at school more likely to commit offences, or are they more likely to be reported to authorities and become the subject of surveillance and intervention? Similarly, are children from single parent families more likely to be subject to welfare/police surveillance because they are already directly connected to regulatory bodies as a result of welfare dependence? Are the young of minority groups more likely to appear in arrest rates because they commit more offences, or because they are members of minority groups and subject to differential treatment and sometimes racism by authorities? In other words, the factors that are often presented as predictors of delinquency may in fact be the predictors of intervention.

New developments in *risk assessment tools* also reflect the types of problems identified above. In Australia, a Canadian risk assessment tool has been imported and adapted as the Youth Level Service Case Management Inventory – Australian Adaptation (YLS/CMI-AA). In 2002 it became mandatory in New South Wales for all young people either on a control order or a community-based supervision order to be assessed to determine their risk of recidivism and level of intervention (Priday, 2006: 346). The tool is presented as objective and scientific in its approach to classification. However, the assessments often require subjective values. For example, the YLS/CMI-AA asks, 'could the young person make better use of their time?'. As Priday (2006: 347) notes, the question implies that young people who are out-of-school, unemployed and not participating in formal recreational activities, are not making 'correct' use of their time. A range of questions (for which points are allocated on a risk scale) require subjective assessments including family relationships, 'normal' parental supervision, lifestyle and living conditions.

There is a strong focus on individual factors to predict risk, and the prediction of future behaviour is heavily weighted by past behaviour. Factors such as age of first court order, prior offending history, failure to comply with court orders, and current offences (particularly those involving house burglary, assault or car theft) are all used to predict risk of future offending. A range of socio-economic factors are also connected to risk including education (such as 'problematic' schooling and truancy) and unemployment. But there is no specific reference in the risk assessment inventory to class, gender, 'race' or ethnicity. Yet it is when we consider the impact of risk assessment on Aboriginal youth that the full cultural and class prejudices of these tools are made transparent. For oppressed minority groups who have lived under racist regimes, the greatest 'risk' may be the institutions of the state itself. In Australia the systematic and forced removal of Aboriginal children from their families by the state has proved to be the greatest 'risk' to the well-being of Aboriginal children, young people and their families throughout much of the twentieth century (National Inquiry into the Separation of Aboriginal and Torres Strait Islander Children from their Families, 1997). As a result, risk assessment tools substitute individual histories for the historical dynamics of societies. The tools reinterpret certain characteristics as representing the failings of individuals rather than the outcomes of inequality, discrimination and the absence of opportunity.

Restorative justice

The ideological climate surrounding juvenile justice has seen policy outcomes which stress both extensive and intensive interventions, and institutional contexts characterised by the expansion of private and public agencies in the areas of policing, prisons and crime prevention. As part of these trends, there have been major changes in the overall sanctioning process:

- From use of a few measures to a broad range (e.g., including cautions, community-based orders, home detention).
- From non-intervention to use of a wider number and variety of interventions (especially at the front end of the system, such as juvenile conferencing schemes).
- From discretionary and parsimonious options to adoption of harsher and non-discretionary measures (e.g., mandatory sentencing).
- From attempts to reduce overall numbers in the criminal justice system to more extensive interventions for some (e.g., expanded use of community sanctions).

It is within this context that restorative justice must be understood. The favoured model of restorative justice in the Australian context is that of juvenile conferencing. The impetus for the adoption of juvenile conferences for dealing with young offenders stems from varying pressures. In some cases, it has been linked to grassroots developments among Indigenous people; in others, to police initiatives; and more generally, new thinking at a theoretical level about juvenile justice (Cunneen and White, 2002: chapter 13). Certainly the rhetoric of this approach has caught on in most jurisdictions within Australia, although it is questionable whether the philosophical basis of the model is necessarily being adhered to in practical programs.

In terms of actual program development, the leading example of juvenile conferencing was provided by New Zealand's Family Group Conference model. The approach to juvenile justice adopted in New Zealand in the late 1980s emphasised the need to keep children and young people with their families and in their communities. In Australia, all States and Territories have now implemented some form of conferencing, although most jurisdictions refer to these forums as juvenile conferences, rather than family group conferences.

The intended outcome of the conferences is that the young offender is expected to complete some kind of agreement or undertaking, including verbal and written apologies, paying some form of monetary compensation, working for the victim or doing other community work, and attending counselling sessions

(Daly and Hayes, 2001: 2). The form of the conference is basically the same, although there are jurisdictional differences in terms of the kinds of offences that are conferenced, the volume of activity that is engaged in via conferencing, the upper limit on conference outcomes, the statutory basis for conferencing and the organisational placement or administration of the conferencing process.

In practical terms, a number of issues relating to juvenile conferencing have been raised that require further attention. Concerns have been raised regarding the denial of young people's legal rights due to the informal nature of some community-based schemes and the prior guilty plea demanded of young people. Net-widening may be a problem, although this does not appear to have occurred in some jurisdictions such as New South Wales where the number of juvenile court appearances has declined proportionately to the number of youth conferences that have been held (Luke and Lind, 2002). A more fundamental problem lies in processes of bifurcation. More marginalised young people are channelled away from options such as youth conferencing and into a justice system more punitive in its sentencing. Biases in the system have been particularly pronounced with Indigenous young people who are less likely to be diverted to a conference and who are quickly drawn deeper and deeper into the criminal justice system (Blagg, 1997; Cunneen, 1997). Community-based programs may not only be unequal in application to specific groups of young people, but they may serve to channel young people into a system that otherwise they might have avoided.

Partly due to the diversity of opinion, values and models under the restorative justice tag, there has been a tendency for specific forms of restorative justice to be implemented in a manner that actively reproduces the dominant forms of social control. For example, juvenile conferencing may be used solely for first time offenders and/or trivial offences and therefore as a filter that reinforces the logic and necessity of the 'hard' end of the system (the 'real justice' of retribution and punishment). The former may well help to legitimate the latter, rather than constitute a challenge to it. Substantial variations in the introduction of restorative justice are apparent across diverse jurisdictions, if we compare legislative, administrative and operational frameworks (see Daly and Hayes, 2001). In almost all cases, however, restorative justice has been blended into existing institutional patterns – part of the continuing hybridisation of criminal justice. How this 'blending' occurs is important, of course, as it makes a major difference in terms of actual operational practices. The degree of expansion of restorative justice into the criminal justice system – to address ever more serious kinds of offences, and to include offenders with extensive criminal careers – provides one indication of potential systemic change.

It is important to note that within restorative justice frameworks the idea of social harm is generally conceptualised in immediate, direct and individualistic terms (and as such ignores the broader social processes underpinning, and patterns of, both offending and victimisation). One consequence of this is that the emphasis on repairing harm tends to be restricted to the immediate violations and immediate victim concerns, thereby ignoring communal objectives and collective needs in framing reparation processes. Thus, the heart of the matter remains that of changing the offender, albeit with their involvement, rather than transforming communities and building progressive social alliances that might change the conditions under which offending takes place (see White, 2002b).

It is possible to re-construct restorative justice in a practice framework that more directly relates to social justice principles. For example, the guiding concepts might be solidarity, compensation and community empowerment. Solidarity implies that the politically and socially weak members of a group need to be included rather than excluded in the sense that tasks are to be performed for and by them, and emotional support is to be given to them. Offenders and victims need to be offered solidarity, and a voice in what affects them and support in the healing process. Compensation refers to the idea that weakness ought to be compensated. The criminal justice system, alongside other general social welfare policies and programs, can play a significant role in helping to address the social disadvantages of people who offend, and the social harms experienced by those who are victimised.

The process of repairing harm has to be re-conceptualised as social rather than solely individual in nature. This involves many different types of state-provided resources as well as input from individuals and groups. For example, it means the development of responses that go beyond simply funding conferencing as such, to include broader social reforms and creative initiatives that can at different points mesh with conferencing processes and opportunities. Community empowerment is about enhancing the welfare and prospects of collectivities, of which individuals are integral members. The point of intervention is to change the material conditions and circumstances of neighbourhoods and family networks, with the active involvement of local people.

Given other current developments in juvenile justice, the approaches based on a restorative justice framework appear to offer an important counter-balance to more retributive and punishment-oriented processes that increasingly seek to breakdown differentiations between adult and juvenile offenders. There is, however, widespread recognition that youth conferencing can be significantly improved in a way which makes it more inclusive and respecting of the rights of offenders and victims (see Australian Law Reform Commission, 1997: 242), as well as relating more directly to community needs and social change (White, 2002b).

Conclusion

We began this chapter by discussing some of the broad changes that are occurring in juvenile justice in Australia. We noted that practices and policies often seem contradictory in their approach to young people. Perhaps the most stark contradiction is between the growth of restorative justice practices, and a growing reliance on risk assessment to apply more punitive approaches in relation to young people. These contradictions find some reflection in current incarceration rates and patterns.

It is important in the Australian context to think through the long-term changes which have occurred in relation to the use of incarceration for young people. In most jurisdictions there has been a long-term decline in levels of incarceration over the last 20 years. Nationally, there is half the number of boys in detention now compared to the early 1980s, and the number of girls incarcerated today is a quarter of that 25 years ago. Overall, the rate of juvenile incarceration today is less than half what it was in the early 1980s (Charlton and McCall, 2004). We suspect a substantial reason for this has been the growth of diversionary options, particularly during the 1990s with the use of youth conferencing.

However, the nature of incarceration has also changed. There is an increased preparedness to transfer some young people into the adult system if they are convicted of serious offences or are otherwise troublesome. Indeed, in New South Wales the institution used to incarcerate the state's most serious juvenile offenders is staffed and administered by the adult correctional system. The composition of juvenile detention centres has also changed, particularly with the growth in the number of indigenous young people and young people from ethnic minority backgrounds. In addition, around half the young people incarcerated in Australia are there because they have been remanded in custody prior to a court hearing and trial, rather than convicted of a criminal offence. This changing nature of incarceration reflects the ideological ascendency of 'risk'.

Across Australia, 'juvenile offender' is basically a code word for 'poor and marginalised'. The most vulnerable sections of the youth population tend to engage with a retributive system, rather than restorative justice, as they negotiate the institutions of authority. For others, there is the promise of redemption through repairing harm and getting on with their young lives. For all, there is the ever present threat of intervention in their personal and group affairs – on the streets, in schools, in their family home. Each and all are subject to varying kinds of risk assessment. But it is the dispossessed, the alienated, the unemployed and the destitute who feel the full brunt of the law, and for whom tolerance has always been pegged at zero.

References

Australian Law Reform Commission (ALRC) and Human Rights and Equal Opportunity Commission (HREOC) (1997) *Seen and Heard: Priority for Children in the Legal Process*, Australian Law Reform Commission Report No. 84, Sydney.

Blagg, H. (1997) 'A Just Measure of Shame?: Aboriginal Youth and Conferencing in Australia' *British Journal Of Criminology*, 37(4): 481–506.

Blagg, H. and Wilkie, M. (1995) *Young People and Police Powers*. Sydney: The Australian Youth Foundation.

Brown, D., Farrier, D., Egger, S. and McNamara, L. (2001) *Criminal Laws: Materials and Commentary on Criminal Law and Process in New South Wales*. Sydney: The Federation Press.

Catalano, R. and Hawkins, J. (1996) 'The Social Development Model: A Theory of Antisocial Behavior', in J. Hawkins (ed.) *Delinquency and Crime: Current Theories*. New York: Cambridge University Press.

Chan, C. and Cunneen, C. (2000) *Evaluation of the Implementation of the New South Wales Police Service Aboriginal Strategic Plan*: Institute of Criminology, University of Sydney.

Charlton, K. and McCall, M. (2004) *Statistics on Juvenile Detention in Australia: 1981–2003, Technical and Background Paper No. 10*. Canberra, Australian Institute of Criminology.

Cunneen, C. (1997) 'Community Conferencing and the Fiction of Indigenous Control' *Australian and New Zealand Journal of Criminology*, 30(3): 292–311.

Cunneen, C. (2001) *Conflict, Politics and Crime, Aboriginal Communities and the Police*. Sydney: Allen and Unwin.

Cunneen, C. and White, R. (2002) *Juvenile Justice: Youth and Crime in Australia*. Melbourne: Oxford University Press.

Daly, K. and Hayes, H. (2001) *Restorative Justice and Conferencing in Australia*. Trends & Issues in Crime and Criminal Justice, No. 186. Canberra: Australian Institute of Criminology.

Developmental Crime Prevention Consortium (1999) *Pathways to Prevention: Developmental and Early Intervention Approaches to Crime in Australia*. Canberra: National Crime Prevention, Attorney General's Department.

Farrington, D. (1996) 'The Explanation and Prevention of Youthful Offending', in J. Hawkins (ed.) *Delinquency and Crime: Current Theories*. New York: Cambridge University Press.

Fitzgerald, J. (2000) 'Knife Offences and Policing, *Crime and Justice Statistics*, Bureau Brief No. 8, June. Sydney: New South Wales Bureau of Crime Statistics and Research.

Luke, G. and Lind, B. (2002) 'Reducing Juvenile Crime: Conferencing versus Court', *Crime and Justice Bulletin*, No. 69. Sydney: New South Wales Bureau of Crime Statistics and Research.

Murray, G. (1995) 'The Authoritarian Exclusion of Young People from the Public Domain – Prevention or Provocation?'. Paper presented at the Youth and Community Preventing Crime Conference, Brisbane, 27–28 September.

National Inquiry into the Separation of Aboriginal and Torres Strait Islander Children from Their Families (1997) *Bringing Them Home*. Canberra: Commonwealth of Australia.

NSW (New South Wales) Office of the Ombudsman (1999) *Policing Public Safety*. Sydney: NSW Ombudsman.

Priday, E. (2006) 'New Directions in Juvenile Justice: Risk and Cognitive Behaviourism', *Current Issues in Criminal Justice*, 17(3): 343–359.

Simpson, B. and Simpson, C. (1993) 'The Use of Curfews to Control Juvenile Offending in Australia: Managing Crime or Wasting Time?', *Current Issues in Criminal Justice*, 5(2): 184–199.

Walsh, T. (2004) 'Who is the "Public" in "Public Space"? A Queensland Perspective on Poverty, Homelessness and Vagrancy', *Alternative Law Journal*, 29(2): 81–86.

White, R. (2002a) 'Indigenous Young Australians, Criminal Justice and Offensive Language', *Journal of Youth Studies*, 5(1): 21–34.

White, R. (2002b) 'Communities, Conferences and Restorative Social Justice', *Criminal Justice*, 3(2): 139–160.

White, R. and Wyn, J. (2004) *Youth and Society: Exploring the Social Dynamics of Youth Experience*. Melbourne: Oxford University Press.

Belgium: From Protection Towards Accountability?

Johan Put and Lode Walgrave

Introduction

In its complicated politico-administrative structure, Belgium is divided into three 'regions' (Flanders, Brussels and Wallonia), with autonomous responsibilities focused on economics, environment and labour, and into three 'communities' (Flanders, including the Dutch speaking population in Brussels; the French community in Belgium, including the French speaking population in Brussels; and a smaller German speaking community), whose responsibilities concern especially welfare, education and culture. The Federal State still holds important responsibilities in the field of, among others, defence, justice, social security and foreign affairs. About 23% of the population is younger than 18. This is not only the age of majority, but also the end of compulsory school attendance. About half of the population continues to study after the age of 18. As in most other Western societies, youth crime and the reform of youth justice are currently hot topics. They have been important issues in recent election campaigns, including dramatising rhetorics on 'explosively growing and more violent youth crime', and promises to 'act tough'. The facts do not justify such panic. However, youth justice reform is also instigated by typical Belgian politics, that is, the complex organisation of the Belgian State and the differences in views between

Flanders and the French speaking part of Belgium, and between the different political parties.

In this chapter, we first survey the history of youth justice in Belgium; then we describe the current situation; and finally comment on several topics.

History of Youth Justice in Belgium[1]

The history of the Belgian juvenile justice system is in many ways parallel to the histories of the systems in the other Western European countries. It resulted nevertheless in a system that may be considered as the most consequentially welfare oriented of all.

From philanthropy to legal protection of children

When Belgium became independent in 1830, the new Belgian State adopted the French penal law system. It made it possible to take security measures (instead of penalties) towards juveniles younger than 16 years old if mental capacity for *discernement* was considered to be missing.

Soon after its independence Belgium had to reckon with serious economic problems, aggravated by an agricultural crisis, followed by typhus and cholera epidemics that severely affected the rural areas between 1845 and 1849. As a result there was an increase in vagrants, groups begging and stealing including many children, which caused unrest in the middle classes. Begging and crime were tackled and treated more severely. More and more people were confined to *dépôts de mendicité*, workhouses or prisons. From 1844 onwards, special penitentiaries and other closed facilities were created for children.

Around the 1860s, the economy had passed the worst of the crisis. The industrial revolution gave rise to two separate worlds, the *Belle époque* of the bourgeoisie, and the miserable living conditions of the proletariat in the urban quarters. The latter was a fruitful soil for the rise of socialism. Concern for the poor and in particular for their children grew among the ruling classes, based on religious motives, philanthropic drives and a concern for keeping 'the masses' under control by making them dependent on charity. The movement issued three main fields of institutionalisation. First, child labour laws gradually regulated children in the economic labour market, finally, in 1914, prohibiting child labour until the age of 14. Second, an increasing offer of basic schooling resulted in the law of 1914 on compulsory education, which made school attendance general up to the age of 14. Third, philanthropic concern about morally abandoned children and children in the justice system inspired several committees and commissions. In many judicial districts, judges and lawyers established, often together with (mostly female) philanthropists,

---

1. A more elaborated version of this historical part can be found in Walgrave 1993.

'Committees for the Defence of Children into the Justice System'. The establishment of the first youth court in Chicago (1899) was followed in Belgium, by an experiment with a children's court in Leuven from 1908 onwards.

The Belgian Children's Protection Act was passed on 15 May 1912. At about the same time neighbouring countries passed comparable laws, subjecting children to special (penal) procedures. The underlying idea was that children or youngsters are not capable of taking responsibility for their offences, and that, consequently, judicial intervention had to be more educative rather than purely punitive. Of all neighbouring countries, Belgium had the strongest educative tendency. A specialised children's judge would deal with all cases of delinquency, misconduct, vagrancy and school absenteeism committed by minors under the age of 16. The children's judge could only enforce measures for the protection of minors and had to take account of the 'dangerous situations' in which the children lived. Punishment *sensu stricto* was excluded. The court's work was supported by Comités de Patronage, consisting mostly of middle-class women, who made social reports and supervised and supported families at risk. In 1913 two residential clinical observation centres became operative, to inform the judges on the personality and social environment of the juveniles, and to help to orient the individualisation of the measures 'in the best interests of the child'.

From the protection of children to the protection of youth

Problems arose, however, for the implementation of the law. 'Restrictivists' complained about a growing interventionism on vague legal grounds, whereas 'maximalists' were of the opinion that the Children's Protection Act was too restrictive and excluded preventive judicial intervention. The latter tendency was much stronger. After the First World War, Belgium developed gradually into a welfare state. In such a climate, socio-clinical sciences flourished and supplied new arguments for further expansion of intervention against juveniles and families 'at risk'. In 1937 for example, Aimée Racine, the then director of the Research Centre on Juvenile Delinquency, funded directly and entirely by the Ministry of Justice, wrote: 'The field of juvenile delinquency is no longer reserved for penalists only, but is now subjected also to control by pedagogues, medical doctors, psychologists and social workers. Would not the statement 'nulla poena, nullum crimen sine lege' lose its meaning in a system that obviously is not repressive, but educative and protective?' Between 1939 and 1959, the number of children referred to the justice system doubled to more than 31,000. Individualisation and the clinical approach to delinquency blurred the concept of delinquency. Delinquency was considered an illness, requiring preventive care.

After several commissions and three bills, a new Youth Protection Act (YPA) was finally passed on 8 April 1965. The exclusively protective option was extended and additional organisations were established for preventive actions.

The law included a social protection section and a judicial protection section. In each arrondissement,[2] a 'Committee for the Protection of Youth' offered voluntary aid and assistance to 'endangered' minors (up to 21) and to their families. The Youth Court, also per arrondissement, could: 1) pronounce civil measures (for example, on emancipation or permission to marry), 2) impose measures on parents neglecting their parental duties, and 3) impose measures on minors, who were considered to be 'endangered' (up to the age of 21), or who had committed 'acts defined as offences' (up to the age of 18). Under the age of 18, no punishment was pronounced. A few exceptions existed (and still exist) though, which will be explained later on.

It can be noted that Belgium set the highest age of criminal responsibility (18) in Europe. The YPA of 1965 has been presented as a product of a consensus model, as the synthesis of a whole range of pre-existing proposals, comments and drafts, responding to the main inadequacies of the 1912 Act and its application. The post-war social context, with its belief in a new welfare society and its humanist criminal policy, produced optimism regarding rehabilitation, reintegration and assistance. This led to a far-reaching state interventionism, and more specifically to the enlargement of the 'protection model' both to delinquent minors up to 18 and to endangered minors up to the age of 21.

The Youth Court can refer minors to residential and ambulant psycho-medical centres for observation. Minors also can be placed in private institutions or in states' facilities for observation and re-education; the latter having a more closed and disciplining character.

The Youth Court was given its own social service for social investigation beforfe the measurement is taken and for follow-up of the measurements ordered.

Criticism and political pressure to change the system

Quite soon the solely rehabilitative character of the law was criticised. The implementation of an individualistic concept of prevention in the judicial context resulted in fact in a judicial control system that itself became uncontrollable: in Youth Court, elementary legal rights, due process or proportionality were hardly safeguarded. Moreover, the instrumental effectiveness of the re-educative measures appeared to be highly questionable, if not non-existent. These discussions remained on a relatively academic level until political changes in the Belgian State in the 1980s gave them a more pragmatic turn.

The law on the State reform of 1980 passed on the responsibility of youth protection to the Belgian Communities. An exception was made for matters of civil law, penal law, and judicial law. The implementation of the law resulted in a

2. Belgium is divided into 26 arrondissements (judicial districts). The number of inhabitants per district can vary from 200,000 to 1,500,000.

long dispute between the Flemish and French Communities and the Federal Government, which led to a clarification in 1988, extending still more the competencies of the Communities. General responsibility was given to the Communities to regulate the assistance to minors in problematical situations and the execution of all measures (including the measures imposed on youthful offenders). The Federal State remained responsible for the organisation of the Youth Courts, as well as the definition of delinquent behaviour and determined the range of measures that can be imposed on youthful offenders.

Meanwhile, the European Court of Human Rights condemned the Belgian State for several inadequacies in the youth justice system, concerning the lack of certain procedural guarantees and concerning the way preventive custody was used in practice (1988)[3]. The age of majority was lowered from 21 to 18 in 1990.

The three Communities finally passed their Decrees in the beginning of the 1990s[4] on their own systems for prevention and assistance with regard to all behaviours and situations that are considered detrimental to the positive development of young people. Each of these systems has its own peculiarities, but they all can refer to Youth Courts when youngsters and/or their families refuse voluntary co-operation, and assistance is considered to be indispensable in the interest of the child. They can also take initiatives of 'general prevention', that is, actions that aim at structural and/or (sub)collective levels, in order to prevent behaviour and/or situations that could be detrimental to the positive development of youth.

The 'hard core' of the social reaction against youthful offending remains in control of a specialised court, organised within the judicial structure of the Federal State. The Youth Protection Act of 8 April 1965, and as adapted by later Acts (in particular the Act of 2 February 1994), introduced enhanced rights of defence. It remains a system which is purely protection-oriented. The 1994 reform has been presented as being transitional, pending a more fundamental reform, which has not yet happened.

Contemporary youth justice in Belgium

Belgian Youth Courts deal with all offences committed by minors under the age of 18. According to Belgian law, 18 is the age of 'penal majority'. Youth Courts impose protection measures only, 'in the best interest of the child', and there are no criminal sanctions. The legislator therefore refers to minors having

3. European Court of Human Rights, 19 February 1988, Bouamar v/ Belgium, *Series A*, nr. 129.

4. The 'Decreet inzake Bijzondere Jeugdbijstand' [Decree on special youth assistance] of the Flemish Community of 4 April 1990, as a co-ordination of the Decrees of 27 June 1985 and 28 March 1990; the 'Decret relatif à l'aide à la jeunesse' [Decree concerning youth assistance] of the French Community of 4 March 1991; the 'Dekret über die Jugendhilfe' [Decree concerning youth assistance] of the German speaking Community of 20 March 1995.

committed 'an act defined as an offence', and not just 'an offence'. Presuming the minor's moral incompetence, s/he cannot be guilty of an offence, but only of committing an act which would be defined as an offence if it were committed by an adult.

There are two exceptions to this principle:

1 Adult courts deal with traffic offences committed by minors of 16 and older.
2 If the Youth Court concludes that youth protection measures are no longer appropriate for a minor, it refers him/her to the common criminal procedures. This possibility of relinquishing jurisdiction only holds for acts committed between the age of 16 to 18.

In both concluding observations of the Committee on the Rights of the Child regarding Belgium, the Committee expressed its concern that persons under the age of 18 may be tried as adults.[5] This is problematic in the light of Article 37(a) of the Convention on the Rights of the Child, by which State Parties have to ensure that neither capital punishment nor life imprisonment without possibility of release shall be imposed for offences committed by persons below 18 years of age. However, capital punishment was officially abolished in Belgium in 1996 (after almost a century in which it was not applied in peacetime), and the possibility of release exists for all those sentenced to imprisonment (albeit with stricter conditions for certain types of crimes).

Procedure

As in most continental European countries, the Belgian judicial system is ruled by a civil law regime. That means that the procedures are centralised and strictly legalised. Whereas common law countries offer flexibility and margins for discretion at all stages of the procedure, this is not the case in civil law regimes. Theoretically, for example, the police do not have any discretionary power, but have to refer all registered offences to the public prosecutor's office. Only the public prosecutor decides whether a case will be referred to the Youth Court or not. The decision is based on whether the facts are established and on the so called 'opportunity principle', meaning that, even if the facts are established, referral to court may not be considered appropriate.

Preparatory investigative phase

The procedure starts with a preparatory investigative phase. Its maximum duration is, in principle, six months; the public prosecutor then has two more months to decide whether or not to submit a subpoena. The public prosecutor

---

5. CRC/C/15/Add.38 of 20 June 1995, nr. 11; CRC/C/15/Add.178 of 13 June 2002, nr. 31–32.

controls the criminal investigation. He/she can undertake all steps to establish the facts. In serious cases, the dossier can also be passed on to an investigative judge. During the criminal investigation, the public prosecutor can advise (but not oblige) the juvenile and/or their parents to consult a psychosocial or medical centre, and can refer the case to a mediation agency. In the meantime, it is the Youth Court judge who orders social examinations to establish the personality of the minor and the living environment in which s/he is raised, in order to determine the minor's own best interest and the appropriate means for their education and treatment. These examinations are carried out by the youth court's social service. If necessary, an additional medico-psychological investigation can be ordered (e.g. by a psychiatrist). The results of the social examinations are communicated to the public prosecutor, who will then decide what to do.

Provisional measures

During the preparatory phase the Youth Court judge can take provisional 'measures of care'. Apart from the reprimand, the provisional measures are mainly the same as the definitive measures (see below).

If the juvenile is placed under a closed regime in a public institution, some additional restrictive rules apply with regard to the age of the minor, the duration of the provisional measure and the regime of confinement.

Preventive custody

On 1 January 2002, the possibility to place the juvenile for a maximum of 14 days in prison (house of custody) was abolished, if the judge could not find an appropriate other place for immediate admission. This happened partly as a result of the Bouamar judgement by the European Court in Strasbourg (1988). Immediately afterwards, the measures taken by Belgian Communities to increase the number of places in institutions for youth assistance, appeared to be insufficient.

After several sensational media releases and alarm signals by judges, the Federal Government created – with unprecedented speed – a Federal detention centre at Everberg (near Brussels). The Act of 1 March 2002[6] was approved by both Chambers of the Federal Parliament in only two days. It prescribes that boys (no girls!) can be entrusted to this centre for a maximum period of two months and five days. There are a few cumulative conditions: the juvenile has to be at least 14 years of age at the time of the offence; there must be sufficient serious indications of guilt; the offences under consideration would mean at

---

6. Act of 1 March 2002 concerning the preventive placement of minors who committed an act defined as an offence, Belgisch Staatsblad [Belgian Bulletin of Acts, Orders and Decrees] 1 March 2002.

least five years imprisonment if committed by an adult; there must be urgent, serious and exceptional circumstances concerning public security; and the preventive measure of placement in another appropriate institution is impossible (due to lack of room).

As all responsible authorities understood, this detention centre is in fact typical of the existing protective Belgian youth justice system. It was agreed that efforts to create a fundamentally renovated youth justice system should be speeded up in order to include such a centre more coherently. So far, however, this has not occurred. The Committee on the Rights of the Child voiced its concern about the creation of the Everberg Centre, and recommended that Belgium ensure, in accordance with article 37 of the Convention on the Rights of the Child, that the deprivation of liberty is only used as a last resort measure, for the shortest possible time, that guarantees of due process are fully respected and that persons under 18 are not detained with adults.[7] It should be noted, however, that stricter legal conditions and more elaborate procedural guarantees apply to temporary detention under the Act of 2002 than to the general provisional measures (including deprivation of liberty) under the YPA.

The preparatory phase ends with the public prosecutor's decision to bring the case before court or not. He can in the latter case still refer the minor and his/her family to the agencies of the Community in view of voluntary assistance.

Judgment

As stated above, all measures taken by the Youth Court are 'measures of care, preservation and education'. The measures are not retrospectively intended as a proportional sanction for the committed offence. On the contrary, they are prospective, aimed at dealing with the underlying situation of the minor (and his/her family) through adapted measures, and, as far as possible, to achieve social rehabilitation.

In theory, there is no gradation in the measures: they are not more or less severe, but more or less adapted to the situation of the minor. In real terms, the seriousness of the facts obviously influences the kind of measures imposed. The theoretical model of protection often has to yield to a more sanction-oriented approach and one which holds the minor to account.

Four types of measures can be imposed:

1   The reprimand. This is an admonition for the act committed and an order to act differently in the future. The judge can also warn parents to supervise the minor in a more disciplined way.

2   'Placement under supervision' of the social service. The social service monitors the compliance with the conditions laid down by court. Possible conditions are:

---

7. CRC/C/15/Add.178 of 13 June 2002, nr. 31–32.

- attend school on a regular basis (in a boarding school if necessary);
- follow the pedagogical and medical guidelines of an educational centre;
- perform an activity of educational or philanthropical nature, in proportion to age and means. This is the only legal basis to impose 'alternative sanctions'.[8] Despite the limited legal alternative, these sanctions have become a widespread practice.

3 Placement with a reliable person (a foster home) or in a suitable institution, under supervision of the social service. The broad formulation of this measure allows for (semi) residential placement in different kinds of institutions, including psychiatric institutions, as well as ambulant support by a welfare service. These institutions or services are based on private initiative, but are subsidised. They have to be recognised by the Communities and have to comply with extensive quality regulations imposed by the authorities.

4 Placement in a public institution for observation and education under supervision. In this case, the juvenile court has to set down the duration of the measure and point out whether the placement is in a closed or a (half)open ward of the institution. This measure can only be imposed on minors over 12, unless in very exceptional circumstances. The public institutions are organised by the Flemish or the French speaking Community.

It must be observed that placement in a psychiatric institution in fact happens very (too) rarely, because of the lack of places for offending minors in psychiatric institutions. So far, these juveniles often end up in the regular services and institutions of youth protection, where the adequacy of their treatment is in question. Currently, efforts are being made so as to provide sufficient placement facilities for young offenders with a psychiatric disorder.

An appeal can be lodged with the Youth Chamber of the Court of Appeal against the judicial orders during the preparatory phase as well as against the judgments of the Youth Court during the judgment phase. The appeal can be entered by the Public Prosecutor and by each of the parties in the first instance within the term of 15 days from the day after the judgment.

Execution of the measures: particularities

While the Federal Legislator is entitled to stipulate the measures to take against offending juveniles, the Communities must execute them. The Communities classify, acknowledge and subsidise the various institutions and services in the

---

8. In a ministerial circular of 7 March 1995, diversion measures are however promoted for minors, instead of judicial intervention. These measures consist of compensation for the damage, the execution of a service for the community or the participation in a measure with a social educational character. The public prosecutor decides not to take the case to court when the minor accepts to carry out such a measure. Nevertheless, different authors estimate that this circular does not have the necessary legal basis to be valid and raises serious questions regarding procedural guarantees. Moreover, this initiative does not lead to diversion, but to net-widening, since the Public Prosecutor mainly selects those cases he formerly did not prosecute.

area of juvenile assistance. The Federal Government and the judges are thus dependent on the Communities for the creation of the necessary facilities and agencies, and for the carrying out of the measures. This is a source of a permanent tension in the field of juvenile justice.

Most of the institutions and services are established on a private basis, but they have to be accredited to admit or guide juveniles. The Communities themselves organise a few public institutions, which are the only ones with closed sections. As mentioned already, a recent addition is the Federal detention centre at Everberg. Here, the Federal Government is the founder and the organiser, but an agreement of co-operation has been concluded with the Communities about their contribution to guidance and the pedagogical staffing.

A juvenile who has been subjected to a measure of placement remains under the supervision of (the social service of) the juvenile court until their age of majority. The youth court supervises the execution of the measures. The judge can decide, for example, about visiting and leave arrangements of the minor. According to the law, the Youth Court judge is supposed to visit each minor placed by her/him at least twice a year.

The Youth Court can 'revise' the provisional, as well as the definitive, measures, so that the judge can change a measure subsequently and adapt it to the development of the juvenile's personality and/or of his/her environment. Each year, the public prosecutor has to introduce a procedure in order to examine a current placement and possibly to confirm, withdraw or modify it. Finally, the parents (or equals) and the juvenile can also ask for a revision, but not until after one year from the beginning of the measure.

Youth crime as a 'hot issue' and pressure for more repression

At the time of writing, juvenile crime is a hot issue. Especially in the bigger cities such as Brussels, Antwerp, Liège, Ghent and Charleroi, a debate is going on about an assumed 'increasing unsafety' on the streets, which is attributed for a great part to youths, especially from Moroccan or Eastern European minorities. The debate is boosted by some sensationalist media and, especially in Flanders, by an extremist right-wing political party. Pressured by its considerable electoral response, the other political parties are being dragged down in a panicky play with regard to safety and immigration. In recent election campaigns youth crime and street crime were focal concerns. Local police initiatives have introduced some kinds of 'curfew' for children under the age of 14: *streetrazzias,* or local imitations of zero-tolerance policies. Public prosecutors and police forces have established special sections for dealing with youth gangs or with collective youth violence. Even insurance companies now offer special policies for teachers victimised by school violence. The speed, mentioned earlier, to create the Federal detention centre is illustrative of the current climate of panic and repression with regard to youth crime.

Poor statistics

Paradoxically, there are no statistics to support this focus on youth crime. Gathering good statistics on youth crime in Belgium is a very frustrating undertaking. Police figures are incomplete and show diverse pictures per municipality or district. They also often reveal decreases in registered crime. Moreover, it is unclear whether the fluctuations are due to the public's changing degrees of tolerance or of confidence in police, to a change in effectiveness in police registration, or whether they must be attributed to norm erosion, or reflect real developments in criminality. Belgian judicial statistics on youth crime are a mess (Walgrave, 2002). The reform of the Belgian State described earlier, including the reshuffling of the competencies over youth justice and protection, has completely disorganised the collecting of data. Some centralised data are available until 1988 – the figures showed a remarkable stability. Between 1988 and 1993, the Flemish community took over the collection of data, but only with regard to the Flemish districts. The data in fact seem to suggest a (slight) decrease, certainly no increase. They stopped in 1993 because the Ministry of Justice decided to restart with a new centre for statistics. Currently, that centre does not function. There is only some preparatory research with a view to 'integrated statistics' on registered youth offending and its judicial proceedings, which has so far yielded partial data.

The Ministry of Justice has issued, among others, a study on developments in Brussels between 1980 and 1997 (Vanneste et al., 1999). These statistics are not representative for the whole of Belgium. Brussels is the largest and the most urbanised arrondissement, with the most heterogenic population, including the highest proportion of immigrant families, and with the highest mobility. After a steady increase in the total number of offences reported, a sharp decrease occurs after 1994. Violent offences, however seemed to increase in 1994 and 1995, and then to remain stable at that higher level. But the changes are not statistically significant enough to know whether they are due to changes in recording practices or whether they reflect any actual change in violent behaviour.

In recent years, several self-report studies have been undertaken on offending committed by sections of Belgian youth. Due to differences in questionnaires and in questioned samples, comparisons are very difficult. The largest and most representative study was undertaken by Goedseels in the frame of a larger project on 'Youth in Flanders' (Goedseels, 2000). In 1998 a representative sample of 4,829 students in secondary schools (age 12 to 17 years old, and a few older students who doubled classes) were questioned on a broad spectrum of issues, including their self-reported delinquency. Table 8.1 overleaf displays the result.

The prevalence rate was 52%. More than half of the Flemish sample thus reported having committed at least one of the questioned offences in the last year. These 52% admitted an average of 2.3 offences in the last year. The age distribution showed a systematic rise till the age of 16, followed by a slight decrease. As

Table 8.1 Self-reported delinquency by secondary school students in Flanders (% of sample)

	Boys	Girls	Total
Fare dodging	28.5	22.6	25.5
Theft	29.1	18.1	23.4
Vandalism	31.9	9.8	20.6
Drug use	21.5	13.5	17.4
Physical violence	19.6	5.8	12.7
Carrying a weapon	22.2	3.4	12.6
Running away from home	6.8	6.3	6.5
Selling drugs	8.5	3.0	5.7
	N = 2,375	N = 2,435	N = 4,829

the questions were selected (and slightly adapted) from an international study on self-reported delinquency (Junger-Tas, 1994), some cautious comparisons are possible. Flemish juveniles appear all in all not to be strikingly different from Dutch, English and Welsh, Portuguese, Swiss and Spanish juveniles. The prevalence rate varied between 44–72.2%. The age distribution was as in the Flemish study.

Ethnic minorities

Most of the public concern about youth crime is focused on offending by ethnic minorities, especially Moroccans and (illegal) Eastern Europeans. At first sight, this might be justified. For example, 44% of the juveniles presented in 1999 at the Brussels' Youth Court for offences were from non EU origins (Vanneste, 2001). Additionally, a study of police data demonstrated an over-representation of foreign youths, especially Moroccans and Eastern Europeans (Van San and Leerkes, 2001). Due to the way it was presented and (mis)used in media and politics, this study created considerable great turmoil. Critics especially pointed to the selectivity of police registration and the naive and incomplete interpretation of the data.

Another more sophisticated scientific research has uncoupled street crime from ethnicity. An intensive research programme in Brussels questioned 4,347 minors, and analysed 2,580 dossiers of youthful offenders signalled at the public prosecutor's office. A superficial quantitative comparison reveals an over-representation of ethnic minority groups, especially Moroccans, in self-reported and registered crime. In a series of statistical multi-variate analyses, however, the ethnicity variable was absorbed completely by socio-economic and school variables. It was not ethnicity as such that appeared to be the problem, but the socio-economic and educational exclusion which especially hits children from Moroccan families. It also appeared that with equal seriousness and type of crime committed, the risks of being arrested by the police were more than three times higher for Moroccan boys than for boys from Belgian origin (Vercaigne et al., 2000).

Obviously, the public rhetoric on 'increasing youth crime', committed especially by 'ethnic minority youths' is not supported by firm and reliable data on increasing criminal behaviour, or on its increasingly violent character. This apparent (at least partial) independence of public concerns from statistical facts seems to be true also in other (European) countries (Mehlbye and Walgrave, 1998). Presumably, the concerns are stirred up by a general cultural climate, characterised by existential uncertainty and loss of mutual understanding leading to more intolerance. The question remains: how far is such a climate a good base for developing constructive, preventive and interventionist policies?

Which kind of juvenile justice reform?

Since the end of the 1980s, Belgium has been embroiled in an ongoing process of juvenile justice reform. After the transfer of many responsibilities to the Communities, the Federal State has been left with responsibility to organise the Youth Courts and to indicate the specific measures (or sanctions) that can be taken against juvenile offenders. Some minor adaptations of the YPA were made in 1994, but more fundamental reform is expected.

In 1995, a Commission for the Preparation of the Reform of the YPA published its final report (Cornelis, 1995). The proposals took into account the many criticisms about the losses of legal safeguards in the old Act, and tried to conform to the available international standards. The model of pure protection was left behind and so-called 'educative sanctions' were proposed, which were meant to be a compromise between an educative measure and a punishment. The report was subjected to criticism that leaving the protection model did not lead to a coherent new approach. There were some 'repressive make ups' and procedural improvements, but the shadow of education was still chased and in particular the potentials of a restorative approach were exploited insufficiently.

In 1996, the 'Research Unit of Youth Criminology' at the Leuven University was invited by the Minister of Justice to write a new report on what a juvenile justice system would look like if it were based consequentially on the principles of restorative justice (Geudens et al., 1997). The report relied on strengthening the international restorative justice tendency, based on practice, research and theorising, and on the expanding practice in Belgium with victim/offender mediation and community service. Moreover, an exploration of recent reforms in most European juvenile justice systems revealed a general tendency to consider juvenile offenders more responsible than in the protective approach; to focus more attention on the victim's harm and suffering; and to avoid the purely repressive response which is dominant in traditional criminal justice approaches. Most European countries have turned to varieties of restorative justice such as restitution, mediation and/or community service (Schelkens, 1998). The Leuven report proposed a system wherein priority would be given to voluntary settlements outside of the judicial system, but under its control, and wherein judicial coercion, if needed, would be exerted primarily in service of possible restitution or compensation. Within the framework of restorative actions or sanctions, reintegration of the offender would be the most important additional goal. Only in cases of very serious threats to public safety, incapacitation instead of reparation could be a primary objective. The report was taken seriously, and it was one of the basic documents for a ministerial working group to prepare a proposal for reform. The group made good progress.

In 1999, however, a new government came into power, with a new Minister of Justice. The earlier proceedings were abandoned and a new proposal was prepared. At the time of the urgent establishment of the Federal detention centre, the Minister also introduced his more comprehensive proposal which was said to be a new pragmatic approach, giving Youth Court judges a mix of adapted solutions. The proposal was rejected by the government in May 2002 as a result of clearly differing opinions within the Federal Government, between the Federal level and the Communities. Meanwhile, restorative justice practices are increasingly being implemented. The Communities recognise and fund private agencies specialised in monitoring community service and mediation. Community service is now a common measure taken in more than 20% of cases, including serious delinquency. In Flanders especially, mediation is on the increase. The number of youthful offenders referred to mediation services increased from 1,277 in 2001 to 1,604 in 2002. Since the end of 2001, an experiment in Family Group Conferences is running in five Flemish districts. These developments are being supported and oriented by university centres to underpin it with restorative justice theorising and empirical evaluation. There is no doubt that Flanders is currently one of the most restorative justice oriented regions in Europe.

After the election of 2003, a new government was formed, with, again, a new Minister of Justice. She wrote another proposal for reform in which the fundamentals of the protective approach would be preserved, but combined with restorative justice practices. The draft has been accepted by the Government and the Bill is currently being treated in Parliament. Flemish commentators express their scepticism as the proposals are too ambiguous: the protective philosophy is said to be dominant, but the possibilities for waiver are maintained so that number of juveniles will be handed over to the punitive justice system. Also, legal safeguard would be insufficiently assured, and the potential for restorative justice should be used more.

All in all, it remains uncertain when the reform of the juvenile justice system will find a new foundation in a comprehensive legal text. It is badly needed because social problems and youth problems have changed considerably since 1965, and the cultural, administrative and structural context of dealing with youth crime is now incomparable to the situation when the YPA was accepted. Also, the Committee on the Rights of the Child recommended that Belgium establish a system of juvenile justice that fully integrates the provisions of the Convention on the Rights of the Child, taking into consideration the holistic approach to addressing the problem of juvenile crime advocated in the Convention.[9]

Meanwhile, the 'creativity' and goodwill of judges and practitioners keep the system working, but without a coherent set of adequate legal guidelines. Belgium has to rebuild its system from the bottom. The country was indeed one of the very few in the world to provide a purely rehabilitative system for its young offenders. While protection has now lost a great deal of its credibility, any belief in returning simply to a traditional punitive system for juveniles is very low. Belgian authorities are confronted with a vacuum in principles on which to base a coherent new system, but hesitate to opt between restorative justice, promoted mainly by Flemish politicians, practitioners and academics, a revised model of rehabilitative justice, defended especially in the French speaking part of Belgium, and a tendency to more punitive and repressive measures for what is called 'serious' youth crime, which is popularly demanded by some in both parts of the country.

Maybe there is only one thing certain for the moment: any new system will be less purely welfare oriented or protective, but will be based on a concept of accountability of the offender. As such, the new system will very probably be based more on restorative (and/or punitive) sanctions and focus more on the harm and suffering caused by the offence to victims.

References

Cornelis, P. (1995) *Eindverslag van de Nationale commissie voor de hervorming van de wetgeving inzake jeugdbescherming*. Brussels: Min. van Justitie.

De Terwanghe, A. (2001) *Aide et protection de la jeunesse*. Liège: Ed. Jeunesse et Droit.

Dupont-Bouchat, M. S., Christiaens, J. and Vanneste, C. (2004). Jeunesse et Justice (1830–2002), in D. Heirbaut, X. Rousseaux and K. Velle (eds). *Politieke en sociale geschiedenis van justitie in België van 1830 tot heden/Histoire politique et sociale de la justice en Belgique de 1830 à nos jours*. Brugge: die keure, pp. 125–159.

Geudens, H., Schelkens, W. and Walgrave, L. (1997) *Op zoek naar een herstelrechtelijk jeugdsanctierecht in België. Een denkoefening in opdracht van de Minister van Justitie*. Leuven: Onderzoeksgroep Jeugdcriminologie, K.U.Leuven.

Goedseels, E. (2000) 'Delinquentie', in H. De Witte, J. Hooge and L. Walgrave (eds). *Jongeren in Vlaanderen: gemeten en geteld*. Leuven: Universitaire Pers, pp. 210–235.

Junger-Tas, J. (1994) 'Delinquency', in Thirteen Western Countries: Some preliminery Conclusions', in J. Junger-Tas, J. Terlouw and M. Klein (eds). *Delinquent Behavior Among Young People in the Western Countries*. The Hague/Amsterdam: RDC/Kugler, pp. 370–380.

Mehlbye, J. and Walgrave L. (eds) (1998) *Confronting Youth in Europe*. Copenhagen: AKF Forlaget.

Put, J. (2002) '[Jugendstrafrecht in] Belgien', in H.-J. Albrecht and M. Kilching (eds) *Jugendstrafrecht in Europa*. Freiburg: Max-Planck-Institut für ausländisches und internationales Strafrecht, pp. 1–26.

9. CRC/C/15/Add.178 of 13 June 2002, nr. 31–32.

Put, J. (2006) *Handboek Jeugdbeschermingsrecht.* Brugge: die keure.

Schelkens, W. (1998) 'Community Service and Mediation in Juvenile Justice Legislation in Europe', in L. Walgrave (ed.) *Restorative Justice for Juveniles: Potentials, Risks and Problems for Research.* Leuven: Leuven University Press. pp. 159–183.

Smets, J. (1996), *Jeugdbeschermingsrecht.* Deurne: Kluwer.

Tulkens, F. and T. Moreau (2000) *Droit de la jeunesse.* Bruxelles: Larcier.

Van San, M. and A. Leerkes (2001) *Criminaliteit en criminalisering van alllochtone jongeren in België.* Amsterdam: Amsterdam university press.

Vanneste, Ch. (2001) Een onderzoek over de beslissingen genomen door de parketmagistraten en de jeugdrechters. *Tijdschrift voor Jeugdrecht en Kinderrechten*, 2: 5, 193–202.

Vanneste, Ch., Amrani, L. Minet, J. F. and Neyt, N. (1999) *Evolution de la délinquance des mineurs. Analyse des données statistiques existantes.* Bruxelles: Institut National de Criminalistique et de Criminologie.

Vercaigne, C., Mistiaen, P., Kesteloot Chr, and Walgrave, L. (2000) *Verstedelijking, sociale uitsluiting van jongeren en straatcriminaliteit.* Brussel: DWTC.

Walgrave, L. (1993) 'The Making of Concepts on Juvenile Delinquency and its Treatment in the Recent History of Belgium and the Netherlands', in A. Hess and P. Clement (eds) *History of Juvenile Delinquency.* Aalen (Germany): Scientia, 2: 655–692.

Walgrave, L. (2002) 'Juvenile Justice in Belgium', in J. Winterdyk (ed.) *Juvenile Justice Systems: International Perspectives.* Toronto: Canadian Scholars' Press. pp. 29–59.

Welfare in Crisis? Key Developments in Scottish Youth Justice

9

Lesley McAra

Introduction

From the 1970s until the mid-1990s, the Scottish juvenile justice system exhibited a high degree of stability, both in terms of its institutional framework and policy ethos. Based on the welfare values enshrined in the Kilbrandon philosophy, the 'children's hearings system' became emblematic of a distinctively Scottish approach to youth crime and justice. This commitment to welfarism was in direct contrast to developments in many other Western jurisdictions (not least the system south of the border in England and Wales).

The stability of the Scottish system has, however, been somewhat shaken by a series of recent policy developments, set in train by the Children (Scotland) Act 1995 and culminating with the anti-social behaviour legislation, which came into force during 2004. These policies are predicated on a broad set of competing and somewhat contradictory rationales (they are variously punitive, managerialist, actuarial and restorative in orientation, as well containing some vestiges of older style penal welfarism). They have also created a wider range of audiences to whom the youth justice system now speaks (including victims of youth crime, 'failing' parents and local communities). Taken together, these developments are indicative of a degree of policy convergence with the youth justice system in England and Wales, as successive Justice Ministers in Scotland have gradually embraced the New Labour crime agenda (McAra, 2004a). A particular irony is that the pace of change has gathered momentum in the period since devolution (1999 onwards), with the reinstatement (after almost 300 years) of the Scottish Parliament.[1]

The history and development of youth justice in Scotland

Prior to the implementation of the hearings system in 1971, the juvenile justice system in Scotland was underpinned by an ambiguity in penal aims between concerns to 'rescue' children and also to punish them. Children were dealt with by the same types of criminal court as those which dealt with adults, although court officials were obliged to have regard to the welfare of the child (McAra, 2002). The tension that beset the courts between the requirement to look after the needs of the child and also act as formal courts of law, precipitated a major review of juvenile justice conducted by the Kilbrandon committee in the early 1960s. The recommendations of this committee were enshrined in the Social Work (Scotland) Act 1968, the preamble to which gave an explicit commitment to the promotion of 'social welfare'. The act, *inter alia*, abolished the existing juvenile courts and established a new institutional framework for youth justice, the children's hearings system.

Ethos

The children's hearings system was based on (what became known as) the Kilbrandon philosophy. According to this philosophy, the problems of children who were involved in offending or who were in need of care and protection (as a consequence of factors such as victimisation from sexual or violent offending or parental neglect) stemmed from the same source, namely failures in the normal upbringing process and/or broader social malaise (Kilbrandon, 1964). The system advocated early and minimal intervention based on the needs of the child, with the best interests of the child to be paramount in decision-making. It aimed to be as destigmatising as possible, a central principle being to avoid the criminalisation of children.

Key institutions

A characteristic feature of the new system was the separation of the judgment of evidence from the disposition of a case. The former lay in the hands of the

---

1. Prior to devolution, Scotland was wholly subject to the rule of the UK national Parliament at Westminster, although Scotland did have its own legal and education system. Policy specific to Scotland was administered by the 'Scottish Office' – a government department which had its headquarters in St. Andrew's House in Edinburgh.

Reporter whose principal task was to investigate referrals and decide if there was a prima facie case that one of the statutory grounds of referral to the system had been met[2] *and* whether the child was in need of compulsory measures of care. The principal task of a hearing was to consider the measures to be applied.

Before a hearing could take place both the child and his/her parents had to accept the grounds for referral (in the case of an offender there had to be an admission of guilt). If the grounds were disputed, the case would be referred to the sheriff court for a proof hearing.[3] Participants at a standard hearing were: the lay panel, who were the principal decision-makers (panels comprised three members drawn from the wider panel in each local authority area); the child and his/her parents; the Reporter (to advise on legal and procedural matters and to record the reasons for the decision); a social worker (to provide expert advice and assessment); and, where relevant, a range of other professionals (for example, a teacher, psychologist or psychiatrist). While the child and/or their parents could be accompanied by a lawyer (or indeed another supporter) no legal aid was available for this in the early years of the system.

The hearing aimed at participatory and consensual decision-making. The main disposals available to the panel were (and continue to be) residential and non-residential supervision requirements – both of which ensured statutory social work supervision based on needs of the child.[4] Supervision requirements normally lasted up to one year but were subject to review and could be extended up until the child's 18th birthday.

While it was possible for anyone to refer a case to the reporter, in practice the overwhelming majority of referrals always came from the police (McAra, 2002). Children could be referred to the system from birth until age 16 on care and protection grounds and from age 8–16 on offence grounds (8 currently being the age of criminal responsibility in Scotland). While most offenders aged 16–18 were dealt within the adult court system, the courts did have the power (little used, see McAra, 1998) to remit such cases back to the hearings system for advice or disposal.

Although the aim of the system was to focus on the needs of the child, it is important to remember that the Crown did reserve the right to prosecute children

---

2. Initially there were nine grounds for referral: (a) beyond the control of a relevant person, (b) moral danger, (c) lack of care, (d) and (dd) victim of or living in household of victim or perpetrator of schedule 1 offence (sex offence or one involving cruelty to children), (e) female child in same household as incest victim, (f) failed to attend school regularly without reasonable excuse, (g) committed an offence, (h) a child who has moved to Scotland from England, Wales or Northern Ireland whose case has been referred to the Reporter by the juvenile court (see Murray, 1982). These grounds have now been extended to include substance misuse (drugs, alcohol or volatile substance) and being in the care of the local authority.

3. The standard of proof in the case of an offence referral was 'beyond reasonable doubt' and for other non-offence referrals 'on the balance of probabilities'.

4. A residential supervision requirement specified some form of local authority residential care which in the early years of the system could include residence in a List D school. If a child was made subject to a non-residential supervision requirement, they would remain in their own home.

who had committed the most serious offences (such as rape or homicide) as well as certain motor vehicle offences[5] in the courts. While some commentators have argued that this went against the grain of key tenets of the Kilbrandon philosophy (that the more serious the offending the more deeper seated the needs), the decision to retain prosecution was justified on the grounds that such cases raised matters of public interest (McAra, 2004a). Moreover, it was a necessary compromise to ensure the support of key elites (including the police, the prosecution service and the judiciary) for the children's hearings system (Morris and McIsaac, 1978). In practice such prosecutions were (and continue to be) extremely rare (around 140 in a typical year, a high proportion of which are remitted back to the hearings for disposal) and require the express and personal permission of the Lord Advocate (the head of Scotland's prosecution service).

Assessment of early years

The implementation of the children's hearings system placed Scottish youth justice on a completely different trajectory from youth justice in England and Wales. During the 1980s and early 1990s England and Wales underwent what Hall has termed, 'the great moving right show' (with skilled working-class voters abandoning traditional Labour party politics to realign with new conservatism and the concomitant election of the Thatcher Government in 1979 on a monetarist and law and order ticket) (Hall, 1979). By contrast Scotland sustained a commitment to left-of-centre politics and a civic culture underpinned by communitarian values (see Paterson, 1994). This disjuncture between Scotland and Westminster resulted in a growing constitutional crisis within Scotland and pressures for home rule. In such a contested political arena, core institutions such as the children's hearings system became inextricably linked to a sense of Scottishness, with a foundational element of national identity being 'other-to England' (McAra, 2004a).

Critique of ethos and practice of system

While the distinctive nature of the children's hearings system was a source of national pride (see Morris and McIsaac, 1978), the practice of the system in its early years points to a number of the more pernicious tendencies to which welfare systems are prone: paternalistic decision-making; overzealous and indeterminate intervention; and greater levels of social control (see Allen, 1981).

For example, while the new institutional arrangements were intended to increase community participation in the system (through the lay panel), in practice panel membership was dominated by those from more affluent social

---

5. This relates only to children aged 15 or over for offences which would involve a penalty of disqualification from driving (see Moore and Whyte, 1998).

backgrounds (Moody, 1976; Hallet et al. 1998). A key concern of early commentators on the system, was that panel members would attempt to impose middle-class notions of morality on an unreceptive and socially distant client group (Martin and Murray, 1981). Concerns were also expressed about the high level of influence which social workers appeared to have on lay panels and the highly discretionary nature of decision-making at both the referral (reporter) and hearing stage (see Hallet et al. 1998).

The system also had a major potential for net-widening. By viewing offending as a symptom of need rather than as an end in itself, this provided the scope for large-scale intervention in the case of very trivial offences, as well as referral of children whose offending may formerly have been seen as too minor as to be in the public interest to prosecute. Official criminal justice statistics provide some evidence that net-widening may have occurred. Over the four years prior to the implementation of the hearings system, there had been an increase of 11% in the numbers of children coming to the attention of official agencies by virtue of their offending. By contrast, over the four years following implementation there was an increase of 45% (HMSO, 1974).

Concerns were also expressed that the system was better at tackling the problems posed by children referred on care and protection grounds rather than those posed by offenders (especially older repeat offenders) (Hallett et al., 1998; Waterhouse et al., 1999). There was, however, limited hard evidence for this. Indeed, very little research was undertaken on the process and outcome of supervision and in the early years no information systems were in place which would allow cases systematically to be tracked and monitored. Where research did identify shortcomings in the existing system, these tended to be failures of implementation (such as gaps in services, social work shortages and failure to allocate cases) rather than a failure of ethos (see Murray et al., 2002; Hallett et al., 1998).

Recent developments

In the period from 1995 until the present, the youth justice system in Scotland has undergone major transformation, particularly in respect of its policies and procedures for dealing with child offenders.[6] One of the main catalysts for change has been the transformation of early anxieties about system effectiveness into a full blown moral panic about the problems posed by persistent offenders and a perceived increase in anti-social behaviour amongst young people (a panic which runs counter to all published indicators which suggest stable or falling levels of youth crime over the past decade, see McAra 2004b). A further contributing factor has been the greater ideological congruence between the Labour/Liberal Democratic coalition governments in Scotland and

---

6. The chapter does not deal with major changes made to the system in respect of care and protection cases. For a detailed overview see Edwards and Griffiths, 2006.

Table 9.1   Key developments in youth justice 1995–2005

1995	• Children (Scotland) Act; decisions do not have to be taken in best interest of child where child poses risk to public; sheriffs empowered to substitute own decision for that of panel in contested decisions.
1998	• Scotland Act (Devolution)
1999	• Partnership for Scotland
	• Safer Communities in Scotland
2000	• Response to report of Advisory Group on Youth Crime ('It's a Criminal Waste'):

  – National strategy based on core objectives
  – Local multi-agency Youth Justice Teams
  – Focus on persistent offending (expanded range of programmes based on 'what works' principles for young people up to age of 18 for use in hearings and courts)
  – Expand bail information/supervision and diversion schemes for all 16/17 year olds
  – National resource to disseminate best practice

• Communities that Care pilots (early intervention programmes to diminish risks of school failure, teenage pregnancy; sexually transitted disease; drug misuse; violence and other crime)

2001   • Grant for SACRO to develop pre-hearing diversion based on restorative principles

2002   • Action Plan to Reduce Youth Crime

  – Reiterating focus on persistent offending and effective practice
  – Increase public confidence (building on community and neighbourhood safety programmes to reduce offending)
  – Victims as stakeholders (information sharing, restorative justice programmes)
  – Easing transition between hearings and adult system
  – Enable young people to fulfil potential (promotion of educational, cultural sporting activities, social inclusion programmes)
  – Early intervention (parenting skills, education, etc.)

• National Objectives and Standards for Youth Justice focus on:
  – Methods of assessment and quality of information (to ensure uniformity in use of assessment tools; action plan etc.)
  – Range and availability of programmes aimed at tackling offending
  – Timescales
  – Information provided to victims and local communities
  – Appropriate targeting of secure care and its effectiveness at tackling offending
  – Management and organisation of youth justice services (annual reporting by youth justice strategy teams)
  – Local Youth Justice Strategy Groups: to ensure progress in meeting standards

• Intensive Support Fund (to develop residential and community based programmes for persistent offenders and additional secure care places)

2003   • Pilot fast track hearings (persistent offenders)
    • Pilot Youth Court (persistent offenders)
    • Youth Crime Prevention Fund (supports voluntary sector projects for those at risk of offending and their parents)
    • Support and Information for Victims of Youth Crime (pilot projects)
    • Criminal Justice (Scotland) Act 2003 provisions for Principal Reporter to give information to victims
    • Police restorative cautioning (full roll out Summer 2004)

Table 9.1 (Continued)

2004	• Glasgow Restorative Justice Initiative (multi-agency early intervention initiative, to raise victim empathy and awareness)
	• Anti-social Behaviour etc. (Scotland) Act 2004:
	  – Extend use of ASBOs to 12–16 year olds (implemented from October 2004)
	  – Police powers to disperse groups (implemented from October 2004);
	  – Community Reparation Order (via courts for those aged 12+)
	  – Extension of remote electronic monitoring (tagging) to under 16s (implemented from April 2005)
	  – Parenting Orders (implemented from April 2005)

the Blairite, New Labour governments at Westminster. It is also arguable that the fledgling Scottish Parliament has been using crime control and penal practice more generally as a means of building political capacity (see Cole, 2005), reconstructing social solidarity and mobilising communities (see below). One of the fall-outs from this has been a gradual erosion of the child-centred ethos of Scottish youth justice policy.

Limitation of space prevents detailed consideration of each of the recent changes (which are summarised in Table 9.1). Rather, this section of the chapter focuses on five key themes which underpin these developments:

1. Managerialism and accountability
2. Public protection, risk management and effective practice
3. Social inclusion and crime prevention
4. Individual rights and responsibilisation
5. Restorative justice and victims as stakeholders.[7]

1 Managerialism and accountability

The period since devolution has seen a major overhaul in the organisation and management of youth justice in Scotland. Local multi-agency youth justice teams (which include representatives from social work, the police, the local community, health services, the voluntary sector and the reporter) are now involved in strategic planning, setting targets and expanding the range of services for offenders. New national objectives and standards have been developed to improve the efficiency and effectiveness of the system and to ensure evenness of service provision across Scotland. The standards set targets in respect of timescales, risk assessment and reductions in the number of persistent offenders. With regard to the latter, the Scottish Executive has now produced a base-line

---

7. This section of the paper is drawn from an article first published in the Cambrian Law Review 2004, Vol. 35 (McAra, 2004a).

figure of 1,201 persistent young offenders which the system is required to reduce by 10% by 2006 and a further 10% by 2008 (see PA Consulting 2004).[8]

In recent years too the range of institutions to which the youth justice system is accountable has grown in complexity. The Scottish Parliament has added new layers of scrutiny – particularly through the work of the two justice committees (which can scrutinise bills before Parliament, conduct enquiries and call on expert witnesses, etc.). Moreover the policy developments (described in more detail below) have together created a diverse set of audiences for the institutions of youth justice, including victims of crime, parents and local communities, whose needs the system must now satisfy.

2 Public protection, risk management and effective practice

The increased levels of managerialism have also been accompanied by a shift in the underlying ethos of the system.

The Children (Scotland) Act 1995 enabled the hearings to place the principle of public protection above that of best interests in cases where the child posed a risk to others. This led to the beginnings of a bifurcated discursive framework within the hearings – with the panel considering issues of public protection in high risk cases and welfare needs in the case of low risk offenders and those referred on care and protection grounds.

The bifurcated framework gained momentum in the early months of the Scottish Parliament (in 1999) with the publication of a major review of the youth justice system which took the problems posed by persistent offenders as its central focus (*It's a Criminal Waste: Stop Youth Crime Now*, 2000). A key recommendation of the review (taken forward in the subsequent *Action Plan to Reduce Youth Crime*, 2002) was that 'what works' principles should be incorporated into an expanded range of social work programmes for persistent offenders and that a national centre be established to disseminate best practice.

What works programmes are focused on tackling criminogenic needs rather than generic welfare needs (as per the former supervision requirement). They involve careful calibration of programme intensity to level or risk posed and advocate the use of cognitive behavioural methods (see McGuire, 1995). A core task of social work is now to provide risk assessments for all hearings referrals, using standardised assessment tools (ASSET/YLS-CMI) (Scottish Executive, 2002a). Although what works programmes are aimed at behavioural change (and thus can be regarded as rehabilitative in orientation), by making offending, rather than the offender, the focus of intervention they have the potential to undermine the holistic and child-centred approach traditionally adopted by social workers.

---

8. This has been based on the definition of persistence set out in the national standards, namely five or more offending episodes in a six month period (an offending episode comprises one referral to the Reporter with an offence component).

The drive to deal more effectively with persistent offenders has culminated with the pilot fast track hearings (2003) and pilot youth court (2003) initiatives. Fast-track hearings are targeted on offenders with a record of five or more offence referrals to the reporter in a six month period. The pilots place strict time targets for the various stages in the referral process (police to Reporter, Reporter to panel), with the aim of bringing persistent offenders before a hearing within a maximum of 53 working days.[9] As part of the pilot schemes, resources are also being directed to the further expansion of specialist community programmes for these offenders. Although the fast track hearings should comprise experienced panel members only and are required to take a holistic view of the child, for the first time deeds rather than needs have become the core driving force behind the hearings referral process.

The pilot youth court in Hamilton (and now Airdrie) is aimed principally at older persistent offenders (charged with summary offences), aged 16–17 who normally would be dealt with in the adult courts, as well as children aged 15 who would otherwise have been dealt with in the sheriff summary court. The criterion for referral to the Youth Court is three or more police referrals to the procurator fiscal (prosecutor) in a six month period. As with the fast-track hearings, timescales have been set for the referral process[10] and local authority social work departments have been charged with developing a portfolio of specialist community-based programmes for these offenders. An important element of the new court procedures is the review hearing, in which certain offenders are required to return to court some time after the initial sentence, to discuss progress in addressing offending with the sheriff.

Arguably the Youth Court is underpinned by somewhat ambivalent penal aims. On the one hand the pilot is explicitly aimed at the promotion of social inclusion, citizenship and personal responsibility as well as enhancing community safety and reducing harm to victims (see McIvor et al., 2004). On the other hand it functions to divert older children away from the adult court system and thus could be seen as a more humane way of dealing with them. However, a key recommendation of the *Youth Crime Review* (2000), was that 16 and 17 year old offenders should be dealt with by the hearings system rather than the courts and a bridging pilot was proposed as a means of facilitating this. That Ministers opted for a court-based setting instead, serves to reinforce the more robust, punitive approach which has now been adopted towards persistent offenders. Indeed when the Youth Court pilot was launched, Cathy Jamieson, currently Minister for Justice, commented that 'punishment is a key part of the youth justice process' (Scottish Executive, 2003a).

---

9. Timescales as follows: police referral to Reporter within 10 days; Reporter decision within 28 days of receiving police referral (Local Authority Initial Assessment Reports and Social Background Reports to assist Reporter decision-making to be made available within 20 days); once decision made to have hearing this should be held within 15 days.

10. Youngsters should make their first appearance in court, 10 days after being charged.

3 Social inclusion and crime prevention

Policy documents produced in the earliest days of the Scottish Parliament: *Partnership for Scotland* (Scottish Executive, 1999a) and *Safer Communities in Scotland* (Scottish Executive, 1999b) contained proposals to reduce youth crime through promoting safer, more empowered communities as well as to confront the causes of crime as linked to unemployment and social isolation (see Hogg, 1999). These policy aims were also taken forward in the *Action Plan to Reduce Youth Crime* which reiterated the need for: more developed neighbourhood and community safety programmes; early intervention to promote parenting skills; and programmes to enable young people to fulfil their potential through the promotion of educational, cultural and sporting activities (see Scottish Executive, 2002b).

Specific initiatives which have come on-stream in recent years include: additional funding for Community Safety Partnerships (2003) to improve access to sports and leisure facilities for young people; the action plan for youth football to divert youngsters away from the streets and into meaningful, structured activity (2004); and the Youth Crime Prevention Fund (launched 2003) which has funded projects such as the Aberlour National Parenting Project (to improve parent–child relationships, prevent or reduce offending and assist parents with problems such as drug use, domestic abuse or mental illness) and the NCH Renfrewshire project (which works with youngsters under the age of 12 and their families where the child shows signs of anti-social or violent behaviour or where there are concerns about parenting skills).

In tandem with these inclusionary policies, however, the emphasis on community safety has recently been give a more punitive edge. This is exemplified, in particular, by a number of the proposals contained in the Anti-Social Behaviour Act 2004. This Act, inter alia, extends the use of anti-social behaviour orders to children aged between 12 and 15 (previously only available in Scotland to people aged 16 or over), gives the police additional powers to disperse groups in designated areas where behaviour is causing or likely to cause alarm and distress to others, and introduces electronic tagging for children (in cases where the child has a history of absconding, where there is evidence that the child's mental, moral or physical welfare is at risk, or where the child is likely to injure him/herself or others).

4 Individual rights and responsibilisation

Recent policy changes have also led to increased focus on both 'rights talk' and responsibilisation. This has been given particular momentum with the incorporation of the European Convention on Human Rights into Scots Law (ECHR) (through the Human Rights Act, 1998).

Major concerns have been expressed by some commentators that ECHR could pose a number of challenges to the youth justice system both of substance and of principle (see Edwards, 2001). One of the earliest tests of compatibility occurred in the *S* v. *Miller* case 2001 (SLT 53). A central aim of this case was to test whether the hearings complied with procedural guarantees set out in article 6 and in particular whether it was unfair that a child had no access to legal aid at the hearing. (Article 6 states that everyone charged with a criminal offence has the right to legal assistance and to be given it free of charge if he/she does not have sufficient means to pay for it.) The court affirmed the right of children to legal representation. A key justification for the decision was that legal aid would enhance the participation of young people in the proceedings (participation being a key element of the Kilbrandon ethos), especially those who were extremely young and those who had limited intelligence or poor social skills. Now a legal representative (from a panel of suitably experienced lawyers, safeguards and curators *ad litem*) can be appointed free of charge in cases where the disposal is likely to involve restriction of liberty, where the case is of unusual complexity, or where the child is not able to understand proceedings (for example due to lack of maturity).

A ruling was also sought in *S* v. *Miller*, as to whether the detention of children in secure care was compliant with the child's right to liberty. (Article 5 states that the only lawful detention of a minor is for the purpose of educational supervision or for the purpose of bringing him before the competent legal authority.) The court held that educational supervision included 'the exercise ... of parental rights for the benefit and protection of the person concerned'. Where a child is detained in secure care these rights are exercised by the local authority, thus in the view of the court, secure care has an educational purpose.

The ruling in *S* v. *Miller* is testimony to both the pliability of the principles underpinning the hearings system and to the reasoning skills of the judges who contrived both to enhance the rights of the child while at the same time upholding the central ethos of the system (ensuring that decision-making is both participatory and in the best interests of the child.) Many commentators are of the view, however, that greater legal input into hearings decision-making will lead to tensions within the system, rendering the hearings process more adversarial in the longer term, and that the status of secure care as an educational disposition may yet undergo further challenge (see for example Edwards, 2001).

The corollary to the increasing emphasis on rights talk has been an increased focus on responsibility, both in respect of child offenders and their parents. This is exemplified in the continued Scottish Executive stalling over raising the age of criminal responsibility within Scotland. At the time of writing the age of criminal responsibility continues to be 8, one of the lowest in Europe. Both the Scottish Law Commission (SLC, 2001) and the youth justice review group (2000) recommended that consideration be given to raising the age of criminal responsibility to 12. Although this recommendation was accepted in principle by the Scottish Executive it has yet to act upon it. The low age may only be tolerated because so few children under the age of 12 are actually prosecuted in court (see McAra, 2004c). Nonetheless, the age of criminal responsibility has enormous symbolic significance, suggesting that extremely young children know right from wrong and are capable of taking full responsibility for their own wrongdoing: an ethos which is slightly out of kilter with the model of offending informing the Kilbrandon philosophy.

Parents are also included within central government's responsibilisation strategy. The Anti-Social Behaviour Act 2004 has introduced parenting orders for the first time in Scotland. These are aimed at parents who 'deliberately and recklessly fail' their children (Scottish Executive, 2004). An order will require parents to take action to deal with their child's offending or anti-social behaviour (although it will still be possible for an order to be sought on welfare grounds, such as extreme neglect). While parenting orders are civil orders, a breach will constitute a criminal offence.

5   Restorative justice and victims as stakeholders

Finally, victims of youth crime are increasingly being seen as key stakeholders in the youth justice system. Indeed pilot schemes were introduced in 2003 aimed at providing support and information to victims of youth crime, reinforced by the Criminal Justice (Scotland) Act 2003 which empowered the Principal Reporter to give information to victims.

The victim focus has been given particular momentum by an increased emphasis on restorative principles in youth justice policy. SACRO has been at the forefront of this – receiving grant aid from central government in 2001 to develop pre-hearing diversion schemes. These schemes offer a range of programmes including restorative conferencing, face-to-face meetings with victims and shuttle mediation (see Brookes, 2004 for an overview). In addition there are now plans to roll out restorative police cautioning across Scotland (initially introduced in a small number of police divisions in 2003, with full roll out by April 2006). Restorative cautioning is delivered by specially trained police officers, in front of the child's parents, and aims to explore why the offence occurred and the impact of the offence on victims and the wider community.

The restorative theme also frames the new community reparation orders, introduced by the Anti-Social Behaviour Act 2004 (and currently being piloted). These orders are a sentence of the court (not a hearings disposal) and involve the offender in some work of benefit to either the victim or the community.

Future prospects

The final part of this chapter turns more briefly to an assessment of the future prospects for the system as they relate to its key audiences: persistent offenders; victims; failing parents; local communities and the wider public.

Persistent offenders

The system may find it difficult to meet the newly specified targets for reductions in persistent offending, not least because it is sending out a set of rather mixed messages to children. Policy is aimed at restoring/building citizenship among young people and reintegrating offenders back into the community, at the same time as it is aimed at the exclusion of youngsters for 'anti-social' behaviour (a form of behaviour which has no legal definition other than that which causes alarm and distress to others, and this may of course vary according to culture, location and individual tolerance levels).

As in the early years of the system, there is also major potential for netwidening, given the expanded range of interventions now available at each stage in the system, from police restorative cautioning and pre-hearings diversion to the recent expansion in the secure estate (see Table 9.1 on pages 132–3). There is also some evidence that the cumulative effects of system contact are as likely to amplify as diminish offending. Research has found that early experience of hearings contact predicts later and more intense referral on offence grounds and that early experience of adversarial police contact amplifies serious offending in later years and inhibits desistence from it (see Waterhouse et al., 1999; McAra, 2005, Smith, 2005).

Furthermore, policy targets take no cognisance of the highly discretionary nature of police decision-making practices which currently have a key role to play in shaping the client group of the hearings system. Research has found that the police tend to target certain categories of youngsters – those who have 'previous form' (being known to the police in previous years) and, of the children who regularly hang out in the street, those who live in a low socio-economic status household (importantly this is a selection effect at the individual level, *not* the result of police targeting of specific areas) (McAra and McVie, 2005). These youngsters become propelled into a repeat cycle of adversarial contact, not always warranted by their current level of offending. Consequently they are more at risk of referral to the reporter than other, sometimes, more serious offenders.

Finally, there is evidence that policy-makers may have made over-optimistic assumptions about what specialist programmes, based on 'what works' principles, will be able to deliver. The research on which 'what works' principles were based (namely meta-analytic studies) only ever claimed that offending could be reduced by a small amount. Given that there are no guarantees that all (or indeed any) of the identified persistent offenders in Scotland will participate in the new specialist programmes, the current targets (of a 20% reduction in the number of persistent offenders by 2008) may be over ambitious.

Victims

A major challenge facing the system is to engage victims in the youth justice process, both in terms of encouraging high levels of participation and ensuring that any involvement has a positive rather than damaging effect. Research suggests that the system, to date, has not been wholly effective in this regard (see Sawyer, 2000;

Skellington et al., 2005). Indeed victim participation may be increasingly difficult to achieve because of the manageralist principles which frame the youth justice process. Lessons from other jurisdictions (see Newburn et al., 2002) would indicate that the current emphasis within Scotland on speed through the system and the reduction of delay (through fast tracking and the introduction of time limits) could minimise the time available to contact victims, to prepare them for involvement in restorative or support initiatives and to follow-up cases.

A more fundamental problem posed by the victim strategy in youth justice, however, is that victims and offenders are generally conceptualised as discrete groups, with the former comprising a more 'morally deserving' group. Research evidence from a range of sources suggests that this may be rather short-sighted, principally because it is young offenders who are most likely to be the victim of youth crime (see Smith, 2004a; Hayward and Sharp, 2005). The close relationship between victimisation and offending means that when the system is addressing offenders it is more often than not speaking to victims (and vice versa) and this of course muddies the principles upon which many restorative programmes are based.

Failing parents

The youth justice system also faces a number of challenges in engaging with 'failing' parents. This is primarily because of tensions between the punitive and preventative dimensions of current policy. On the one hand social inclusion policies are aimed at destigmatising problem families and reintegrating them into the community, whereas the newly implemented parenting orders have the potential to restigmatise families – and increase the risks of criminalisation (given that a breach of a parenting order will constitute a criminal offence). The challenges posed by these mixed messages are compounded by research on parenting and offending which indicates that the most effective model of parenting in terms of controlling offending, works least well in the context of neighbourhood deprivation (Smith, 2004b). Unless the environmental and cultural context is propitious, then attempts to teach parenting skills or indeed force parents to take greater control over their children (through measures such as parenting orders) are likely to fail.

Local communities

Turning to communities, a major difficulty facing the youth justice system is that the conception of community which underpins recent policy is inherently an elastic one. To borrow Clarke's classification (2002), community is variously invoked as a site of governance (through efforts to police the physical space within which a community is located as exemplified in the new dispersal orders); a mode of governance (as exemplified by the efforts to involve the community in the youth justice process, through youth justice teams and the lay panel), and an effect of governance (with many interventions aimed at mending fractured and impoverished communities). Arguably there are major tensions here – for how can a community function as a site or mode of governance if it is not already an effect of governance, in other words if it is not already mobilised as a functioning entity?

The mobilisation of a community is of course an enormously difficult challenge in the face of the concentration effects of poverty and social exclusion in some areas. Currently around 14% of the population in Scotland live in the top 10% most deprived wards, areas blighted by poor health and housing and fragmented by high crime levels and sectarian violence (NFO Social Research, 2003a; Scottish Executive, 2003b). That such areas lack the capacity to mobilise themselves is evident from the recent evaluation of the 'Communities that Care' pilot projects. These projects were implemented in three areas of high social deprivation across Scotland and were intended to involve local residents along with statutory and voluntary agencies in the planning and development of risk prevention programmes for young people. However, the evaluation found that while the programmes had promoted some degree of partnership working, they had been impeded by a 'lack of a fully inclusive and consistent range of contributors' (Bannister and Dillane, 2005: 3). A particular concern was the low number of local residents who took part in the programmes, especially young people.

The wider public

The wider public is invoked as an audience of youth justice policy in two ways: as audience for the mechanisms for audit which now pervade the youth justice process and as audience for pronouncements about serious and persistent offending, when policy is at its most punitive and exclusionary (with ASBOs, electronic tagging and risk management being justified as mechanisms better to protect the public). These invocations arguably play against each other: the rational and bureaucratic language in which audit is conducted contrasting strongly with the more emotional and expressive language of punitiveness.

A fundamental difficulty the system faces in *demonstrating* that it can protect the public is that many of the factors which feed into public perceptions of safety are outwith the control of youth justice agencies. A number of commentators argue, for example, that certain so-called 'signal crimes' (often low level incivilities such as graffiti or burnt-out cars – not always committed by children) can magnify a person's perception of risk. Thus people living or working in a low street-crime area may be erroneously more fearful of attack if some of the surrounding buildings are covered in graffiti (see Murray, 2004).

The construction of the persistent offender as a contemporary folk-devil allows politicians to tap into public fears and use these to justify a tougher stance on young offenders. However this is a strategy which risks the further exclusion and alienation of young people from the neighbourhoods within which they live, with damaging consequences in terms of both community cohesion and the more inclusive and nurturing elements of the youth justice policy frame.

Conclusion

The Scottish youth justice system has undergone significant transformation in recent years. Formerly predicated on a welfare-based ethos it is now under-pinned by a more complex set of penal rationales. As Scottish Ministers have embraced the New Labour crime and justice agenda, so too have institutions of youth justice begun to lose their distinctive Scottish identity. Many of the changes have been driven by a moral panic about persistent offending and anti-social behaviour not based on particularly strong evidence. There is, however, a danger that this moral panic may turn into a self-fulfilling prophecy as a result of police gate-keeping practices (which serve to recycle the usual suspects back into the system time and again) and the potential for deviancy amplification which system contact brings.

Research continues to be supportive of core elements of the Kilbrandon philosophy and in particular its holistic approach to troubled and troublesome children, the links made between social malaise and offending and the need for support to be offered in ways which do not stigmatise recipients. This philoso-phy is now under threat as a new range of services and programmes are grafted on to existing institutions which uncouple the victim from the offender and which have begun to place deeds rather than needs at the forefront of decision-making processes.

Youth justice has become a central plank in the new Scottish Executive's efforts to build political capacity and regenerate communities. In doing so the Executive has created a broader set of audiences whose needs the system must satisfy: persistent offenders; victims; failing parents; local communities; and the wider public. The evidence would suggest that the youth justice system is a rather risky mechanism through which to carry forward any vision of polity building: predicated as it now is on both inclusionary and exclusionary forms of practice, which work against each other in complex ways. Carrying the weight of political expectation, undergoing a process of 'de-tartanisation', the Scottish system of youth justice faces an uncertain future.

References

Allen, F. (1981) *The Decline of the Rehabilitative Ideal: Penal Policy and Social Purpose.* New Haven: Yale University Press.

Bannister, J. and Dillane, J. (2005) *Communities That Care: An Evaluation of the Scottish Pilot Programme Crime and Criminal Justice Research Findings No. 79* www.scotland.gov.uk/Publications/2005/06/01163534/35373.

Brookes, D. (2004) 'Restorative Justice in Scotland's Youth Justice System', in J. McGhee, M. Mellon and B. Whyte (eds) *Addressing Deeds: Working with young people who offend*. London: NCH.

Clarke, J. (2002) 'Reinventing Community? Governing in Contested Spaces', paper delivered at Spacing for Social Work Conference (Bielefeld, November 14–16).

Cole, A. (2005) *Beyond Devolution and Decentralisation: Building Regional Capacity in Wales and Brittany*. Manchester: Manchester University Press.

Edwards, L. (2001), '*S v. Miller*: The End of the Children's Hearing System as We Know It', *Scots Law Times* 41, 23 May.

Edwards, L. and Griffiths, A. (2006) *Family Law*. Edinburgh: W. Green, Sweet and Maxwell.

Hall, S. (1979) 'The Great Moving Right Show', *Marxism Today* 23.

Hallet, C. Murray, C. Jamieson, J. and Veitch, B. (1998) *The Evaluation of the Children's Hearings in Scotland, Volume 1 'Deciding in Children's Interests'*. Edinburgh: The Scottish Office Central Research Unit.

Hayward, R. and Sharp, C. (2005) *Young People, Crime and Anti-Social Behaviour: Findings from the 2003 Crime and Justice Survey*, Home Office Research Findings no. 245.

Hogg, K. (1999) *Youth Crime in Scotland. A Scottish Executive Policy Unit Review* http://www.scotland.gov.uk/library3/law/youth.pdf

Kilbrandon Committee (1964) *Report on Children and Young Persons, Scotland*. Edinburgh: HMSO.

Martin, F., Fox, S. and Murray, K. (1981) *Children out of Court*. Edinburgh: Scottish. Academic: Press.

McAra, L. (1998) *Social Work and Criminal Justice Volume 2: Early Arrangements*, Edinburgh: The Stationery Office.

McAra, L. (2002) 'The Scottish Juvenile Justice System: Policy and Practice', in J. Winterdyk (ed.) *Juvenile Justice Systems: International Perspectives*, second edition. Toronto: Canadian Scholars Press.

McAra, L. (2004a) 'The Cultural and Institutional Dynamics of Transformation: Youth Justice in Scotland and England and Wales' Cambrian Law Review 35: 23–54.

McAra, L. (2004b) 'Youth Crime and Justice in Scotland: Perception and Reality', *Children, Young People and Crime in the United Kingdom and Ireland, Fourth Biennial Conference: Perception and Realties, Conference Report*.

McAra, L. (2004c) *Pre-Inquiry Seminar on Youth Justice in Scotland: Report and Recommendations* http://www.scottish.parliament.uk/justice2/inquiries-04/yji/yji-seminar.htm

McAra, L. (2005) *Patterns of Referrals to the Children's Hearings System for Drug or Alcohol Misuse*, Edinburgh Study of Youth Transitions and Crime, Research Digest No. 6.

McAra, L. and McVie, S. (2005) 'The Usual Suspects? Street-life, Young Offenders and the Police', *Criminal Justice*, 5(1): 5–35.

McGuire, J. (ed.) (1995) *What Works Reducing Offending: Guidelines from Research and Practice*. Chichester: Wiley.

McIvor, G., Brown, A., Eley, S., Malloch, M., Murray, C., Piacentini, L. and Walters, R. (2004) *The Hamilton Sheriff Youth Court Pilot: The First Six Months*, Scottish Executive, Social Research Findings No. 77 www.scotland.gov.uk/socialresearch

Moody, S. (1976) *Survey of the Background of Current Panel Members*. Mimeo: Scottish Home and Health Department.

Moore, G. and Whyte, B. (1998) *Social Work and Criminal Law in Scotland*, third edition. Edinburgh: Mercat Press.

Morris, A. and McIsaac, M. (1978) *Juvenile Justice? The Practice of Social Welfare*, Cambridge Studies in Criminology, Cambridge: Heinemann.

Murray, C., Hallett, C., McMillan, N. and Watson, J. (2002) *Home Supervision*, Scottish Executive Social Research, Research Findings No. 4.

Murray, K. (1982) 'Structure and Operation' in F. Martin and K. Murray (eds.) *The Scottish Juvenile Justice System*. Edinburgh: Scottish Academic Press.

Murray, P. (2004) *Signal Crimes: Risk Perception and Behaviour*, Working Paper No. 5. www.odpm.gov.uk/stellent/groups/odpm_science/documents/page/odpm_science_028389.hcsp

MVA (2002) *The 2000 Scottish Crime Survey Overview Report*, The Scottish Executive, Central Research Unit.

Newburn, T., Crawford, A., Earle, R., Goldie, S., Hale, C., Hallam, A., Masters, G., Netten, A., Saunders, R., Sharpe, K. and Uglow, S. (2002) *The Introduction of Referral Orders into the Youth Justice System, Final Report, Home Office Research Study 242*. London: Home Office.

NFO Social Research (2003) *Sectarianism in Glasgow* http://www.glasgow.gov.uk/NR/rdonlyres/DA614F81-4F1B-4452-8847-F3FDE920D550/0/sectarianism03.pdf

PA Consulting Group (2004) *Scottish Youth Justice Baseline* http://www.childrens-hearings.co.uk/pdf/Scottish%20Youth%20Justice%20Baseline.pdf

Paterson L. (1994) *The Autonomy of Modern Scotland*. Edinburgh: Edinburgh University Press.

Sawyer, B. (2000) *An Evaluation of the SACRO (Fife) Young Offender Mediation Project Edinburgh*, The Scottish Executive Central Research Unit.

Scottish Executive (1999a) *Partnership for Scotland* www.scotland.gov.uk/publications.

Scottish Executive (1999b) *Safer Communities in Scotland* www.scotland.gov.uk/publications.

Scottish Executive (2000) *It's a Criminal waste: Stop Youth Crime Now: Report of Advisory Group on Youth Crime* http://www.scotland.gov.uk/youth/crimereview/docs/agyc-00.asp

Scottish Executive (2002) *Scotland's Action to Reduce Youth Crime*. Edinburgh: HMSO.

Scottish Executive (2002a) *National Standards for Scotland's Youth Justice Services* http://www.scotland.gov.uk/library5/justice/nssyjs.pdf

Scottish Executive (2002b) *Scotland's Action to Reduce Youth Crime*. Edinburgh: Her Majesty's Stationery Office.

Scottish Executive (2003a) 'Scotland's First Youth Court Opens', Press Release www.scotland.gov.uk/pages/news

Scottish Executive (2003b) *Scottish Indices of Deprivation 2003* www.scotland.gov.uk/library5/social/siod-07

Scottish Executive (2004) *Putting our Communities first: A Strategy for Tackling Anti-social Behaviour* http://www.scotland.gov.uk/consultations/social/pocf-00.asp

Skellington Orr, K. McCaig, E. and Leven, T. (2005) *An Assessment of the Support and Information for Victims of Youth Crime Pilot Scheme*, Scottish Executive www.scotland.gov.uk/publications/2005/04/11105447/54484

Smith, D. J. (2004a) *The Links between Victimisation and Offending*, Edinburgh Study of Youth Transitions and Crime, Research Digest No. 5.

Smith, D. J. (2004b) *Parenting and Delinquency*, Edinburgh Study of Youth Transitions and Crime, Research Digest No. 3.

Smith, D. J. (2005) 'The Effectiveness of the Juvenile Justice System', *Criminal Justice* 5(2): 181–195.

Waterhouse, L., McGhee, J., Loucks, N., Whyte, B. and Kay, H. (1999) *The Evaluation of the Children's Hearings in Scotland, Volume 3 Children in Focus*. Edinburgh: The Scottish Executive Central Research Unit.

Japan: From Child Protection to Penal Populism

Mark Fenwick

Introduction

In May 1997 in the city of Kobe, Western Japan, an 11 year old boy was reported missing after leaving home to visit his grandparents. Several days later his severed head was discovered in front of the main gate of a local school. With the head was a note, apparently written by the killer, expressing his hatred of society and extolling the pleasures of killing another person. The investigation soon focused on a 14 year old boy from the same school who was known to have been bullying the victim. Within days, the police had arrested the suspect, whom the media came to refer to as *Shonen A* (young person A). Shonen A was later implicated in the earlier murder of a 10 year old girl as well as three other violent attacks on schoolgirls (for more background on this case, see Schreiber 2001: chapter 4).

The Kobe case, along with a series of high-profile juvenile murders that followed, focused public attention on youth offenders and instigated an ongoing process of law reform that has transformed juvenile justice in Japan. Of particular importance was a package of measures passed by the Diet in November 2000 that amended the Juvenile Law. A traditional concern with the welfare of youth offenders was supplemented by a new emphasis on punishment, the rights of the victim, and parental responsibility. Emboldened by the apparent popularity of these measures, the government has pursued the issue with a further round of reform proposals in January 2005. As such, the last decade has witnessed an important break in the rhetoric and practice of Japanese youth justice. This chapter will examine this change by introducing the Juvenile Law 1948, outlining the main features of the 2000 reforms, and conclude with a brief description of the issues that are currently dominating discussion of youth justice.

The broad contours of this narrative will make familiar reading to anyone who follows global trends in youth justice. The impact of the Kobe case echoes similar high profile juvenile murder cases in the USA or UK. Moreover, the eclipse of welfare based approaches and the recourse to punishment as a tactic for the re-legitimation of political clites has become a recurring theme in the criminological literature (Garland, 2001: chapter 5). That such events are occurring in Japan is interesting not least because it provides the opportunity for the kind of 'East–West' comparison that is unfortunately quite rare within comparative criminology. However, it is of particular interest since Japan has often been regarded as a 'crime-free' society that has successfully overcome its crime problem without recourse to formal systems of criminal justice (for a representative and influential illustration of this view, see Braithwaite, 1989). The study of recent developments in youth justice can thus contribute to a more nuanced picture of the role of crime and criminal justice in contemporary Japan. And yet, in engaging in research of this kind, a delicate balance must be sought between identifying similarities and differences with trends occurring elsewhere. As many commentators on contemporary penality have observed, it is important to exercise caution when utilizing notions such as punishment or welfare as 'general logics' outside an understanding of their place within substantial political programs and their associated moral and cultural contexts (Garland, 1990: chapter 10; O'Malley, 1992; Sparks, 2000). This exhortation to be sensitive to the specificities of time and place has particular resonance when discussing developments that are being played out in criminal justice systems, such as in Japan, that have a distinctive history and culture. This chapter will, therefore, attempt to identify in a preliminary way some of the distinctive features of contemporary Japanese debates on youth justice, as well as identifying trends that, in many cases, parallel developments elsewhere.

The Juvenile Law 1948: the primacy of child protection

The post-war system of youth justice was established by the Juvenile Law of 1948, which was drafted under the influence of the US occupation forces and was, until the late 1990s, widely regarded as one of the most successful aspects of penal policy (Johnson 1996: chapter 7; Yokoyama 1997). The law is a comprehensive one that along with the Rules of Juvenile Proceedings establishes the basic principles and procedures governing youth justice in Japan. The stated purpose of the Juvenile Law, as found in Article 1, is 'the wholesome rearing of juveniles' and 'to carry out protective measures relating to the character, correction and environmental adjustment of delinquent juveniles'. The system is thus founded on notions of protection and tolerance towards juvenile offenders (on this point see Izumida-Tyson, 2000: 2–3). In keeping with the so-called 'protection principle', Article 1 makes no explicit reference to punishment. In this respect, Japanese criminal justice established a clear distinction between adult and juvenile justice. The latter embodied a distinctly modern conception of childhood and adolescence based on notions of innocence, malleability and dependence. Youth justice was designed to protect juveniles both from the social environment that had produced their delinquent behavior and from the possible harmful effects of the youth justice system itself. The exclusive emphasis on the welfare of the offender is particularly significant when one considers that the law defines juveniles as any person under 20 years of age (Juvenile Law, Article 2).

The Juvenile Law deals with three categories of young person: (1) any juvenile aged between 14 and 20 who is alleged to have committed a crime; (2) any juvenile under 14 years of age who is alleged to have committed a crime; and (3) any juvenile who, in the opinion of the authorities, has the potential to commit a crime or perform an act in violation of a criminal law given the juvenile's character or surroundings. The three groups are designated juvenile offenders, law-breaking children, and pre-delinquent juveniles, respectively (Juvenile Law, Article 3). The categories are important as they affect the way the authorities may proceed with a case and limit the available dispositions. For example, a juvenile under the age of 14 cannot be held criminally liable for their acts (Criminal Code, Article 41).

In cases involving juvenile offenders, the police and prosecutors are obliged to refer the case to the family court (Juvenile Law, Articles 41–2). This procedure was designed in part to protect suspects from the kind of vigorous investigative techniques described by Miyazawa (1992) and other commentators on Japanese criminal justice. Moreover, the mass media are prohibited from reporting the name or personal details of juvenile offenders (Juvenile Law, Article 61). In the family court, an extensive investigation of the suspect's background, family, school life and psychological condition is carried out before the judge decides whether to hold a hearing (Juvenile Law, Articles 8–9; Berezin 1982). The law gives the judge a discretionary power to dismiss a case without a hearing if, after the investigation stage, such a hearing is deemed unnecessary (Juvenile Law, Article 19). The judiciary utilized this discretionary power in a significant number of cases. In 1999, for example, 39.6% of all offenders had their cases dismissed without such a formal hearing (see Table 10.1). The system thus parallels the practice of adult criminal justice in that significant numbers of offenders are released without being formally indicted even though enough evidence exists to secure a criminal conviction (see Foote 1991, 1992; Hayley 1999: chapter 6). In the case of young offenders, however, this was a

Table 10.1 Disposition of juvenile cases at family court, 1999

FAMILY COURT DISPOSITION	Number of cases
Dismissal before hearing (without imposing measures)	117,085
Dismissal after hearing (without imposing measures)	74,617
Protective measures (probation or committal to a training school)	56,092
Referral to prosecutor (for prosecution in ordinary criminal court)	16,349
Referral to Governor or Child Guidance Center	155
Other settlement	31,004
High Court – complaint (against imposition of protective measure)	452
Total	295,754

Source: Ministry of Justice, Crime Statistics, 2000

practice that has been justified on the grounds that it was the best means of implementing the protection principle as required by Article 1.

In those cases that resulted in a hearing, the protection principle dictated that such a proceeding should avoid the danger of stigmatizing offenders. Hearings were not open to the public and, under the 1948 version of the law, were to be conducted in a 'cordial atmosphere' (Juvenile Law, Article 22). Hearings tended to be relatively informal, at least in the sense that few procedural restrictions were in place. The symbols of authority so typical of adult criminal trials in Japan – for example, the shackling of defendants – were dispensed with and hearings were conducted in small rooms rather than open court. Normally present at the hearings would be the judge, the court appointed investigator, the suspect and the parent or guardian. Under the original law, neither the prosecutor nor the victim or their families were entitled to participate in the hearing. Moreover, many suspects did not feel the need to have formal legal representation, often preferring an attendant, typically a respected member of the local community who at the court's discretion would speak on the juvenile's behalf (Juvenile Law, Article 10). Such attendants would also assume some responsibility for the subsequent behavior of offenders.

In disposing of cases that reached the hearing stage, family courts judges had a number of options. In numerical terms non-conditional dismissal was the most important: by the 1990s, around 25–30% of all offenders had their case dealt with in this way. The legal standard for such a disposition is if, after the hearing, the judge feels that further measures are unnecessary (Juvenile Law Article 23(2). This practice meant that 60–70% of all cases would be dismissed without formal sanction either before or after the hearing stage (Johnson 1996: 164). When considering this figure it is important to emphasize that a lack of evidence would only account for a small minority of cases. Diverting the overwhelming majority of offenders out of the system and placing them back in the community was a considered policy on the part of the judiciary based on an acknowledgment of the potential dangers of formally labeling them a juvenile offender. Moreover, this seems to reflect a distinctly Japanese conception of rehabilitation in that the state primarily relies upon informal social actors and mechanisms for the reintegration of offenders into communities rather than a professionalized probation service, social workers or other 'psy' professions (on this point, see Braithwaite, 1989: 61–9).

Various forms of so-called 'protective measures' could also be taken. Conditional discharges, involving regular contact with a probation officer (most of whom are volunteers) or training programs designed to offer guidance in a normal life setting, accounted for the majority of cases (Juvenile Law, Article 25). A custodial option, in one of several different types of juvenile training school or reformatories, was used in a very small number of cases involving repeat offenders or serious crimes, typically less than 5% of all cases in the 1990s (Johnson, 1996: 164). These institutions were seen as rehabilitative institutions that educate offenders and prepare them for their return to society. Although some stigma clearly attaches to juveniles who receive such a custodial sentence, these institutions are generally regarded as effective in reforming juveniles and preventing further delinquency (Thornton and Endo, 1992: 116–18; Hardung, 2000).

Finally, the judge had the option, in certain instances, to refer a case back to the prosecutor with a view to prosecuting the juvenile in a criminal court. In such a case ordinary rules of (adult) criminal procedure would apply, subject to certain exceptions (Juvenile Law, Article 40). Examples of exceptions include the separate detention of such offenders (Juvenile Law, Article 49) and the mitigation of the death penalty to life imprisonment for those crimes where capital punishment exists (Juvenile Law, Article 51). In practice, many of the cases referred back to the prosecutor for criminal prosecution involved juveniles who were found to have been over the age of 20 at the time of the offence. However, under the 1948 law, this discretionary power also applied to particularly serious crimes committed by juveniles aged between 16–20 (Juvenile Law, Article 20). Significantly, it did not extend to offenders aged 14–16, i.e. it did not cover Shonen A who was aged 14 at the time of his alleged offences. Moreover, it was an option that the judges were increasingly unwilling to take, even in serious cases involving offenders in the upper end of the 16–20 age bracket. In the 1950s, 10% of all cases were referred back to the prosecutor, by the 1990s this figure had fallen to less than 5% (Johnson 1996: 164). Again this stance was justified on the grounds that formal prosecution in a criminal court was difficult to reconcile with the protection principle.

The 2000 reforms: punishment, victim's rights and parental responsibility

Although reform of the Juvenile Law had been on the agenda for several years (Murai, 1988), it took events in Kobe to prompt the government into more concerted action. Soon after the Kobe murders, the government established a legislative committee to investigate possible changes to youth justice. In April 1998, this committee made the first of a series of recommendations, which after a long and protracted process of negotiation and compromise between politicians, bureaucrats, lawyers, prosecutors and other interest groups resulted in the passing of Law no. 142 amending the Juvenile Law in November 2000. This law was by far the most significant set of changes made to the Juvenile Law since its original promulgation. The following discussion will not offer a comprehensive review of every aspect of the legislative process or of all aspects of the enacted reforms, but rather will focus on some of the most salient points.

In the public debate that preceded the enactment of the amendments, various aspects of the Juvenile Law were identified as problematic. Firstly, youth justice was perceived as unfair in that it was exclusively oriented towards the protection of the interests of the offender rather than society more generally or the victim. In fact, the exclusion of the victim from the process became one of the key issues in the ensuing debate. There were horror stories of parents of murder victims, receiving almost no information on the details of their child's death, of the murderer's identity or motive, or of the outcome of the judicial process. Secondly, it was argued that assumptions of childish innocence embodied in the law were widely perceived as out-dated and naïve given the type of offences that juveniles were committing (on this last point, see Sato, 1996). Offenders were not forced to take responsibility for their actions. This issue assumed special significance as a result of the relatively high age of offenders subject to the Juvenile Law. Thirdly, the fact that criminal records were erased when the suspect reached 20 combined with the guarantees of anonymity to create a sense that the law failed to have any real value as a deterrent. On the contrary, the system was seen as providing an open invitation to commit crimes safe in the belief that there would be minimal consequences for those that did so. Finally, there was the absence of a punitive moment, symbolized by the limited use of custodial sanctions, the exclusion of the prosecutor from the hearings and the unwillingness of the judges to exercise their discretionary power to refer cases, even serious ones, back to the prosecutor for prosecution in a criminal court.

Critics of youth justice drew upon widespread public anger to discredit a law that was seen as out of touch with popular attitudes towards criminal wrongdoing, as well as the realities of youth in 1990s' Japan. Other aspects of the law that might reasonably have been criticized, namely the broadly defined powers to detain so-called pre-delinquents who had not committed any criminal offence and the lack of due process protection for juveniles, were rarely, if ever, raised in the media discussion. Nor did the fact that reforming the law in a punitive direction might violate Japan's obligations under the UN Convention on the Rights of the Child receive any media attention. In this sense, the dominant rhetoric in public discussion was one of penal populism rather than due process, and it was the protection principle that was identified as the key issue that needed to be addressed.

It is worth noting that Juvenile Law reform became a prominent political issue from the late 1990s (Izumi-Tyson, 2000). In particular, the Prime Minister of the time, Yoshiro Mori, and the Liberal Democratic Party utilized the issue in an attempt to muster popular electoral support in the 2000 national elections. This was unusual as the politicization of crime so typical of the USA or UK is still relatively uncommon in national level Japanese politics, although there have been prominent examples of gubernatorial elections – most obviously in Tokyo – being influenced by politically fuelled anxieties about crime (Fenwick, 2004). Moreover, swift legislative action that aims to appease public concerns in the wake of high profile offences has, at least in comparative terms, been relatively unusual, perhaps as a result of the prominence of unelected bureaucrats in the legislative process (Johnson, 1995: chapter 6). A final feature of the public discussion was the extent that the political class relied on popular support to discredit the concerns of lawyers, juvenile justice workers, and academics – many of whom were opposed to reform on the grounds that it avoided serious consideration of the underlying causes of the youth crime problem. Again this displacement of criminal justice expertise through an appeal to broader populist concerns has been unusual in Japan where criminal justice expertise is still accorded a great deal of respect.

The amendments to the Juvenile Law completed their passage through the Diet in November 2000 and came into effect from April 2001. Interestingly, the law was passed with the support of the three Government coalition parties and also the two main opposition parties, the left of center Democratic Party (who had earlier opposed the changes), and the more conservative Liberal Party. The shift in attitude on the part of the Democratic Party highlights the degree of popular support that the proposed reform was perceived to have and echoes similar policy shifts on the part of left of center political parties in the USA and UK. Only the Communist Party and Social Democratic Party voted against the bill, arguing that it would destroy the principle of protection on which the juvenile justice system was predicated.

The 2000 reforms introduced a number of significant changes. Symbolically, the most important change was the lowering of the minimum age at which juveniles can be held criminally responsible for their acts in an adult criminal court (from 16 to 14) (Juvenile Law, as amended, Article 20). It is now possible for a 14 year old who has committed a serious offence to have their case referred to the prosecutor for criminal prosecution. The most obvious consequence of this change is that if a crime were committed in the same circumstances as in Kobe in 1997 the offender would face the very real possibility of formal criminal prosecution. The decision to refer such a case to the prosecutor resides with the family court judge, and is discretionary. Post-2001, the judiciary has exercised this option in a very small number of serious cases. In practice, the more significant change concerns the rules relating to 16–20 year olds. The revised law requires that the family court should, in principle, refer all juvenile murder suspects aged 16 or older to the prosecutor so that they can be put on criminal trial

(Juvenile Law, as amended, Article 20(2)). As was noted above, prior to 2001 this was at the discretion of the court and the general tendency was not to do this even in serious cases.

The revised law thus places a new emphasis on punishment and expressive justice in cases involving allegations of violent criminal wrongdoing. The rehabilitative ideal may not have been entirely displaced, but it has lost its preeminent status. Figures released by the Secretariat of the Supreme Court for the period April 2001 (when the revised law took effect) to February 2002 illustrate the immediate impact of the reform. In that period, there were 59 cases of serious crimes in the 16–20 age category: 9 murder cases, 8 cases of robbery resulting in death, and 42 cases of bodily injury resulting in death. Of these, 6 of the murder cases, all 8 of the robbery-death cases and 28 of the bodily injury-death cases were referred to the prosecutor for criminal prosecution (Yomiuri Shinbun, 15 March 2002).

This impression of a shift towards a more punitive approach is further compounded by a series of significant changes to family court procedures. Firstly, Article 22 was amended. The previous emphasis on the 'cordiality' of the proceedings was supplemented by the requirement that juvenile offenders engage in 'soul-searching' over the crimes they have committed (Juvenile Law, as amended, Article 20). Lawmakers seem to have accepted the criticism that unrepentant offenders were taking advantage of the informal nature of proceedings under the previous system. The rationale now appears to be that protection of offenders can only occur after offenders have recognized their responsibility and expressed remorse for their victims.

A newly added section (Juvenile Law, as amended, Article 22 (2) (i)) gives the family court the discretionary power to allow the prosecutor to participate in hearings. Again it only applies to serious cases, but it does point to a change to a more adversarial type of proceeding in the family court. In such cases, a panel of three judges will preside over the hearing – not a single judge as was previously the case. Critics of these changes point to the fact that the mere presence of the prosecutor disturbs the delicate search for truth characteristic of the judge–court investigator relationship under the former system. Significantly, prosecutors have also been given a right to 'complain' to the high court if they are dissatisfied with the outcome (prosecutors enjoy a power to appeal in adult criminal cases). Post-2001, prosecutors have been cautious in exercising this power: the first appeal of this kind was lodged in June 2004 by the Shizuoka District Prosecutors in a rape case involving an 18 year old boy whose case was dismissed by the family court even though several co-accused were found to have been involved. The amended law requires that a lawyer for the defendant be present if a prosecutor is participating in the hearing (Juvenile Law, as amended, Article 22 (3)) and a system of state-appointed lawyers for juveniles was created. This confirms the impression of a shift from a more welfare-oriented to legalistic style of proceedings. Supporters of the reform process have justified these procedural changes on the grounds that they are to ensure that multiple perspectives are incorporated into the fact-finding stage of the judicial investigation. However, critics argue that they serve to undermine the protection principle. At the very least, it is suggested that these changes have changed the mood within which judges deal with all cases, even perhaps the less serious ones.

Also of significance, the amended law strengthens the rights of the victims and their relatives. For example, victims and their relatives now have the right to be notified of the family court's findings (Juvenile Law, as amended, Article 31(2)) and are to be given access to copies of investigation records (Juvenile Law, as amended, Article 5). Victims or relatives are also given an opportunity to present their views at the hearing (Juvenile Law, as amended, Article 9(2)). The law does not however, go as far as many victims groups wished. Victims are not allowed to attend hearings in their entirety, although such a measure was strongly urged by victim's groups. It even seems to have enjoyed the support of the dominant Liberal Democratic Party (LDP). However, one of the LDP's coalition partners – the Buddhist New Komei party – insisted that the privacy of suspects would be inevitably violated if details of the trials were leaked, as they might be if victims were permitted to attend the whole hearing. There were also concerns that the presence of victims might adversely affect the proceedings, thus precluding the family court from ensuring its primary objective, under the law, of protecting the offender. Victims groups were further angered when a scheme introduced in October 2001 to provide notification to crime victims when the offender is to be released from prison was not extended to victims of juvenile crime. Not withstanding these issues, the strengthening of victims' rights in 2000 was a significant change.

Finally, under the revised law, judges have been given the power to issue warnings and instructions to parents of juveniles falling under their jurisdiction (Juvenile Law, as amended Article 25(2)). This renewed emphasis on parental responsibility reflects broader concerns about socially irresponsible parenting as a possible cause of the current problem. A government sponsored TV advertisement from 2002 focused on the same issue. In one ad, a woman in her early 30s sits alone in a darkened room with a baby's dummy in her mouth. In another, a man of a similar age sits staring at the TV, also sucking a dummy. In both cases the caption reads: 'just because you have a child, it doesn't mean you are a parent'. The changes to the law and such publicity campaigns send a clear message to parents that they need to take responsibility for their children's acts. Again this is a theme that has frequently cropped up in political discussion of this issue. Prime Minister Mori's successor, the populist Junichiro Koizumi, on a number of occasions blamed parents for juvenile crime (Mainichi Shinbun, 14 June 2004). Rather than focus exclusively on addressing crime in a direct fashion by means of a punitive sanction against the offender, this approach promotes a different kind of indirect action, which attempts to prevent crime by encouraging parents to acknowledge their role in crime prevention.

Those familiar with the operation of youth justice in Japan have suggested that the practical effect of the 2000 reforms has been to interfere with the system achieving its primary purpose, namely child protection. This results from the tension that commentators suggest now exists between the stated purpose of the law found in Article 1 – which it is important to note remained unchanged by the reforms – and much of the new content, which has set a more punitive and adversarial tone. Such a critique of the reforms has merit, based as it is on an assessment of the implications for youth justice practitioners and it highlights the fact that this was a legislative exercise that was, to a large degree, detached from a considered engagement with the day-to-day realities of youth justice.

And yet, many critics of the law have failed to engage with the broader issue of public support for the general direction that the reform process has taken. In focusing on this question, one needs to examine the symbolic force or communicative aspects of youth justice reform. After all, the changes were a response to anxieties about youth crime and public safety and were intended to appease those concerns. The reforms gave expression to a particular conception of youth crime that seems to resonate with the common-sense perceptions of many ordinary Japanese. In that sense, the 2000 reforms were clearly populist in nature. More specifically, the reforms articulated a conception of youth offending detached from that found in the 1948 law. The broad thrust of the changes has been to expand the scope of criminal prosecution, but also to make the family court hearings more like a proceeding in a criminal court. The reforms have introduced a new moral rhetoric into youth justice, namely one of criminal responsibility, culpability, guilt and condemnation of the offender. This line of thinking raises several important socio-political questions, namely why does this moralistic approach to youth offending resonate with ordinary conceptions of youth crime, and, perhaps more importantly, why are Japanese elites now responding to these concerns?

It is beyond the scope of this chapter to offer a systematic answer to these issues, but it is no coincidence that the pervasiveness of these new attitudes to youth crime have coincided with the protracted downturn in Japan's economic fortunes post-1990 and increased geo-political tensions in north-east Asia. In that sense a distinctive narrative of 'ontological insecurity' provides the broader context for current changes in criminal justice policy. Moreover, country-specific institutional filters have to be considered in order to explain why these kinds of social pressures are now being transformed into more punitive crime control measures. For the most part, the post-war Japanese system of governance was based on a model that placed unelected bureaucrats at the centre of the state apparatus (Johnson, 1995). The luxury afforded by this form of state–civil society integration was that the bureaucrats who governed Japan were relatively detached from the needs of the populace and were far less attuned to public opinion than would be the case in other liberal democracies. Although the power of the bureaucracy within Japan is still largely intact, the kind of economic and political crises alluded to above have clearly shaken public confidence in their ability to govern. Sidelining criminal justice expertise and making recourse to more punitive criminal justice policies can be regarded as one example of how the more populist (and in other spheres, nationalist) policies are being utilized in an attempt to re-legitimize these discredited elites.

Conclusion: the 2005 proposals

The 2000 reforms were populist measures that re-introduced the rhetoric and values of punishment and criminal responsibility into the family court as a way of demonstrating to the public that the interests protected under the revised system would be the interests of the victim and the community more generally, as well as – and in some cases, instead of – the interests of the offender. In January 2005 a further series of proposals were announced. These proposals follow the same trajectory as the earlier ones in that they weaken the protection principle by introducing counter-veiling values that will seemingly further blur the distinction between adult and youth justice.

The issue at the top of the legislative agenda is child offenders. Once again, the political discussion has been influenced by events, notably a series of high profile offences involving offenders under the age of 14. Two crimes, in particular, grabbed national attention; the first in Nagasaki involving a 12 year old boy who abducted and murdered a 4 year old in December 2003 and a second case in Sasebo in which an 11 year old girl stabbed her 12 year old classmate. A widespread perception has grown that Japan is experiencing a rapid increase in child crime. In 2003, police recorded 212 serious cases involving juveniles who had committed serious crimes, such as homicide and robbery, figures that were up 47% on 2002 (Mainichi Shinbun, 8 September 2004). Whether this represents a long-term trend is less clear, but the government has responded by adopting proposals that would significantly change how cases involving those under the age of 14 would be dealt with. Under the new recommendations, a family court will be able to send younger offenders who are found to have committed serious offences to reformatory institutions. Once again distinctions that differentiate between offenders are being blurred as a result of public concerns.

A further illustration of changing attitudes to juvenile crime came in December 2003 when the National Police Agency established guidelines for identifying juvenile suspects in the course of criminal investigations. Article 61 of the Juvenile Law does not contain an explicit provision about whether investigators can identify teenage crime suspects before they are referred to the court, i.e. during the investigation phase. However, the majority of legal experts have always interpreted Article 61 as prohibiting the police from such actions on the grounds that the publication of a name during the investigation would render the protection afforded by Article 61 meaningless. The police also seem to have taken this view, as under the previous 1998 guidelines investigating authorities were, in principle, only permitted to disclose the identities of suspects aged 20 or over. Under the new guidelines, however, police can, subject to certain strict conditions, disclose the identities of juvenile suspects aged 14 or over during a criminal investigation. The alleged suspect must have committed a heinous crime, there must be the possibility of further offences and there must be the real possibility of serious public unrest. The fact that this significant change in policy was widely welcomed – by academic commentators as well as the public – indicates the extent of the shift in perceptions of youth crime.

In December of 2004, Shonen A was released on parole from detention at the age of 21. Significantly, the Ministry of Justice decided to make the parole decision public. This was the first time this had occurred in a case involving a juvenile offender. Although the man's name and new address were withheld in order to protect his privacy, the disclosure of the fact that he was being released was significant. The justification given for this decision was that it was necessary to respond to public concerns and dispel apprehensions about the release of someone who had committed such violent criminal acts (Asahi Shinbun, 13 December 2004). As with the changes to police guidelines mentioned above, it once again highlights how new values have being introduced into youth justice policy. The victims' families urged the government to reveal further information to them about the perpetrator, specifically concerning what progress has been made in his rehabilitation. The government declined to do so. Although the public mood may have compelled those who govern Japan to take unprecedented measures in responding to youth crime, it also seems clear that a gap still exits between public perceptions – or at least, victim's perceptions – and the realities of youth justice. One suspects that there was always a gap of this kind. What has changed, however, is that the government have shown a willingness to address these anxieties about youth crime and to enact populist laws that may not be in the best interests of either individual juvenile offender or society more generally. In that sense, recent events do seem to mark the end of an era in the modern history of Japanese youth justice.

References

Berezin, E. P. (1982) 'A comparative analysis of the US and Japanese juvenile justice systems', *Juvenile & Family Court Journal*, November: 1.

Braithwaite, J. (1989) *Crime, Shame and Reintegration*. Cambridge: Cambridge University Press.

Fenwick, M. D. (2004) 'Crime talk and crime control in contemporary Japan', in J. Ferrell and K. Hayward (eds.) *Critical Criminology Unleashed*. London: Cavendish Press.

Foote, D. H. (1991) 'Confessions and the right to silence in Japan', *Georgia Journal of International and Comparative Law*, 21: 415–88.

Foote, D. H. (1992) 'The benevolent paternalism of Japanese criminal justice', *California Law Review*, 80: 317.

Garland, D. (1990) *Punishment and Modern Society*. Chicago: University of Chicago Press.

Garland, D. (2001) *The Culture of Control*. Chicago: University of Chicago Press.

Haley, J. O. (1999) *The Spirit of Japanese Law*. Athens: University of Georgia Press.

Hardung, J. (2000) 'The proposed revisions to Japan's Juvenile Law', *Pacific Rim Journal of Law & Policy*, 9: 139.

Izumida-Tyson, M. (2000) 'Revising *Shonenho*: a call to a reform that makes the already effective Japanese juvenile justice system even more effective', *Vanderbelt Journal of Transnational Law,* 33: 739.

Johnson, C. (1995) Japan: *Who Governs? The Rise of the Development State*. New York: Norton.

Johnson, E. H. (1996) *Japanese Corrections: Managing Convicted Offenders in an Orderly Society*. Carbondale: Southern Illinois University Press.

Ministry of Justice (2000) Annual Crime Statistics, Tokyo: Japanese goverment publication.

Miyazawa, S. (1992) *Policing in Japan: A Study on Making Crime*. New York: State University of New York Press.

Murai, T. (1988) 'Current Problems of Juvenile Delinquency in Japan', *Hitotsubashi Journal of Law & Policy*, 16: 2.

O'Malley, P. (1992) 'Risk, power and crime prevention', *Economy and Society*, 21: 252.

Sato, I. (1996) *Kamikaze Biker*. Chicago: University of Chicago Press.

Schreiber, M. (2001) *Infamous Japanese Crimes and Criminals*. Tokyo: Kodansha.

Sparks, R. (2000) 'Perspectives on risk and penal politics', in T. Hope and R. Sparks (eds.) *Crime, Risk and Insecurity*. London: Routledge.

Thornton, R. and Endo, K. (1992) *Preventing Crime in America and Japan: A Comparative Study*. New York: M. E. Sharpe.

Yokoyama, M. (1997) 'Juvenile justice: an overview of Japan', in J. Winterdyk (ed.) *Juvenile Justice Systems*. Toronto: Canadian Scholars' Press.

Italy: A lesson in tolerance?

11

David Nelken

Introduction

Comparative research, whether aimed at advancing theoretical understanding or practical goals, faces demanding challenges (Nelken, 2002; Roberts, 2002). This is well exemplified by collections that invite contributors to describe their different legal systems (Bailleau and Cartuyvels, 2002). Depending on the space allocated one can learn much that is important about each particular system (though there is never enough space even to provide a decent summary of the 'law in books', never mind the 'law in action'). But the point of the exercise can remain somewhat obscure. Often the only purpose of a contribution seems to be to show the evolution of a given system (by comparing it to itself). Sometimes there are just too many potential points of interest, which are difficult to bring into focus unless we are told to what the system described is being compared.

If local experts merely provide a series of unconnected accounts of justice in different places we risk ending up with a somewhat unenlightening 'comparison by juxtaposition' (Nelken, 2000). Authors are rarely encouraged to discuss what goes into their work of description. Yet only in this way can the reader come to recognise that any interpretation is (necessarily) partial and controversial, and easily becomes out of date. More than this, it needs to be better appreciated that such accounts can reflexively form part of the reality that is being described, which they are sometimes even intended to (re) shape.[1]

In any case, systems cannot be satisfactorily described only 'in their own terms'. Many of their elements are likely to be borrowings or imitations of practices and ideas originally found elsewhere. In a globalising world, legal systems find their place in a field of 'inter-cultural legality' whereby other models (or better, models of models) serve as cultural resources for development of our own systems through processes of imposition, imitation or rejection (Muncie, 2005).[2] Likewise, when we set out to describe for others any given system of justice, our account can only be understood in terms of its perceived similarities or differences from the systems with which they are familiar. Hence all descriptions involve dealing with potentially more widely applicable concepts. Success in furthering comparative understanding is largely dependent on the wise choice of such 'framing concepts'.[3]

In line with this aspiration, this chapter sets out to discuss Italian juvenile justice as an example of a system that is alleged to be particularly 'tolerant'. It seeks to explore Italy's relatively tolerant approach to young people's crime against the background of increasing punitiveness in many 'Anglo-American' societies. I shall first discuss what is involved in 'explaining' tolerance, and go on to consider the evidence that justifies describing the Italian approach as one that is relatively tolerant (giving special attention to the methodological problems in showing this). I shall then say something about the conditions that make such tolerance possible.

Explaining 'tolerant' juvenile justice in Italy

The term tolerance has many nuances and, as investigation of relevant dictionaries confirms, there are also subtle differences in Italian and English. But it can serve as a suitable starting point for our purposes because both outside observers

---

1. But this does not mean that all interpretations are equally valid. Some descriptions of the Italian system are just wrong, as where outsiders have explained its leniency in terms of 'alternatives to prison'. More often the danger is of conveying a misleading impression. A recent account of Italian leniency by an insider unfortunately only provides information on cases (some of which are quite unrepresentative) collected from the *pre-trial* stages of the juvenile process, at one of Italy's best resourced Tribunals, and tells us little about the wider conditions of tolerance (Scalia, 2005). For more discussion of insider, outsider, and insider–outsider observers see Nelken, 2000a.

2. See Nelken (forthcoming). Most (though not all) Italian commentators currently use both the UK and the USA systems as negative models of juvenile justice.

3. In his recent pioneering textbook of comparative criminal justice Francis Pakes (2004: 13ff) wrongly cites Nelken 1994 as a source for his claim that the interpretative approach is relativistic, and the search for difference correlates with a lack of interest in practical lessons. The chapter on which he relies, argued, on the contrary, that all comparisons inevitably imply cross-cultural commonalities, and proposed the concept of trust as one example of such a common 'framing concept'.

and inside commentators concur in describing the Italian system as tolerant and lenient.[4] In the UK, leading critical criminologists and specialists in youth justice (including its comparative aspects) such as John Pitts and John Muncie, have held up the Italian case as a model of tolerance and non-punitiveness from which England and Wales has much to learn.[5] In Italy, Duccio Scatolera, for example, has recently spoken of what he calls 'the "benevolent tolerance" that often accompanies the view taken of small-scale criminality by young Italians' (Scatolera, 2004: 400.) He argues that the propensity to tolerate such criminal behaviour increased in recent times once the authors of such behaviour no longer belonged exclusively to the marginalised classes at risk (Scatolera, 2004: 400). And even insiders critical of the system, such as Ricciotti (2001), complain about tolerance (as over-indulgence). Thus he concludes his sharp critique of the relevant 1988 law with these words: 'in simple terms, with respect to crimes when committed by youngsters, it is now thought appropriate to respond not with the penal sanction or with a thought – through exercise of mercy, but only with an offer of help which the subject may even refuse' (Ricciotti, 2001: 56).

Given this consensus, when writing for an English-speaking audience it seems 'natural' that what needs to be explained is the relative leniency of juvenile justice in Italy. But if we were to compare the Italian system to other Continental European or Scandinavian jurisdictions we would find that it would not stand out anything like as much. In Scandinavia prison rates are even lower, in France educational efforts are more thorough.[6] Even in Scotland the Hearings system set out to avoid punishment for most youth crime. So we shall need to keep in mind that comparison is a two-way process: our interest in Italy's lack of punitiveness could tell us more about our obsession with youth crime in Anglo-American cultures than it does about Italy. Rather it may be that it is this obsession which most requires explanation.

This applies not only if we come to praise but also to condemn the Italian 'style' of juvenile justice. One of the best known attempts in English to examine Italian juvenile justice from the outside tells us as much about the author's starting point as it does about the object of his description. And this is all the more remarkable given that it is written by one of the greatest criminologists, Edwin Lemert, the inventor of the social reaction and labelling approach, as well as being a specialist in juvenile justice. In a paper published in 1986 Lemert noted the enormous disproportion between the number of juveniles arrested

---

4. Most authors speak of tolerance as if it simply means leniency in responding to crime by juveniles, but, although the two terms overlap, talking of tolerance rather begs the question whether the behaviour being tolerated is equally problematic in the societies being compared.

5. Likewise, in describing the system in England and Wales, the 1980s are said to mark 'the end of tolerance' (Smith, 2003).

6. As Blatier (1999: 248) explains 'The French legal system for juveniles appears to give priority to educative care, decided on without going to court, which finally becomes what we call "no proceedings" that is leaving the young person in family care, or just a warning'. But the French system is changing.

and processed in the USA and Italy. But, rather than see this as an indictment of the American approach, he offers this as proof that the Italian system was what he called a 'spurious' example of juvenile justice since it could not be seriously considered as trying to implement a welfare system for juveniles on the American model. As a result of this one article, the Italian system was still being classified in a leading American typological textbook of comparative criminal justice as late as 1999 as an exemplar of a 'legalistic' system (Reichel, 1999). The system has been through at least two evolutions since Lemert wrote,[7] including a failed effort in the 1980s to deinstitutionalise and 'administrativise' juvenile justice by placing it in the hands of local government. Ironically, the USA juvenile justice system itself is now well on the way to rejecting most of what Lemert identified as the principal defining characteristics of such systems.

Whatever the truth of Lemert's claims about Italian 'legalism', more recent interest in tolerant systems of justice is closely connected to concern about growing punitiveness and the so called 'punitive turn' (Pratt et al., 2005). But what do we mean by punitiveness and leniency? Are we mainly interested in the causes and conditions of variations in levels of punishment, irrespective of the intentions of those involved? Or are we trying to explain whether and why those working in a given system are actually trying to be punitive- or non-punitive? As in so many other spheres, the objective and subjective do not always coincide. We also need to be clear if we are using the term as an evaluation (on the whole with positive overtones, though occasionally as a pointer to deplorable laxity), or to serve more neutral descriptive and explanatory purposes.

It is not easy to decide how best to measure harshness or leniency. Even if we limit ourselves to the criminal justice process there are a number of different stages and aspects to take into account (see Whitman, 2003). Whether we are seeking to borrow[8] or to learn, it may be important to distinguish leniency at the stage of writing laws, police enforcement, prosecution decision-making, judicial sentencing, the use of prison, the cancelling of convictions etc.[9] In studying the exercise of tolerance it can be useful to distinguish *when* this happens (for what crimes? for what offenders?), *how* it takes place (by diversion from the system? within the system?), *who* is responsible for it (judges? social workers?) and *why* it takes place (under what conditions?).

Comparison becomes even more tricky if we extend our gaze beyond the juvenile justice system to what happens in the larger society (Nelken, 2004). The differences between attributing tolerance to a justice system or to a whole society is that it may not be at all safe to assume that what happens within the juvenile system necessarily reflects wider social tolerance. A given level or type of tolerance cannot be taken to be an 'essential' aspect of a society or culture if it is

---

7. Though published in 1986 much of Lemert's data actually referred to the 1960s.
8. I will not have space to discuss processes of borrowing. But see Nelken and Feest, 2001.
9. Ricciotti's textbook on juvenile justice (2001) is organised in terms of the different types of leniency that the system incorporates.

true that developments in juvenile justice, as in other areas of social policy, go through 'cycles of tolerance' (Bernard, 1982). Both Italian juvenile justice and Anglo-American type systems have gone through such cycles and perhaps each are doing so now, albeit finding themselves in different phases.

Finding evidence of tolerance

How could we show that the Italian system is more tolerant than, say, the one in England and Wales? The basic problem in comparative work is of course ensuring that 'like is being compared with like'. We expect some differences, otherwise there would be no point in comparing. But comparison always involves highlighting differences against a sufficient background of (presumed) similarity in order for the 'differences' to stand out. Ideally all jurisdictions would collect the same information about the same matters. But we cannot assume that different jurisdictions have the same sort of information available for use in describing their operations. They will certainly differ in whether and how they collect information. More importantly, if we are studying tolerance and leniency (or any other given topic) we must make allowance for the possibility that the differences that interest us also affect the process of gathering and using information. In our case, for example, the Italian system is more likely to seek to show that all is 'under control' (Nelken, 2003); the English system by contrast may be just as much concerned to show the *need* for control. Tolerant societies not only treat crime more leniently but may also show less crime going on just because they are tolerant!

Most published information about juvenile justice in Italy involves sophisticated legal and philosophical debate about different interpretations of the meaning and aims of the relevant 'jurisprudence'. For statistical information there is the internet site of the Ministry of Justice from which we can learn how many youths are sent to prison or about the use of different measures.[10] But – crucially – there is relatively little reliable information available on the effectiveness of such measures in relation to the type of cases for which they are used. As in most other countries in Southern Europe, it is also hard to find good qualitative sociological analyses of juvenile justice.[11] The lack of such work means that there is an ever-present danger of taking what people say they are doing or even what they say they should be doing as a description of what is actually happening. To go beyond this requires the careful examination of case files and interviews with different actors involved in the system at a variety of different tribunals. With the help of my research collaborators I have been carrying out

---

10. Gatti's work, which I cite extensively in this chapter, elaborates on these sources.

11. Although there are a number of studies of the operations of specific tribunals, these tend to be relatively straightforward descriptive exercises, often provided by people starting out on their career, or else by those working within the system.

such investigations over the last six years.[12] Although writing-up of the data is still in progress this chapter is informed by this work.

The main source of Italian leniency is to be found in the law itself (both as set out in the 'law in books' and as applied in the 'law in action'). The relatively autonomous Juvenile Tribunals distributed around the country have responsibility for both civil and criminal cases. The system remains firmly in the hands of professional judges, assisted by honorary judges with relevant expertise, and relies mainly on Ministry of Justice social workers for its interventions. The penal work of the court is shaped by the juvenile justice procedural reform act passed in 1988 (DPR 448) that deals with youngsters aged from 14 to 18. This requires that the use of prison be avoided to the utmost, and, more in general, that care be taken in legal proceedings not to interrupt the normal process of education and growing up.

When the criminal case is put forward by the prosecutor (which, under the principle of obligatory prosecution, must be done wherever there is evidence to do so) there are a series of trial stages in which judges seek as far as possible to deal with the offender without the need to arrive at a full trial. Judges have available a variety of ordinances by which to oblige the youth to remain at home at certain times or not to frequent certain places. Otherwise there are three main measures possible – all of which involve interrupting further progress towards a full trial. First, the judge may declare the offence 'irrelevant' (when offences are 'trivial' and 'occasional').[13] Secondly, he/she may confer a 'judicial pardon' (a long-established possibility for adults and youths alike), in the cases of offenders who commit offences punishable up to two years' prison for whom it is possible to make a prognosis that they will not offend again.

Finally, however, he/she may impose a new form of *pre-trial* probation called 'messa alla prova', or 'putting you to the test', which is considered the most innovative of the disposals introduced by the 1988 code. This can run up to a year for crimes carrying punishments up to 12 years (the average is around eight months) and up to three years for those carrying a higher potential penalty. The decision whether to hold a final trial is put on hold to see if the youth complies with a court approved programme focused on schooling, work, voluntary work (often organised by the local Church) and, if necessary, psychological counselling.

---

12. With the research assistance of Dr. Vincenzo Scalia, Dr. Michele Mannoia, Dr. Roberta Rao, Dr. Francesco Ranci, Dr. Letizia Zanier and Judge Pietro Merletti, I have analysed over 700 case files (and interviewed numerous participants) at the Tribunals of Bologna, Milan, Naples, Ancona, Palermo, and Catania. In a later comparative project financed by the ESRC with the help of Dr. Stewart Field, Professor Mark Drakeford and Ruth Holgate, we have examined 208 offence files from 8 Youth Offending Teams in South Wales, and carried out extensive interviews with all involved.

13. This provision, particularly important in a regime of obligatory prosecution, replaced the previous possibility of discontinuing cases on the basis that the offender was 'immature' or 'unable to form criminal intent' (over the years such findings had increasingly come to be used for deflationary purposes).

Whereas about 30% to 40% of cases finish with a judicial pardon, only around 6% of those brought to court overall get messa alla prova (though this is increasing year on year).

One of the most striking features of messa alla prova is the fact that no type of crime is excluded. Cases of murder by young people are therefore also eligible for the scheme and most cases (especially in the North and Centre of Italy) are dealt with in this way. This means not only that most young people in Italy are not sent to prison for this crime but that, because this is a *pre-trial* measure, if they successfully fulfil the requirements of the order they do not even get a criminal conviction. They are not 'getting away' with murder in the sense that nothing is done. But, in the context of thinking about tolerance, there can be little doubt that this shows how the Italian system gives little importance to the need for denunciation, retribution, deterrence or any aim other than putting the child first.

For those who do go to full trial and are found guilty,[14] the only penalty that can be imposed is prison, though this is usually suspended in all but the most severe cases. Fines are rarely used as punishment and, as compared to Anglo-American jurisdictions or even countries such as France or Germany, there is relatively little going on in terms of officially-sponsored positive interventions in children's lives. Arrangements for restitution and compensation to the victim, though theoretically possible, are rare; mediation schemes have recently been introduced in some court districts on an experimental and voluntary basis but their authorisation under the 1988 law is somewhat controversial. The 'putting you to the test' form of probation does involve social intervention but only as a pre-conviction alternative to prison. Such schemes are administered by social workers employed by the Ministry of Justice, often with the help of local government social workers. They can and often do involve some use of (non-secure) community homes.[15] Currently there are just over 1200 cases a year of pre-trial probation. But some judges and social workers are reluctant to apply the measure more generously, and resource considerations limit the use of social interventions especially in the poorer parts of the country.

The Ministry of Justice is encouraging greater use of such interventions, and deems well over 70% of the current measures to be successful. But it is interesting to consider the criterion it uses, especially in the light of the above-mentioned methodological difficulties in studying leniency comparatively. Rather than use the conventional criminological criterion of a two year crime-free period after the application of the measure, the Ministry treats as a success every case where the judge decides at the *end of the programme* that there is no need to go on and stage 'the trial'. This unconventional measure of success is also

---

14. A good number of cases that reach trial are found not guilty on the facts.

15. Community homes (which after the 1988 law can longer be secured) are also independently of any penal measures, especially by tribunals in the South. There were around 1200 cases in 1999.

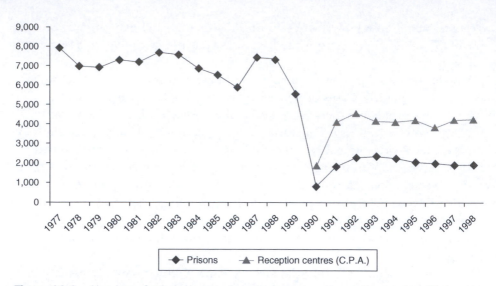

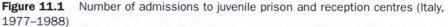

Figure 11.1   Number of admissions to juvenile prison and reception centres (Italy, 1977–1988)

Source: Gatti and Verde, 2002.

problematic in itself. By this point the youngster is almost old enough to go before the adult court and has already received the most thorough intervention available to the system, so there is little reason for the judge to recommend a trial even if there have been (as is frequently the case) failure on one or more of the requirements.[16]

There is no officially sponsored follow up of later recidivism after this measure has been terminated, but the limited evidence available, when juvenile court and adult records are checked against each other, suggests an almost 40% recidivism rate within a two year follow-up period (Scivoletto, 1999). It is debatable whether this should be seen as a high or as a still acceptable rate of recidivism for the sample of cases it deals with. It is also moot whether recidivism rates should play as large a role as they do in shaping juvenile justice, as it does in so many other jurisdictions. The point being made here is that, whatever the answers one gives to such questions, seen cross-culturally, even the measurement of 'success' forms part of a more or of a less tolerant approach to crime.

The main reason why many consider the Italian system to be relatively tolerant is the low number of youngsters who finish up in prison. As Figure 11.1 (taken from Gatti and Verde, 2002) shows, there has been a constant diminution in the use of prison from the late 1970s to the late 1990s, with the main change following the introduction of the new code in 1988/1989.[17]

---

16. There are also many cases where crimes are committed but overlooked during the life of the measure itself.

17. Most of those in prison are there awaiting trial. The average time spent in prison is around five months.

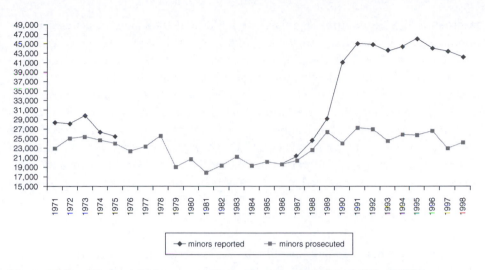

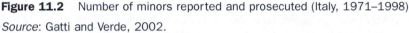

Figure 11.2 Number of minors reported and prosecuted (Italy, 1971–1998)

Source: Gatti and Verde, 2002.

Only around 2,000 young people are sentenced to prison each year, as compared to the 10,000 or more young people in the same age group sentenced to prison in England and Wales (and the proportion in the USA is of course many times higher). At any given time there are no more than around 500 young people in prison, which means Italy has one of the lowest levels of all Western countries (Muncie, 2005). The number of Italian-born youngsters sentenced to prison has in fact declined so as to become almost negligible. Prison is still used by some southern Italian courts for young men convicted of violent crimes such as armed robbery. But since the 1990s it is mainly used for dealing with young unaccompanied immigrants accused of drug dealing or low-grade property offences,[18] as well as gypsy girls accused of pick-pocketing. As Scatolera concludes, 'but for immigrants and drug addicts, penal correctional ideology for young people would be exhausted for lack of human material on which to exercise itself' (Scatolera, 2004: 401).

The low prison numbers are in part the result of the fact that, as compared to England and Wales, many fewer young people face prosecutions and fewer still are convicted. In the 1970s less than 20,000 young people were being reported for crimes. After 1988 this number increased sharply to 45,000, but, remarkably, the number of those being prosecuted (despite this being a system of obligatory prosecution) has remained the same (see Figure 11.2).

It is something of a puzzle how Italy continues to make only residual use of prison despite changes that could arguably have transformed this pattern (given also the continued failure to develop alternatives). In 1988 the Juvenile Tribunal

---

18. By law unaccompanied immigrants are neither allowed to work nor to be deported until reaching the age of 18. Those not made wards of court usually 'disappear' just before that date.

prosecution offices were reorganised, and allocated their own designated police (replacing the fragmented local governmental responsibility for the previous period as seen as the break in the graph in Figure 11.2). This encouraged increased reporting of offences. Following this there was a rise in officially recorded crimes per young person,[19] and especially a three-fold increase in violent crimes (Gatti, 2002). But increasing reports of crime have not led to higher numbers of prosecution (and as Figure 11.2 also shows, nor has the failure to prosecute discouraged the reporting of such cases.)[20] The low use of prison has survived the influx of young unaccompanied immigrants during the 1990s. According to Gatti and Verde the number of crimes reported to court in which young immigrants were involved went up from 18% in 1991 to 27% in 1999. But, although a disproportionate number of such offenders received prison sentences, they have displaced rather than added to the number of Italian-born youths sent to prison.

On the other hand, Italian juvenile justice is not always lenient. It is true that the rate of convictions is low.[21] But the proportion is now rising and went up during the 1990s from 8.5% in 1991 to 15.9% in 1998, largely because of the increasing number of immigrants and gypsies being prosecuted (Gatti and Verde, 2002). It could also be argued that sending 2,000 young people to prison out of a total number of 20,000 prosecutions (plus the use made of reception centres and community homes) is actually quite a high proportion. Above all, the fact that immigrants and gypsies often benefit less from pre-trial probation is the subject of much criticism in Italy. Judges say this is because of the difficulty of organising programmes without the back up of a fixed (and law-abiding) home base, though some tribunals are finding ways to overcome this.[22] But this 'bifurcated' response as between Italian-born youngsters and members of these two groups (who are found mainly in the North and Centre of Italy) suggests to many that the 1988 law was not designed with these outsiders in mind.

Individual cases may also test the limits of tolerance. Since 2000 there have been a series of well-publicised scandals in which teenagers or young adults have murdered their fathers or mothers. The case that attracted most media attention was that of Erica and Omar who together killed Erica's mother and younger brother for apparently the most futile of motives. Both young lovers were from good families in the North of Italy; Erica in particular came from a well off, professional and apparently model religious family background (and attended a

---

19. On the other hand, because the number of young people in the population is declining, the overall number of crimes has not gone up.

20. Half of these crime reports correspond to an increase in cases regarding those under 14 (quite often gypsy children) who are not eligible for prosecution.

21. Though this is to be expected in regimes where prosecution is obligatory but guilt is contested.

22. However, our research suggests that immigrants and gypsies often do benefit from the other two deflationary measures at least as often as Italian youngsters (sometimes even when the legal requirements may not be met). But this could be read less as benevolence than as an unwillingness to invest resources in trying to deal with their behaviour.

religious school). Erica's mother had recently left work to be more available for her children, and her younger brother's last school essay had been full of love for his sister. The sentences they received at first instance were 16 years and 14 years respectively. Public opinion was struck by the way these youngsters had originally tried to blame the crime on foreigners, by the lack of excusing circumstances, and the fact that Erica in particular failed to make the public admission of contrition expected in such cases. It was shocking to think that this crime could have happened to anybody and little protest was heard over the length of the prison sentences handed down.[23]

But even this shocking case has not, so far, had any enduring effects. Roberto Castelli, the Northern League Minister of Justice, hoped he could launch his 'reform' of juvenile justice on the wave of what he thought was heightened public alarm (in the same way that the Bulger case produced a change in legal provisions in England.) His draft law, introduced in 2003, proposed, along with more bipartisan changes on the civil side, to separate civil and penal jurisdiction, to reduce the number of specialist lay advisers in the court and to exclude serious crimes such as murder or sexual offences from the ambit of pre-trial probation. But the bill failed at the first parliamentary hurdle, with even his colleagues in his own parliamentary majority refusing to follow him.

It is also worth underlining the point that systematic leniency in Italy is a result of procedure rather than substance. The 1988 Act was a *procedural* reform (made necessary by a larger procedural reform for adults introduced in the same year). The new measures the law introduced are all, formally speaking, ways of postponing or avoiding the need for trial. No new substantive penalties were introduced. Thus, as for adults, prison remains the 'standard' post-trial sentence (reduced by a third), even if it is usually suspended. One reason the system sends so few children to prison is the difficulty of overcoming the hurdle of deserving a prison sentence. As compared to other jurisdictions, children do not have the opportunity to fail a series of social interventions and thus move up the ladder of penal severity. Delay in dealing with cases, sometimes deliberate, also has the same result.[24] Simply talking of 'tolerance' obscures the importance of this combination of the dichotomisation of sanctioning between pre- and post-trial sentence and the bifurcation of response between Italians and immigrants.

Conditions of tolerance

The characteristics, aims and implementation of the 1988 law explain to a large extent how and why Italy manages to be so relatively tolerant (at least in cases

23. The prison lengths were shaped by the governing legal guidelines. The only alternative, which the defence lawyer did try for, would have been pre-trial probation!

24. Delay may sometimes be used to see whether the child will, or has, 'grown out' of offending behaviour (the guiding assumption being that intervention is itself risky). The contrast with the current emphasis on 'early intervention' in the English and Welsh system could not be more marked.

involving Italian youngsters). But we still need to ask about the wider conditions that make this possible. I shall outline five aspects of the wider context which are relevant in comparing Italy with elsewhere, and in particular with Anglo–American societies. Once again, however, some preliminary points are in order. The factors mentioned here are intended to be illustrative rather than exhaustive, and operate differently in different parts of the country. As important, whereas some are deep-lying, others are much more contingent (which explains why prison rates for juveniles have been much higher in the past).

Here too we need to avoid identifying the legal system with the society, or confusing tolerance as an objective outcome with tolerance as a subjectively pursued goal. The conditions of greater tolerance in the legal system may some-times presuppose *less* tolerance in civil society. Any system of juvenile justice lies at the intersection of the production of 'delinquency' and the imposition of 'accountability'. So the factors responsible for reducing the *incidence* of crime may coincide with those that belong to the *reaction* against crime. Once we acknowl-edge that 'policing' involves more than the police, it can be difficult, and some-times even impossible, to distinguish the phenomenon of youth crime from the nature of the response it receives. In further investigations we might need to specify more carefully which conditions accompany Italian tolerance, which explain why Italy can afford to be tolerant, and which actually show us that Italian judges have no need to be tolerant.

The first factor to bear in mind is whether the problem or threat of 'youth crime' is the same in Italy as in the places with which it is being compared. Published statistics show that in 1999, of roughly 44,000 crimes reported to the juvenile court, as far as crimes against property are concerned, there were around 16,000 for theft, 3,000 for receiving, 4,500 for drug dealing, 3,000 for criminal damage, while, for offences involving violence, there were 3,300 assaults, 500 sexual assaults, 50 murders and the same number of attempted murders (Gatti, 2002).[25] Much of the crime being processed involves little more than the steal-ing and receiving of motor-cycles; there is a much lower incidence of burglary and a much lower level of high-volume recidivist crime generally. To set against that, Southern Italian courts do see a consistent number of cases of armed rob-bery and there is continuing (inconclusive) discussion about the possible recruit-ment of young people into organised crime groups there. Although the only published self-report study suggests little difference in crime rates among young people in Italy (see Junger-Tas, 1994), all the evidence we have seen suggests that young people commit less crime, and especially less serious crime, in Italy than in England and Wales.

Patterns of crime reflect different ways of life. The 14–18 young offender age group being dealt with in Italy has a different significance than in the UK given

---

25. It is worth noting, the purposes of a fair comparison, that while under age driving has been decriminalised, there are other crimes, such as that of insulting those in authority, which are still regularly prosecuted in Italy.

that so many young people live at home until well into their 30s. There is less excessive drinking (though it is on the rise), and, except for around discotheques, still little sign of the drinking culture which plays such a role in youth crime and disorder in city centres over the weekends in Northern Europe. There is much less polarisation in the social organisation of towns with fewer outright ghetto housing estates (except in the largest Southern cities). Newspapers in Italy, unlike those in England and Wales, do not display a continuing 'moral panic' about youth and crime. There is recurrent concern over events such as throwing rocks from motorway bridges, and continued anxiety over entrenched behaviour such as bullying and extortion from schoolmates at school (often attributed to power hungry children from well-off families) or the extent of youthful drug dealing and consumption. But, all in all, youth crime comes very low in the order of national worries. Arguably, therefore, it could be because there is less of a 'problem' that it is so easy for judges and society to be tolerant. But it could also be working the other way round, given that, in general, levels of punishment in different societies are not well correlated with their respective rate of crime.

A second (and related) issue concerns the role of the family and attitudes to young people generally. The strength of the Italian 'family' (with the relatively low level of broken homes) helps reduce crime both through the quality of parenting as well as the exercise of surveillance (usually organised by the omnicompetent Italian mother). The young people who are drawn into the system come mainly from the remaining failing families. The availability of the extended family, in which grandparents play a vital part as secondary carers and socialisers, is also important. Families are even crucial to finding employment, especially in the small businesses that are the backbone of the Italian economy.[26]

There are also subtle differences in what it means to learn to be a responsible adult. It is difficult to exaggerate how much more quickly people in Italy (and in Mediterranean societies in general) display affection towards children, as compared to Anglo-American societies, though (curiously) fewer and fewer children are being brought into the world. The cultural emphasis on putting children first means that children are both seen *and* heard, and are the subject of continual nurturing, high expectations and affective investment. But such expectations are much less focused than in Anglo-American societies on the need to become independent. In educating Italian children, priority is given to learning to collaborate with the groups in which they find themselves. Compared to the UK or the USA, schools are less focused on individuality and competitiveness, and are more reluctant to exclude troublesome pupils.

All of this does encourage government and courts to delegate the work of crime control to families, though they would never say so in so many words.

---

26. This may help reduce the effects of globalisation on increasing youth unemployment and the consequent penal reaction (Bailleau and Cartuyvels, 2003).

Family life gives children powerful incentives to conform, but to describe the family as an agent of 'social control' would be to misrepresent the depth of mutual affection and *reciprocal* obligation that so often characterises these relationships. This said, lengthy widespread economic and emotional dependence on the family does also have its down side. One Italian writer on the family has described this generation of children (for whom prison is ruled out) as living in 'a gilded prison'. Even when adult, family-like methods of co-optation shape inclusion and advancement in Italian society. Calling on group affiliation is often essential for protection of your rights at work or in dealing with official bureaucracy. And there is little or no tolerance of any breaches of the unwritten laws that regulate collaboration in such groups (Nelken, 2004).

A third factor relates to the role of courts, politics and politicians. Whatever its specificities, developments in juvenile justice are also affected by the overall politics of criminal justice. So it is surely relevant that, in general, there is much less politically (and media) exploited public fear of conventional crime as compared to common law countries. Until the 1990s, crimes as serious as robbery, burglary and even rape were actually referred to as 'micro-crimes', so as to contrast them with the forms of crime that threatened the state itself, such as corruption, political terrorism or organised crime (Nelken, 2000b). The term 'juvenile delinquency' is hardly used in Italy.

There has been some change recently, and politicians and the media are beginning to speak of 'street crime' or 'diffuse' crime. Parties forming part of Berlusconi's ruling coalition, such as the Northern Leagues or the National Alliance (former Fascist) party, are now revealing some authoritarian leanings. They tend to minimise police brutality, have recently relaxed the law restricting torture, and are planning to re-criminalise soft drugs. Politicians are well aware that it can be politically popular to pass measures that tighten up the control of unauthorised immigration, even if the practical effects of these measures may only be to make immigrants more vulnerable to economic exploitation. Now that local mayors are elected by direct vote they also have reason to play on the 'fear of crime'.

Yet we are still far from 'law and order' politics. The current Prime Minister has made it much more difficult to obtain convictions for white-collar crime, and his hopes for balancing budgets were largely based on pardoning former financial crimes. Some of the procedural reforms he has sponsored for his own benefit can also make it more difficult to obtain convictions in more conventional crime cases. In addition, there is still remarkable cross-party support for what Anglo-American legal culture would describe as 'due process' legal procedures (the so-called 'garanzie') in the penal process, even if these inevitably exact a price in terms of difficulty in achieving 'crime control' except where criminals are caught 'red handed'.

If governments tend to 'rule through leniency', judges in juvenile tribunals in any case feel an allegiance to the law rather than to government policy as such. There is much less central direction or target-setting than is found in England

and Wales. Judges (and judicial prosecutors) play a much larger role in defining the crime problem as compared to common law countries; the police, by contrast, are given little chance to act as spokesmen. Victims are also rarely the focus of concern. It is the collective values embodied by the constitution, rather than the 'community', as a set of locally based individuals, which vindicates itself through criminal law. No one has yet sought to play up the fact that young people are as likely to be the victims as the offenders. There are localised experiments in victim mediation and it is theoretically possible to insist that young people make restitution. But I have not come across any cases of restitution, and some tribunals explicitly reject a focus on victims as likely to interfere with their welfare aims.

Another matter worthy of investigation is the part played by culture and, not least, the role of the Catholic Church as an active and widely influential institution as well as the source of key ideas and practices. Juvenile court judges do not see themselves as an emanation of the Church. In some respects, though less than in the past, the Church continues to sap legitimacy from the secular State institutions and their law. But they do rely heavily on local priests for organising welfare interventions. And Catholic culture helps shape a large part of Italian thinking and behaviour even among those who see themselves as anticlerical. The reduced status of the victim is linked to religious expectations concerning forgiveness and pardon. Catholic thinking may also help tone down the significance of mere 'actions' as compared to confession and undertaking to make a new start. More broadly, civil society tends to 'overlook' many breaches of legal rules. The undoubted stress on solidarity and inclusiveness that characterises Catholic and ex-communist ideology may also conceal a form of 'repressive tolerance'. In terms of Young's dichotomy (1989), Italy seems better able to tolerate deviance than difference.

A final word should be said about the role of scientific evaluation and criminology itself. 'Scientific' evaluation of 'what works' is not an important part of most social policy initiatives in Italy (as compared to political idealism and party-political point scoring). So it is not surprising that more attention is given to legal processing for its own sake than to the reduction of crime and recidivism. Gaetano di Leo, the academic architect of the 1988 reform, used the language of 'responsibilisation' rather than talking of the intellectually then somewhat discredited goals of welfare or rehabilitation. But there is little real interest in making children responsible to the 'community' and both judges and social workers still subscribe to a bland (but not blind) welfare ethos.[27] As for

---

27. One judge explained his philosophy as follows, '... hence these are all youths with big problems and dealing with these must be the best way of solving the problems youths represent for the legal system. Youth crime is in any case not an urgent problem because there are not so many such crimes. Crimes are not going up; at least to me it doesn't seem that they are. Then there are of course those isolated cases where young people kill their fathers or mothers. But, come to that, there are also cases where parents kill their children!'

the future, in a country where ideas count for so much, support for the 1988 law is more likely to be eroded by international mutations in intellectual fashion than by any perceived failures in its everyday achievements or any major changes in the conditions which underpin current tolerant practices.

Conclusion

In this chapter I have used the Italian system as a case study to show what is involved in speaking of a juvenile justice system as one that is particularly tolerant of juvenile crime. I have argued that there is certainly evidence that supports this characterisation but that it is over-simplistic to describe this as the explicit aim of those running the system. In particular, attention needs to be given to the extent to which the current system is shaped by the fact that its governing law was constructed as a merely procedural reform.

More generally, I have suggested the need for a framework for investigating variations in tolerance that examines this in terms of how, when, and why a system is tolerant. As in any analysis of punitiveness, therefore, the study of *non*-punitiveness also requires us to explore its causes, conditions and consequences (Nelken, 2004; Nelken, 2006). Much of the academic literature tends to attribute the rise of punitiveness to the influence of 'penal populism'. An enlightened or more tolerant approach to crime, on the other hand, is said to reflect the 'value placed on professional expertise in planning penal policy' (see Pratt et al., 2005). This may fit the Anglo-American context as well as having some wider applicability. But, as I have tried to show, it is only once we place juvenile justice in the context of criminal justice and the larger national (and global) society, that we come to appreciate the many other relevant factors that shape its functioning.

The message of this chapter is that we need to learn more *about* tolerance if we are to learn *from* tolerance. What are the conditions which underpin it? When are these conditions relevant? How relevant are these conditions? What are the possible drawbacks of living with such conditions? Too often ideas and practices alleged to be tolerant are abstracted from the context that gives them their sense. On the other hand, the existence of different conditions elsewhere should not be used simply as an alibi. For example, some magistrates interviewed in England and Wales defended their practices by saying that it was easier for the Italians because they were able to rely on the strength of 'the family'. As we have seen, the 'Italian family' is neither a necessary nor sufficient condition for explaining its patterns of juvenile justice. While it is important to appreciate the wider context, it is wrong to suggest that tolerant practices are or must be inevitably anchored in a given and unchanging set of social circumstances. To suggest otherwise is itself a move in the struggle over what models of justice are possible and plausible.

References

Bailleau, F. and Cartuyvels, Y. (2002) Special issue of *Deviance e Societé*, 26: 3.

Bailleau, F. and Cartuyvels, Y. (2003) 'Juvenile penal justice in Europe: issues at stake and outlook', unpublished paper, Council of Europe research group on juvenile justice.

Bernard, T. (1982) *The Cycle of Juvenile Justice*. Oxford: Oxford University Press.

Blatier, C. (1999) 'Juvenile justice in France. The evolution of sentencing for children and minor delinquents', *British Journal of Criminology* 39(2): 240–252.

Gatti, U. (2002) 'La delinquenza giovanile' in M. Barbsgli and U. Gatti (eds) *La Criminalità in Italia*. Bologna: Il Mulino, pp. 159–170.

Gatti, U. and Verde, A. (2002) 'Comparative Juvenile Justice: an Overview on Italy', in J. Winterdyk (ed.) *Juvenile Justice Systems: International Perspectives* (2nd edition). Toronto: Canadian Scholars Press, pp. 297–320.

Junger Tas, J. (ed.) (1994) *Delinquent Behaviour among Young People in the Western World*. Amsterdam: Kugler.

Lemert, E. (1986) 'Juvenile Justice. Italian Style' *Law and Society Review* 20: 509–544.

Muncie, J. (2005) 'The globalization of crime control – the case of youth and juvenile justice', *Theoretical Criminology* 9(1): 35–64.

Nelken, D. (1994) 'Whom Can you Trust?', in D. Nelken (ed.) *The Futures of Criminology*, London, Sage, pp. 220–44.

Nelken, D. (ed.) (2000a) *Contrasting Criminal Justice*. Aldershot: Dartmouth.

Nelken, D. (2000b) 'Telling Difference: Of Crime and Criminal Justice in Italy', in D. Nelken (ed.) *Contrasts In Criminal Justice*, Dartmouth. pp. 233–64.

Nelken, D. (2002) 'Comparing Criminal Justice', in M. Maguire, R. Morgan and R. Reiner (eds) *The Oxford Handbook of Criminology* (3rd edition). Oxford: Oxford University Press, pp. 175–202.

Nelken, D. (2003) 'Corruption in the European Union', in Martin Bull and James Newell (eds) *Corruption and Scandal in Contemporary Politics*. London: Macmillan, pp. 220–33.

Nelken, D. (2004) 'Being there', in L. Chao and J. Winterdyk (eds) *Lessons from International/Comparative Criminology*. Toronto: De Sitter Publications, pp. 83–92.

Nelken, D. (2005) 'When is a Society Non–Punitive? The Italian Case', in J. Pratt, D. Brown, S. Hallsworth, M. Brown, and W. Morrison (eds) *The New Punitiveness: Current Trends, Theories, Perspectives*. Willan: Cullompton, pp. 218–38.

Nelken, D. (2006) 'Patterns of Punitiveness' *Modern Law Review*.

Nelken, D. and Feest, J. (2001) *Adapting Legal Cultures*. Oxford: Hart.

Pratt, J. (eds) (2005) *The New Punitiveness: Current Trends, Theories, Perspectives*. Cullompton: Willan.

Reichel, P. (1999) *Comparative Criminal Justice Systems: A Topical Approach* (2nd edition). Englewood Cliffs, New Jersey: Prentice Hall.

Ricciotti, R. (2001) *La giustizia penale minorile*. Padova: Cedam.

Roberts, P. (2002) 'On Method: The Ascent of Comparative Criminal Justice', *Oxford Journal of Legal Studies* 22: 529–61.

Scalia, V. (2005) 'A lesson in tolerance: Juvenile justice in Italy?' *Youth Justice* 5(1): 33–43.

Scatolera, D. (2004) 'Devianza Minorile e Coercizione Personale,' *Questione Giustizia* 2–3: 397–411.

Scivoletto, C. (1999) *C'è Tempo per Punire. Percorsi di Probation*. Milano: Franco Angeli.

Smith, R. (2003) *Youth Justice: Ideas, Policy Practice*. Cullompton: Willan.

Whitman, J. (2003) *Harsh Justice: Criminal Punishment and the Widening Divide Between America and Europe*. Oxford: Oxford University Press.

Young, J. (1989) *The Exclusive Society*. London: Sage.

Finland: A Model of Tolerance?

12

Tapio Lappi-Seppälä

Introduction

The age of criminal responsibility in Finland is 15 years. Originally the 1889 criminal code gave the courts the right to impose disciplinary penalties and to place 7–15 year olds in reformatory schools. However, the general child welfare reforms of the 1930s and 1940s removed children under the age of 15 from criminal court jurisdiction and placed them under child welfare authorities. Young offenders aged 15 to 17 are dealt with under both the child welfare system and the system of criminal justice, while young adults between 18 to 20 will be dealt only by the criminal justice authorities.

The functioning of these two systems – child welfare and criminal justice – is based on fundamentally differing principles. The criterion for all child welfare interventions is the best interest of the child. All interventions are supportive and criminal acts have little or no formal role as a criterion or as a cause for these measures. The 'criminal justice side', on the other hand, makes much less difference between offenders of different ages. All offenders from the age of 15 years onwards are sentenced in accordance with the same criminal code. Strictly speaking, there is no separate juvenile criminal system in Finland in the sense that this concept is usually understood in most legal systems. There are no juvenile courts and the number of specific penalties only applicable to juveniles has been quite restricted. Nevertheless, young offenders are in many respects treated differently to adults: there are limiting rules for the full application of penal provisions. Offenders aged 15–17 receive mitigated sentences and there are additional restrictions in the use of unconditional prison sentences. They may also be sentenced to a specific community punishment (juvenile punishment). Offenders under the age of 21 receiving a suspended sentence (conditional imprisonment) may be put under supervision and they may be released on parole earlier than adults.

Juvenile justice in Finland has one foot in the adult criminal justice system and another foot in the child welfare system. A balanced overview requires that both dimensions are taken into account.

Trends and changes in criminal policy and child welfare

Sentencing reforms between 1960–1990

In the 1960s, the Nordic countries experienced heated social debate on the results and justifications of involuntary treatment in institutions, both penal and otherwise (such as in health care and in the treatment of alcoholics). The critique of compulsory care merged with another reform ideology that was directed against an overly severe Criminal Code and the excessive use of custodial sentences.[1] The resulting criminal political ideology was labelled as 'humane neo-classicism'. It stressed both legal safeguards against coercive care and the goal of less repressive measures in general. In sentencing, the principles of proportionality and predictability became the central values. Individualised sentencing, as well as sentencing for general preventive reasons or perceived dangerousness were put in the background.

Since the early 1970s Finland has shaped its sanctioning system in the spirit of 'humane neo-classicism'. The overall aim of these law reforms – altogether about 20–25 – was to reduce the use of imprisonment. The reforms started during the mid-1960s, and continued up to the mid-1990s.

Penalties for both traditional property offences and drunken driving were heavily reduced. Amendments were made in the general penalty structure by strengthening the role of non-custodial sanctions. Fines were increased in order to provide a credible alternative to short-term prison sentences. The scope of conditional imprisonment (suspended sentence) was extended, and the number of annually imposed conditional sentences rose from 4,000 (in 1960) to 18,000 (in 1990).

The use of imprisonment as a default penalty for unpaid fines was restricted and the daily number of fine-defaulters fell from over 1,000 to less than 50. In

---

1. The trends in the Scandinavian criminal political thinking in the 1960s are analysed in Anttila 1971. The reform ideology of the 1970s and the 1980s are described in Anttila and Törnudd, 1992. See also Lahti, 2000 and Lappi-Seppälä, 2001.

the early 1970s the number of people held in preventive detention fell overnight from 250 to less than 10. The system of early release was expanded by lowering the minimum time to be served before the prisoner as eligible for parole: first from 6 months to 4 months in the mid-1960s, then from 4 to 3 months in the mid-1970s, and finally from 3 months to 14 days in 1989.

The reform of general sentencing principles in the mid-1970s restricted the role of prior convictions in sentencing, leading to an overall reduction of sentences in offence categories with high recidivism rates. In the early 1990s the scope of non-prosecution was extended especially for younger offender groups. A few years earlier the Conditional Sentence Act was amended by including a provision which allows for the unconditional sentencing of young offenders only if there are weighty reasons calling for this.

The scope of community sanctions was further extended in the early 1990s by the introduction of community service. The number of annually imposed prison sentences fell from between 9,000 and 10,000 to 6,000 while the number of community service orders grew from 0 to almost 4,000 between 1992–1997. Today community service replaces around 35% of short-term (max 8 months) prison sentences.[2]

Prison rates and crime rates 1950–2000

The overall effect of these policy reforms is reflected in a dramatic fall of Finnish prisoner rates. At the beginning of the 1950s the prisoner rate in Finland was four times higher than in the other Nordic countries. Finland had almost 200 prisoners per 100,000 inhabitants, while the figures in Sweden and Norway were around 50. Even during the 1970s, Finland's prisoner rate continued to be among the highest in Western Europe. In the early 1970s Finland had some 120 prisoners/100,000 inhabitants, while the corresponding figures at that time in England and Wales were almost half. Today the situation is the reverse. When most European countries experienced rising prison populations, the Finnish one decreased. By the beginning of the 1990s Finland had reached the Nordic level of about 70 prisoners per 100,000 inhabitants. In 1999 the figures hit an all time low. In 2003 the number of prisoners was the same as in 1990.

Figure 12.1 overleaf shows incarceration rates in Finland, Sweden, Denmark and Norway, from 1950 to 2000. In order to estimate any impact on crime rates, trends in reported crime are included below.

A remarkable feature of this change was that it evidently had no corresponding counter effects in crime rates. There is a striking difference in the use of imprisonment, and a striking similarity in the trends in recorded criminality. That Finland has substantially reduced its incarceration rate has not disturbed the

---

2. The subject has been dealt in more detail by the author in Lappi-Seppälä, 2001. See also Törnudd, 1993.

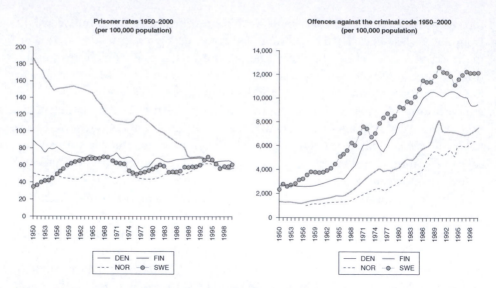

Figure 12.1   Prison rates and crime rates 1950–2000

symmetry of Nordic crime rates. The figures, once again, support the general criminological conclusion that crime and incarceration rates are fairly independent of one another; each rises and falls according to its own laws and dynamics.

Stocks and flows in juvenile imprisonment

Juveniles are basically under the same system as adults, so changes made to the adult system usually affect that of juvenile justice. Reducing the penalty scales for property offences and restricting the role of recidivism were especially influential since property offences are typical juvenile offences and recidivism is especially high among the younger age groups. What one could expect from all this, is that the decline of prisoner rates should have been the heaviest especially for young people. This was precisely what happened.

Prison statistics 1975–2003   The numbers of prisoners in age groups 15–17 and 18–20 years from 1975 onwards are presented in Figure 12.2

The number of prisoners aged between 15 and 17 fell from over 100 in the mid-1970s to less than 10 in the 1990s. Prisoners in the age group 18–20 fell from over 350 to less than 100. The percentage of juvenile and young prisoners in the overall prison population was also dramatically reduced (see Figure 12.3). The male/female ratio is about the same in both age groups: Around 4–5% of young prisoners are female (of all prisoners 5.5% are female).

Sentencing statistics   Similar changes may be traced from court statistics. The absolute numbers of annually imposed prison sentences are presented in Figure 12.4.

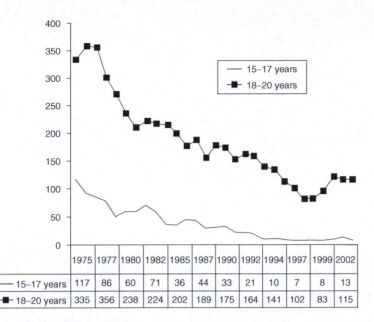

	1975	1977	1980	1982	1985	1987	1990	1992	1994	1997	1999	2002
—— 15–17 years	117	86	60	71	36	44	33	21	10	7	8	13
—■— 18–20 years	335	356	238	224	202	189	175	164	141	102	83	115

Figure 12.2 The number juvenile prisoners 1975–2002 (annual averages, absolute figures, remand included).

Source: Compiled from Statistic Finland.

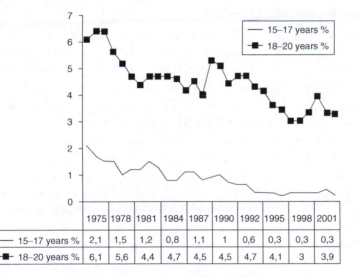

	1975	1978	1981	1984	1987	1990	1992	1995	1998	2001
—— 15–17 years %	2,1	1,5	1,2	0,8	1,1	1	0,6	0,3	0,3	0,3
—■— 18–20 years %	6,1	5,6	4,4	4,7	4,5	4,5	4,7	4,1	3	3,9

Figure 12.3 The number of juvenile prisoners 1975–2002 (percentages).
Source: Compiled from Statistic Finland.

For 15–17 year old offenders these fell from over 400 in the late 1980s to well below 100 in 2003. The corresponding change in the age group 18–20 was from 1,500 to 800. The latter trend seems to have stabilised, as a part of an overall increase of prison sentences, during the latter half of the 1990s (see below). In the younger age group the number of prison sentences has remained stable – or even declined.

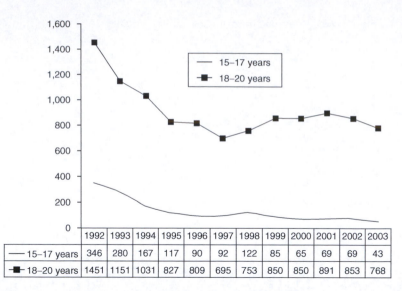

	1992	1993	1994	1995	1996	1997	1998	1999	2000	2001	2002	2003
——15–17 years	346	280	167	117	90	92	122	85	65	69	69	43
—■—18–20 years	1451	1151	1031	827	809	695	753	850	850	891	853	768

Figure 12.4   Annually imposed unconditional prison sentences for young offenders 1992–2003.

Source: Compiled from Statistic Finland.

Institutional treatment in child welfare and health care

The reform movement of the 1960s and the 1970s did not confine itself to prisons and to criminal justice: all compulsory treatment, whether in prisons, mental hospitals or in institutes for alcoholics was closely scrutinised. The child welfare system was no exception. The conditions and the treatment methods in state-run reformatory schools were heavily criticised and the whole existence of the system was questioned. During the following decades the state-run reformatory schools were practically run down and the number of residents fell from 1,500 in the mid-1960s to 750 in the mid-1970s and to around 300 in the early 1990s.

The treatment and working methods in child welfare underwent a profound change. Punitive elements disappeared. Misbehaviour and criminal conduct of the child as major motives for placement were replaced by need-based arguments. During the 1980s the rhetoric of 'in the best interest of the child' was further combined with family centred approaches (see Pösö, 1993). Simultaneously, emphasis was given to 'right-based' arguments. Children became subjects who needed to be heard and whose rights must be appreciated.

Today the whole structure of these institutions looks very different. Large state-run reformatory schools have been replaced by small residential units, with typically only 10 to 20 places. The majority of placements are voluntary. The outspoken motive for placement is the 'best interest of the child'. This, of course, does not preclude the possibility that criminal conduct has relevance in the decision to place children in care (as a factor endangering the child's future mental and physical development). But since 'crime' does not belong to the vocabulary of today's social work, and measures are not recorded on this basis, it is difficult to assess in how many cases the placement has been partly motivated by 'crime related reasons'. Evidently, a substantial number (around 50%) of children placed in reformatory schools have had crime-related problems. However, in only a small minority (around 10%) has the criminal behaviour of the child been the principal reason for their placement (see Kitinoja, 2005.)

In addition one should also take into account the measures taken by the health care authorities, especially the use of psychiatric treatment. Children under 18 can be ordered to undergo treatment against their will if they are deemed to be suffering from a severe mental disorder which, if untreated, would become considerably worse or seriously endanger their health or safety or the health or safety of others, if all other mental health services are unavailable or inappropriate (discussed in more detail below).

Explaining the past

The social-liberal approach adopted in Finland during the 1970s was far from unique at that time. The interesting question is why some countries with fairly liberal (such as the UK) or exceptionally tolerant (such as the Netherlands) policies changed their practices in the opposite direction from the late 1970s onwards; why some countries (such as Sweden, Denmark and Norway) have been able to keep their prisoner rates more or less stable over a lengthy period of time; and why some countries – in this case Finland – managed to adopt a course that ran counter to most European penal systems throughout the 1980s and 1990s? Unfortunately, no simple answers are to hand. In order to explain penal changes one needs to take into account a complex network of structural (economic, social and political), cultural and ideological factors, as well as a number of micro-level professional practices and arrangements.[3] The following observations, therefore, serve only as examples from a longer list of factors worth considering.[4]

Ideological and political background

Ideologically the overall change in penal policy, and the related decline of institutional treatment for juveniles, was a part of a wider social and political reform movement of the 1960s. It grew out of the criticisms of all totalitarian institutions and the widespread mistrust in the effectiveness of imprisonment. The

---

3. As demonstrated so convincingly by Garland, 2001.
4. See in more detail Lappi-Seppälä, 2001.

reform movement was inspired by the belief that crime was predominantly a social problem that could be counteracted by social reform, rather than repression. The decarceration strategies gained additional political support from intensified Nordic co-operation in legal matters from the 1960s onwards. Finland's exceptional position in Nordic prison statistics became politically difficult to explain in an atmosphere which stressed common Scandinavian values and the aims of penal harmonisation. By the early 1970s a political consensus was reached that prison overcrowding and Finland's high prisoner rate was a disgrace and that something should and could be done about it.

While the early years of the reform movement in Finland were inspired by 'radical liberals', the subsequent reform policy during the late 1970s and 1980s was carried out mainly by 'pragmatic practitioners' in the Ministry of Justice, Prison Administration and Research-Institutes. During this phase 'Rational and Humane Criminal Policy' became the official watchword. This combined the pragmatic aims of criminal justice with ideas of fairness and respect for legal safeguards, and emphasised the role of both social and situational strategies in crime control.

Political culture

The decline in Finnish rates of imprisonment was, thus, a long-term result of deliberate policy choices. But one may still ask, what made it possible to carry out these liberal law-reforms? Part of the answer can be found in the political culture. Finnish criminal policy can be described as exceptionally *expert-oriented*. Reforms were formulated by a relatively small group of experts and criminal justice professionals. Their impact was reinforced by close personal and professional contact with some politicians, state officials and academic researchers. Also the *decision-making process* itself offered less political temptation for short-term populist and punitive gestures. It may be argued that the Scandinavian 'consensual democracies' with multi-party systems, large-based coalition or minority governments and high-levels of corporatist participation invite negotiation and compromise. Bi-polarised (majoritarian) political systems, in contrast, create more favourable settings for episodes of penal populism and short-term politically oriented single-case criminal justice legislation.[5] *Consensus and consistency* have, indeed, been cherished values in Finnish (penal) policy. The legislative drafting process seeks to ensure that all interest groups have an opportunity to participate and express their views (and commit themselves to the reforms). Reform also takes time. The slow speed of the drafting process, with several preparatory levels, provides time for cool consideration, which, in turn, diminishes the risk of rapid turnarounds and expressive 'single-case' law-reforms.

---

5. On this see also Green 2004 with references.

These features may partly also explain why crime control has never been a central political issue in election campaigns in Finland. The fact that the media has retained quite a sober and reasonable attitude towards issues of criminal policy is also of principal importance. The Finns have been largely saved from the low-level populism so characteristic of elements in the British media.

Professional practices and social structures   Micro-level institutional arrangements and specific professional practices have contributed to this change. Collaboration with and assistance from the judiciary was a key factor. Different courses and seminars arranged for judges and prosecutors in co-operation with the universities have impacted on sentencing and prosecutorial practices. Judges and prosecutors are also trained career officials who have received teachings in criminology and criminal policy in the law faculties. At the other end of the continuum macro-level social and economic factors may also help to understand some of the wider 'penological-peculiarities' of the Scandinavian countries. The period of penal liberalisation in Finland started when Finland joined the 'Nordic welfare-family'. As a whole, the Scandinavian experience might be used to support Garland's (2001) hypothesis about the associations between social and economic security and solidarity granted by the welfare-state and low levels of penal repression.[6]

Juvenile justice today

Sanctions and sentencing

The Finnish sanction system is fairly simple. General punishments are fine, conditional imprisonment, community service and unconditional imprisonment. Specific punishments for young offenders include supervision connected with conditional sentence and juvenile punishment. In addition the law defines various routes of diversion including non-prosecution and waiver of punishment in the courts (discharge) (see Figure 12.5).[7]

Fines   A fine is imposed as a day-fine. Day-fines are imposed in between 1 and 120 units. The number of day-fines is based on the seriousness of the offence while the amount of a day-fine depends on the financial situation of the offender. One day-fine corresponds roughly to one-third of the gross daily income of the offender. Fines are the most common penalty for all age groups accounting for 74% of court sentences for 15–17 year olds, 62% in the 18–20 age-group and 55% for those over 20.

---

6. While making these kind of comparisons, one must of course take into account the fact that Finland has been culturally and demographically quite homogenous and that there are far less ethnic- and minority-tensions, to be exploited by right-wing parties.

7. On Finnish juvenile legislation, see closer Marttunen, 2004.

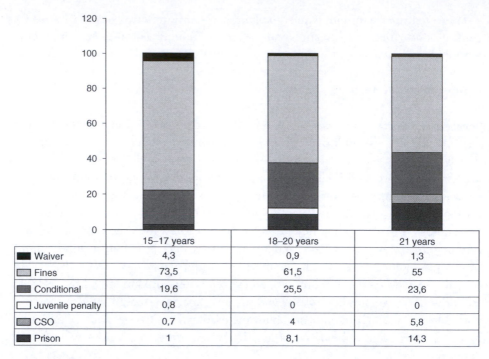

	15–17 years	18–20 years	21 years
■ Waiver	4,3	0,9	1,3
▢ Fines	73,5	61,5	55
■ Conditional	19,6	25,5	23,6
▢ Juvenile penalty	0,8	0	0
▢ CSO	0,7	4	5,8
■ Prison	1	8,1	14,3

Figure 12.5   Penalties imposed by the court for different age groups.

Source: Compiled from Statistic Finland.

Imprisonment   A sentence of imprisonment may be imposed either for a deter-mined period or for life. The general minimum sentence of imprisonment is 14 days and the general maximum is 12 years. Young persons under the age of 18 cannot be sentenced to life imprisonment. Unconditional prison sentence is also seldom used for this age group. The annual number of prison sentences has varied between 50 and 100, corresponding to about 1% of all sentences in this age-group. About 8% of offenders aged between 18–20 are sentenced to impris-onment while the figure for adults (over 20) is 14%.

Conditional imprisonment   Sentences of imprisonment of, at most, two years can be imposed conditionally. The choice between conditional and unconditional imprisonment is based mainly on blameworthiness (harm, culpability and prior convictions). For offenders under 18 there is a clear presumption for imposing prison sentences conditionally. On the other hand, all prison sentences over two years must be imposed unconditionally. For 15–17 year olds this is usually reserved for homicides, aggravated robberies and aggravated drug offences. About half of conditionally sentenced young offenders under 18 are placed under supervision. The role of supervision is basically supportive. A condi-tional sentence may be revoked only because of a new imprisonable offence.

Conditional imprisonment is the 'backbone' of community penalties in Finland. 20% of 15–17 year olds and 25% in other age-groups are sentenced to conditional imprisonment.

Community service Prison sentences up to 8 months may be commuted to community service (from 20 to 200 hours). In order to ensure that community service will really be used in lieu of unconditional imprisonment, a two-step procedure has been adopted. First the court is supposed to make its sentencing decision by applying the normal principles and criteria of sentencing without considering the possibility of community service. Second, *if* the result of this deliberation is unconditional imprisonment (and certain requirements are fulfilled), the court may commute the sentence into community service. In principle, community service may therefore be used only in cases where the accused would otherwise receive an unconditional sentence of imprisonment. Since community service can be ordered only instead of unconditional imprisonment, and since young offenders may receive prison sentences only in exceptional cases, community service has rather limited relevance for offenders under 18. Each year about 1% of offenders under 18 receive community service. The corresponding figures in other age groups are 4% (18–20) and 6% (over 20).

Juvenile punishment Offenders between 15 and 17 at the time of the offence can be sentenced to juvenile punishment if, 'in view of the seriousness of the offence and the circumstances connected with the act a fine is to be deemed an insufficient punishment, and there are no weighty reasons that require the imposition of an unconditional sentence of imprisonment'. Juvenile punishment is rated on the same severity level as conditional imprisonment. The court should favour juvenile punishment if it is deemed 'justified in order to prevent new offences and to promote the social adjustment of the young offender'. In practice, the main criterion is prior convictions. Juvenile punishment was introduced on an experimental basis in seven cities in 1997. After certain modifications, the sanctions were established nation-wide in 2005. Juvenile punishment is something of a compromise between neo-classicist and social and rehabilitative approaches. It creates an additional rung in the system of sanctions and enables any movement towards custodial sanctions to be slowed down. In addition, it also has clear social and re-integrative goals. Enforcement is arranged in co-operation with the social welfare board and the content of the punishment is based on programmes developed by the Probation Service and the social welfare authorities (see Marttunen and Takala, 2002).

Correctional practices and international obligations Most prisoners under the age of 21 serve their sentence in a specific juvenile prison. They can be released on parole after they have served one third (instead of the normal one half) of their sentence. Juvenile prison is a closed institution. However, its daily routines differ markedly from normal adult prisons with much more emphasis on education and professional training. At the end of 2003 there were 62 prisoners in juvenile prison, 59 boys and 3 girls.

About one-third of young prisoners under the age of 21 serve their sentence in other institutions. This results partly from the requirement that prison terms in juvenile prison may not exceed four years. Thus young offenders, sentenced for more serious crimes (homicide and sometimes aggravated drug offences) serve their sentence in adult prisons. On the other hand, those offenders eligible for open prisons usually prefer open adult facilities over closed juvenile prison.

These arrangements indicate that Finland has not been able to comply with the United Nations International Covenant on Civil and Political Rights' requirement that young offenders be segregated from adult prisoners.[8] While ratifying the convention in 1976 Finland filed a reservation that 'although juvenile offenders are, as a rule, segregated from adults, it does not deem appropriate to adopt an absolute prohibition not allowing for more flexible arrangements'. This reservation is still in force. A recent government bill on prison law, however, proposes that prisoners under the age of 18 be held in a ward separate from adults. A derogation from this obligation would only be possible if it was in the best interests of the child.

Table 12.1 opposite summarises the main dispositions available to the Finnish juvenile justice system.

Mediation

Academic and political debate of the 1980s and early 1990s was strongly influenced by the Nordic abolitionist movement. While the critical criminologists' approach was endorsed by a substantial number of young criminologists, a 'victim rights perspective' had less to offer in a system which already acknowledged wide procedural and substantive guarantees for compensation of crime damages (see Lappi-Seppälä, 1996). Of all initiatives, informal victim–offender

---

8. The UN convention entered into force in Finland in 1976 and the European Human Rights Convention in 1990. Finland joined the UN Convention on the Rights of the Child in 1989. All the international agreements that Finland has adopted are part of the Finnish judicial system after having first been incorporated by the decision of the parliament. However, these documents, such as the European Human Rights Convention (ECHR) do not have a general or absolute precedence over other statutory law in Finland. Still, in cases where the provisions of the convention and the contents of national law contradict each other, a doctrine of interpretation known as 'human rights friendly interpretation', was adopted in Finland by the Constitutional Committee of the parliament: the interpretation and application of laws shall always aim at obtaining a result that as closely as possible corresponds to the international obligations of Finland in the field of human rights. The same principle has also been declared in the new Finnish Constitution which entered into force in 2000. According to section 22, the public authorities shall guarantee the observance of basic and human rights. As a result, the Finnish courts have more and more often referred to the articles of the convention in their decisions.

Table 12.1   Statistics on juvenile justice in Finland

		15 to 17 years	18 to 20 years	21 years & over
PROSECUTOR	Summary fines	10,000	25,000	180,000
	Non prosecution due to petty nature of the offence, youth etc (guilt confirmed)	1,000	800	4,000
	Waiver of sentence	200	100	700
	Fines	3,000	6,000	30,000
COURTS	Conditional sentence	800	2,500	12,000
	(with supervision)	(400)	(600)	–
	Juvenile punishment	100	–	–
	Community service	50	400	3,000
	Imprisonment	50	800	7,000
	Daily average 2003 (incl. remand)	7	116	3,455
PRISON	Admissions/year			
	– to serve a sentence	9	105	3,397
	– for remand	26	159	1,700
Population	Total 5,234,000	191,000	194,000	3,937,000

mediation turned out to be a success. After a slow start in the early 1980s, the movement expanded rapidly. Today, all towns with a population over 25,000 and most over 10,000 offer mediation services. Eighty per cent of Finns live in a municipality that has an agency for mediation.[9] Mediation is based on volunteer work. Participation is voluntary for all parties. The municipal social welfare authorities usually have a hand in co-ordinating the mediation services, but the mediators are not considered as public officials. Mediation is possible for all age groups. Its principal importance, however, lies with offenders under the age of 21. Mediation has not been integrated into the criminal justice system as a form of 'specific penal measure'. However, the criminal code mentions an agreement or settlement between the offender and the victim as possible grounds for waiving of charges by the prosecutor, or waiving of punishment by the court and as grounds for mitigating the sentence.

Mediation process   Mediation can start at any time between the commission of the offence and execution of the sentence and by any of the interested parties. Three-quarters of the cases are referred to mediation either by the prosecutor or by the police; the remainder are initiated by the parties or social authorities. The mediator's principal role is only to mediate and act on a neutral basis. Once the process has started it normally leads to a written contract. The contract contains the subject (what sort of offence), the content of a settlement (how the offender has consented to repair the damages), the place and date of the restitution as well as consequences for a breach of the contract. What happens after a

---

9. See in more detail Grönfors, 1989, Lappi-Seppälä, 1996 and Iivari, 2000.

successful mediation depends largely on the category and seriousness of the offence. In complainant offences a successful mediation automatically means that the prosecutor drops the case. In non-complainant offences it is under the discretion of the prosecutor whether he/she is willing to drop the charge. This would be possible if prosecution would seem 'either unreasonable or pointless' due to a reconciliation, and if non-prosecution would not violate 'an important public or private interest'. In mediation cases non-prosecution is, thus, always discretionary. Unlike in some other countries, mediation does not automatically divert the case from the criminal justice system. This may narrow the diversionary effect of mediation. On the other hand, it also prevents mediation from becoming restricted to trivial cases.

Experiences and reform plans   A rough estimate of the total number of cases in all mediation schemes yields about 4,000 referrals each year. Eighty per cent of the cases consist of either minor property offences or minor forms of assault and battery. Agreement is reached in about 60% of the referrals. On average, 90% of the contracts will be fulfilled. The majority of the contracts contain monetary compensation, but may also include an apology or a promise not to repeat the behaviour. Mediation clearly provides a workable channel of restitution. In addition to material compensation, mediation may serve as a means for repairing some of the emotional and psychological damage caused by crime.

Studies report predominantly positive results (see Iivari, 2000). Major criticism has been directed to unequal distribution of services. There are still regions in the country – especially smaller rural communities – where mediation is not available. To change this, a law was passed in 2006 which obliged all of the provinces to organise mediation in their area. In practice this means the mediation services will be available throughout the country. The law did not change the informal character of the activity. However, the act introduced a number of precisions dealing with the preconditions of mediation, qualifications and tasks of the mediators, as well as procedural rules and organisational issues. Mediation is still not classified as a sanction, but it may be taken into account in sentencing either as a mitigating factor or as a ground for waiving from penal measures (see above).

Child welfare and children in trouble

Child welfare measures   The criterion for all child welfare interventions is the best interest of the child. These interventions comprise in the first instance support interventions in community care. The authorities should undertake community-based supportive measures without delay if the health or development of a child or young person is endangered or not safeguarded by their environment or if they are likely to endanger their own health or development. In more serious cases measures include taking into public care, transfer of guardianship and placement in a foster home or in residential or other (institutional) care. 'Taken into care' may be voluntary or involuntary. In most cases all parties (the child and the parents) agree on the matter. Annually some 8,000 children are in public care, of which 1,500 (20%) are placed involuntarily.[10] The available data suggests that on any given day, there are some 400 14 to 17 year olds placed in residential care against their or their parent's will. Half of these are in family-group homes and one quarter in children's homes. About 100 are placed in closed juvenile homes or in state-run reformatory schools. About half of these children have been involved in criminal activities, but only in 10–20% of the cases has crime been the principal cause for placement.

The psychiatric hospitals had a patient-flow of 2,044 children between the ages of 12 and 17 in 2003, and the average duration of treatment varied between 30–50 days. In all, the annual average of children aged between 14 and 17 in mental care institutions has been around 350. Of these placements about 20–22% are involuntary (in age-group 10–17). No official data is available of criminal history. Basically treatment is based on medical reasons, as stipulated in the law. In practice the systems overlap, as placements change between psychiatric units and other institutions. Psychiatric and mental health related reasons also seem to play an increasing role in care-taking orders and placements in reformatories (see also below).

Causes of concern   In the light of international standards the Finnish child welfare system has managed fairly well. The comments from the UN Committee on the Rights of the Child have been basically positive. In its 2000 report, the Committee reiterated its satisfaction at the comprehensive social security system and the wide range of welfare services for the benefit of children and their parents, in particular free health care, free education, extended maternity leave, parental leave, and an extensive day-care system. It also welcomed the efforts taken to reduce the impact on children of the economic recession in the first half of the 1990s.[11]

However, there are also causes of concern. There are clear signs of decreased physical and mental well-being of children, young people and their families. The child-welfare authorities have reported a steep rise in emergency interventions. The number of children taken into foster care increased by some 30–40% during the 1990s. Also, the number of children in need of psychiatric treatment and the number of placements in psychiatric hospitals has been increasing.

This may be the post-effects of the 1990s recession. The increase in the number of children in trouble reflects to a large extent the deteriorating social and

---

10. Either against the will of the parents and/or the child. The true extent of 'involuntariness' is hard to confirm, since the parties may feel that the use of statutory rights to oppose the placement could in practice be futile (see Pösö, 2004).

11. The comments may be obtained from http://www1.umn.edu/humanrts/crc/finland2000.html.

economic position of their parents with more demanding and more insecure work-relations and with less time and less resources for parenthood. The UN Committee on the Rights of the Child pointed out these same concerns and 'strongly recommended' the State to allocate more funds to families with children. In its third national report for the Committee (2003) the Finnish government was able to report increased funds targeted for mental health services and for children and young people at risk of social exclusion.[12]

Justice for juveniles tomorrow

Trends within the juvenile justice system

Over a 30 year period, the Finnish Penal Code and its system of sanctions has undergone total reform. In the 1990s, some of its neo-classical assumptions were contested through the introduction of community service in 1991 and the new juvenile punishment in 1997. Neither of these reforms though can be characterised as 'repenalisations'. The outspoken motive of community service was to replace short-term prison sentences. The aims of juvenile punishment were more mixed but undoubtedly initiated by political motives to introduce a more 'tangible and credible' alternative to the conditional prison sentence.

Causes of concern Current Finnish debate however contains worrisome elements familiar to most Western jurisdictions. Youth violence has attracted considerable media attention, and contributed to public demands for government action to 'do something'. Isolated serious violent offences committed by juveniles with mental health problems was a cause of general concern during the early 2000s. In 2001 a majority of Finnish parliament members signed a (subsequently rejected) proposal to reduce the age of criminal responsibility – a topic that seems to be a recurring theme of discussions in parliament every two to three years. General public dissatisfaction towards the 'repeated use of conditional imprisonment for young recidivist offenders' has also fed demands for 'more tangible and effective juvenile sanctions' such as new short-term prison sentences. So far these initiatives have not led to concrete legislative action. Research evidence showing that, in general, juvenile crime has been in decline during the last 10 years, has served as an efficient back-up argument against the expansion of the criminal justice system.

Still, Finnish juvenile justice may well be facing changes in the near future. The main concerns deal with pragmatic issues, such as, how to improve co-operation between different actors and how to avoid unnecessary delays in judicial processing. Efforts have been made to 'speed up' the criminal process, especially by improving and enhancing the co-operation between different

---

12. The report may be obtained from http://www.unhchr.ch/html/menu2/6/crc/doc/report/srf-finland-3pdf.

officials. Another debate has pondered the issue whether the distinctive needs of young offenders should be taken into account to a greater extent within the criminal justice system, or whether rehabilitative aims should still be channelled mainly via the social welfare system. The need for more immediate action in the case of evident risk of re-offending has also been a subject of political concern.

In 2001 the Ministry of Justice launched a commission to address these issues. The commission had a general mandate 'to establish a more rehabilitative perspective in the Finnish juvenile criminal system'. The main part of the commission's proposals concentrated on improving co-operation between different officials and in speeding up the juvenile criminal process. The commission also proposed expanding the use of juvenile punishment to include 18–20 year olds. It also drafted plans for a new preventive oriented 'liberty restricting juvenile arrest'. The group rejected the idea of 'custodial arrest' and proposed electronically monitored house arrest and a locally defined restraint-order ('target arrest'). The new sanctions would not be classified as punishment, but as measures of security to be used mainly instead of remand.

The proposals of the juvenile committee are, for the most part, well considered and recommendable. But some risks are involved: one-sided managerialist aims to speed up the criminal process may undermine the more substantial values of dealing with offenders with proper depth and with required expertise. And the faster the cases go through the system, the sooner one may expect the juvenile to return. This may mean more cases, more court decisions and, eventually, more prisoners. Increased co-operation and increased exchange of information may also lead to more breaches of client confidentiality and decreased feelings of trust and confidence. Reborn optimism in rehabilitation also has its inherent risks. As long as rehabilitative measures are in the hands of child welfare authorities, the deep rooted and uncontested principle of voluntariness in social services is a solid guarantee against hidden coercion and punishment under the label of treatment. Once rehabilitation becomes incorporated into a system that is based ultimately on coercion, the more tempting it becomes to get led by good intentions and start to use coercive measures for the 'good of the clients'.

Broader trends within the general penal system Proposals with manifestly punitive aims or those based on risk assessments and incapacitation are hard to find in current Finnish juvenile justice debate. However, the threats may also come from the 'outside'. In the past, the juvenile justice system has benefited from favourable developments in adult criminal justice. But this door swings both ways. The bond is still there and possible changes in the adult criminal justice system may, again, have corresponding repercussions in the juvenile system.

The general international risk factors within adult criminal justice include the general tendency to politicise criminal justice policy and the increased pressure towards harmonising criminal law within the European Union. Traces of these trends are beginning to be seen in Finnish penal policy. The overall number of prisoners has started to rise although this change has yet to touch younger age groups (see Figures 12.2 and 12.3 on page 181). However, it is evident that the previous downward trend in imprisoning young offenders has now stabilised. Taking into account that very few of the social, political, economic and cultural conditions which explain the rise of mass imprisonment in the USA and England and Wales apply to Finland, there may still be room for some optimism. Social equality and the demographic homogeneity of Finnish society may mitigate against unfounded repression. There are less racial and class tensions/distinctions, less fear and less frustration to be exploited by marginal political groups and less extreme demands for control and exclusion. Related to this, the welfare state was never openly discredited in Finland, not even during the deepest recession of the 1990s. The social and economic security granted by the Nordic welfare state can still function as a social backup system for a tolerant criminal justice policy. Trust in, and legitimacy of, the legal and political system may also play an important part. The fact that the Finns have, by international standards, a high level of confidence in their political and legal system may partly explain why there has been no need for expressive gestures in penal policies. The political culture still encourages negotiations and appreciates expert opinion. And, regarding especially juveniles, in Finnish public policy, juvenile crime and 'children in trouble' are still viewed as problems arising from social conditions; and these problems should be addressed by investing more in health services and in general child welfare – not in penal institutions.

References

Anttila, I. (1971) 'Conservative and radical criminal policy in the Nordic countries', *Scandinavian Studies in Criminology* 3: 9–21.

Anttila, I. and Törnudd, P. (1992) 'The Dynamics of the Finnish Criminal Code Reform', in R. Lahti and K. Nuotio (eds) *Criminal Law Theory in Transition. Finnish and Comparative Perspectives* Tampere: Finnish Lawyers' Publishing Company.

Garland, D. (2001) *The Culture of Control: Crime and Social Order in Contemporary Society*. Chicago: The University of Chicago Press.

Green, D. (2004) 'Repairing Damaged Democracy? Toward an improved model of public consultation in penal policy making'. ASC draft paper. Nashville, 19 November.

Grönfors, M. (1989) 'Mediation: Experiment in Finland', P.-A. Albrecht and O. Backes (eds) *Crime Prevention and Intervention*. Walter de Gruyter Berlin – New York.

Iivari, J. (2000) 'Victim-offender mediation in Finland', in *Victim-Offender Mediation in Europe. Making Restorative Justice Work*. Leuven: Leuven University Press.

Kitinoja, M. (2005) 'Kujan päässä koulukoti (At the end of the road, a reform school, a study of the child welfare clienting and school history of children placed in reform schools)'. Stakes 150/2005.

Lahti, R. (2000) 'Towards a Rational and Humane Criminal Policy: Trends in Scandinavian Penal Thinking', *Journal of Scandinavian Studies and Crime Prevention*. 1: 141–155.

Lappi-Seppälä, T. (1999) 'Reparation in Criminal Law. Finnish National report', in A. Eser and S. Walther (eds) *Wiedergutmachung im Strafrecht* Max-Planck-Institut, Freiburg im. Br. 1996.

Lappi-Seppälä, T. (2001) 'Sentencing and Punishment in Finland: The Decline of the Repressive Ideal', in M. Tonry and R. Frase (eds) *Punishment and Penal Systems in Western Countries*. New York: Oxford University Press.

Marttunen, M. (2002) 'Youth Criminal Procedure: Evaluation of the Practice of the Youth Criminal Process'. The National Research institute of Legal Policy, 193/2002. (English summary) http://www.om.fi/optula/19527.htm

Marttunen, M. (2004) 'European Youth Involved in Public Care and Youth Justice Systems. ENSA-Youth Project: A Collection of Papers from three European Symposia'. http://www.cjsw.ac.uk/servlet/page?_pageid=952&_dad=portal30&_schema=PORTAL30

Marttunen, M. and Takala, J. P. (2002) 'Juvenile Punishment 1997–2001. Evaluation of a new punishment'. The National Research Institute of Legal Policy, 192/2002. (English summary) http://www.om.fi/optula/15811.htm

Pösö, T. (1993) 'Kolme koulukotia (Three reformatory schools)'. Acta Universitatis Tamperensis. Ser A. vol. 388. Tampere.

Pösö, T. (2004) 'Vakavat silmät ja muita kertomuksia koulukodista (Serious Eyes and Other Experiences of Reform Schools)', Stakes 133: Helsinki. 2004.

Törnudd, P. (1993) *Fifteen Years of Decreasing Prisoner Rates in Finland*. National Research Institute of Legal Policy. Research Communication 8/1993.

Törnudd, P. (1996) *Facts, Values and Visions. Essays in Criminology and Crime Policy*. National Research Institute of Legal Policy. Research reports 138/1996.

States of Transition: Convergence and Diversity in International Youth Justice

John Muncie and Barry Goldson

Introduction

It is no longer necessary to make the case for a comparative approach to understanding systems of youth and juvenile justice. It is increasingly assumed that developments in any single nation state cannot be fully explored without reference to sub-national, regional and local diversity as well as acknowledging the impact of international and global forces. The advantage of an international focus (even though this volume is restricted to 12 'significant' cases in Western societies only) is that it encourages debate of the structural, cultural and political constraints and dynamics within which juvenile justice was constructed in developed capitalist countries during much of the 20th century and which have then been challenged, and in some cases overturned, since the 1980s. Comparative analysis makes it possible to begin to unravel the relative import of internal, national dynamics and external, international contexts and constraints. But equally it must be recognised that, as a result of competing internal and external pressures, such systems are continually in transition and flux. Whatever future trajectories appear likely on the basis of a reading in the first decade of the 21st century may not hold for a decade in the future. As a result, rather than simply seeking apparent similarities and differences, this volume recognises the increasing complexity of the mix of different interventions and acknowledges that in all jurisdictions such a mix is likely to increase. Rather than proceeding with a state by state descriptive analysis of powers and procedures, this concluding chapter identifies multiple overlapping and contradictory themes in contemporary international juvenile justice reform – such as repenalisation, adulteration, welfare protectionism, differential justice, restoration, tolerance, decarceration and rights – and applies them to particular exemplary cases.

The collapse of welfare protectionism?

The principle that children and young people should be protected from the full weight of 'adult' criminal jurisdiction underpins the concept of welfare in youth justice. For much of the 20th century most Western systems of juvenile justice have sought legitimacy in a rhetoric of child protection and 'meeting needs'. Custodial institutions were criticised as stigmatising, dehumanising, expensive, brutalising, and as criminogenic rather than rehabilitative agencies. 'Justice' for juveniles was considered best delivered through the establishment of a range of community-based interventions. The care and control of young offenders was thought best placed in the hands of social service agencies and professionals. This 'ideal' found a quite remarkable international consensus until at least the 1970s. Beginning with the first juvenile courts established in South Australia in 1895, in Illinois, USA in 1899 and in England and Canada in 1908, through to the likes of Belgium's Children's Protection Act of 1912, France's 1945 edict prioritising protection and education, or Japan's Juvenile Law of 1948, child welfare models of juvenile justice have been paramount.

But by the 1980s this consensus began to unravel. First, conservative critics argued that the primary function of the youth justice system should be to *control* young offenders rather than to *care* for them. The concept of welfare was widely to be regarded as evidence that juvenile justice had become or was becoming 'too soft'. Second, academic commentators and radical youth justice practitioners questioned the legitimacy of imposing wide-ranging interventions on the basis of 'need', and challenged individualised notions of 'rehabilitation' and 'treatment'. They argued that channelling ostensibly 'welfare' interventions through a youth justice system often produced 'more harm than good'. Third, rights advocates and legal professionals, argued that wide-ranging discretionary judgements in respect of 'welfare' undermined the child's *right* to 'justice'. Young people, particularly young women and girls, were considered in double jeopardy, sentenced for their 'vulnerability' and background as well as for their offence (Hudson, 1987; Goldson, 2004). As a result it has become widely assumed that, by the late 20th century, welfare had been all but formally expunged from most Western systems of juvenile justice. In its place has emerged a series of diverse 'justice-based' principles more concerned with responding to the 'deed' of the offence rather than the 'need' of the offender. Discourses of support and protection have indeed become increasingly challenged, but not always eclipsed by discourses of accountability, responsibility and the primacy of punishment.

This storyline has played itself out differently across Western jurisdictions. For example, in Scotland the juvenile court was abolished in 1968 and the system has been operating with a welfare tribunal for the majority of under 16 year old offenders for the past 30 years. As a result it has long been maintained that the childrens hearing system ensures that child welfare considerations hold a pivotal position for younger offenders and provide a credible alternative to the punitive nature of youth justice pursued in many other jurisdictions (Bottoms, 2002). It has, however, not been without its critics, not least because of the lack of legal safeguards and the apparent tendency for the adult courts to deal with those aged 16 and over with undue severity. Scotland has a relatively high rate of under 21 year olds admitted to prison. Moreover, the Scottish Executive decided in 2003 to pilot the re-establishment of youth courts for 16 and 17 year olds. Ostensibly this was to deal with 'persistent offenders' but would also overcome the Scottish anomaly of being the only Western European country to routinely deal with this age group in the adult courts. Re-introducing youth courts, rather than extending the remit of the children's hearing system, also appears driven by an ensuing moral panic about 'neds': labelled by the media as 'drug fuelled youths' who are 'the scourge of Scottish society' (see McAra, Chapter 9 of this volume).

Belgium, it is claimed, has developed a system that is the 'most deliberately welfare-oriented of all' (see Put and Walgrave, Chapter 8 of this volume). The Youth Protection Act 1965 established principles of social protection and judicial protection to apply to all those under the age of 21. With a few exceptions, no punishments are available to those under 18 (18 being the age of criminal responsibility). All judicial interventions for this group continue to be legitimated through an educative and protective, rather than punitive and responsibilising discourse. In principle it is the needs of the young person that determine the nature of the intervention. The powers of the Youth Court which include reprimand, supervision, community service and fostering, however, also allow for placement in a public institution for the purposes of observation and education. From 2003 the temporary placement of juveniles in closed centres run by the federal Ministry of Justice (rather than the Community run public institutions) has been allowed. For these reasons, Put and Walgrave remain suspicious of Belgian welfarism which 'leads not to justice without punishment but punishment without guaranteed justice'. Moreover they note a developing politicisation of juvenile and street crime in Belgium fuelled by media sensationalism and extremist right-wing vitriol directed at Moroccan and Turkish minorities. Challenges to welfare protectionism appear imminent through a growing emphasis on offender responsibility and accountability.

In Finland juvenile justice policy continues to prioritise an understanding of 'children in trouble' grounded in socio-economic explanations rather than in individual pathology. As a result there remains a remarkable political consensus that investing in health and social services is more likely to deliver positive outcomes than developing penal institutions. Yet even here warnings emerge that such a consensus may soon unravel in the face of a growing international politicisation of the 'youth crime' issue (see Lappi-Seppälä, Chapter 12 of this volume).

'Adulteration': treating children as adults?

A shift from welfare to justice based philosophies not only opened a door to a consideration of judicial due process but also allowed justice and rights to be usurped, particularly by political conservatism, as a means of delivering 'just deserts' and enforcing individual responsibility. Rather than rehabilitation and meeting needs, a growing international (particularly North American, Australian and English) discourse is now one of risk management (Farrington, 2000) and zero tolerance with an obsession for public safety (Wacquant, 1999). Retribution and deterrence have taken precedence over positive rights agendas. Special consideration given to young offenders is being undermined in favour of adult style justice (Fionda, 1998; Schaffner, 2002). The emphasis has become one of fighting juvenile crime rather than securing juvenile justice.

Certainly this storyline is again pertinent to unravelling the contemporary twists and turns of youth justice in many jurisdictions. But in itself it remains significant that throughout Europe the term *juvenile* justice is preferred to that of *youth* justice, while the UN advocates the formulation of a *child-centred* criminal justice. The UK countries stand out as having some of the lowest ages of criminal responsibility. In the European Union these ages range from 8 in Scotland, and 10 in England and Wales to 15 in Denmark, Norway, Finland and Sweden and 18 in Belgium and Luxembourg. Ireland legislated to raise its age of criminal responsibility from 7 to 12 with its Children Act 2001 (O'Dwyer, 2002) but to date this has not been enacted and a more limited rise to the age of 10 appears more likely (*Irish Times*, 16 June 2003). Spain though has recently moved in the same direction by increasing the age of responsibility from 12 to 14 with its Juvenile Responsibility Act 2001 (Rechea Alberola and Fernandez Molina, 2003). In contrast, England and Wales abolished the principle of *doli incapax* for 10 to 14 year olds in 1998 despite recurring complaints from the UN, and in 2000 Japan lowered its age of criminal responsibility from 16 to 14 (see Table 13.1 overleaf).

In Holland, too, the conditions governing the possibility of transferring juvenile cases to an adult court have been recently relaxed along with early intervention projects, such as STOP, which effectively lowers penal responsibility from 12 to 10 year olds (Junger-Tas, 2004 and see uit Beijerse and van Swaaningen, Chapter 5 of this volume). Similarly Canada's recent youth justice reforms are based on the core principle that the protection of society be uppermost. Under its Youth Criminal Justice Act 2002, the Youth Court has been

Table 13.1   Ages of criminal responsibility

Scotland	8
England and Wales	10 (*doli incapax* abolished 1998)
Northern Ireland	10
Australia	10
Canada	12 (established in 1984)
Ireland	12 (raised from 7 in 2001 but yet to be implemented)
Netherlands	12
Turkey	12
France	13
New Zealand	14
Germany	14
Italy	14
Spain	14 (raised from 12 in 2001)
Japan	14 (lowered from 16 in 2000)
Denmark	15
Finland	15
Norway	15 (raised from 14 in 1990)
Sweden	15
Belgium	18
Luxembourg	18

renamed the Youth *Justice* Court and discretion has been afforded to provincial governments to impose adult sentences on those aged 14 and above (see Smandych, Chapter 2 of this volume).

Such 'adulteration' is most marked in the USA which has witnessed the widespread dismantling of special court procedures that had been in place for much of the 20th century to protect young people from the stigma and formality of adult justice (see Krisberg, Chapter 1 of this volume). Since the 1980s (but beginning in Florida in 1978), most American states have expanded the offenses for which juvenile defendants can be tried as adults in criminal courts, lowered the age at which this can be done, changed the purpose of their juvenile codes to prioritise punishment, and resorted to more punitive training and boot camps. A renewed emphasis on public safety (rather than a child's best interests) has also meant that confidentiality has been removed in most states with the names of juvenile offenders made public and in some cases listed on the internet. Equally, in many states, children below the age of 14 and as young as 7 can have their cases waived by the juvenile court and be processed as if they were adult. Forty-six states can require juvenile court judges to waive jurisdiction over minors and 29 states have laws that do not allow certain cases to be heard in a juvenile court at all. As a result, around 200,000 children under 18 are processed as adults each year (Snyder, 2002). The tendency in the USA to prosecute and punish children as if they were adults is inconsistent with the approach encouraged by international standards adopted by almost every country in the world; that governments should establish laws, procedures, authorities and institutions specifically for children. Since 1997, four countries – the USA, Iran, Pakistan, and the Democratic Republic of Congo – have executed individuals for crimes committed before they were 18. But the practice is in worldwide decline due to the express provisions of the UN Convention on the Rights of the Child. The USA stubbornly held on to this power into the 21st century. Five US states, notably Texas and Florida, continued to allow execution for 17 year olds and a further 17, notably Alabama and Louisiana, were able to authorise the death penalty for children aged 16 (Streib, 2003). Since 1976 there were 22 executions of juveniles. But in March 2005 the US Supreme Court abolished the practice ruling by a slim majority of 5 to 4 that it amounted to 'cruel and unusual punishment' (see Krisberg, Chapter 1 of this volume).

States of incarceration

One widely acknowledged problem in comparative analysis is that of interpreting the experience of other countries through the experiential lens of those countries with which the researcher is most familiar. This is compounded by any tendency to use the 'home' country as the norm against which others are judged. One way out of this impasse has been to turn to the study of aggregated data which are becoming increasingly available from international agencies. The main global comparative statistics on the stock, flow and rates of imprisonment are those collected by the United Nations *Surveys on Crime Trends and the Operations of Criminal Justice Systems* dating back to 1970 and by the *World Prison Population Lists* produced by the Home Office and the International Centre for Prison Studies at King's College London. The sixth edition of the latter details the numbers of prisoners held in 211 countries and in doing so estimates that over 9 million people are being held in penal institutions worldwide at any one time (Walmsley, 2005). The United States has the highest penal population with some 714 incarcerated per 100,000 population. This is followed by the likes of Russia (532) and Belarus (532). The UK rate of 142 places it as the highest in the European Union. The lowest in Europe appears to be Iceland (39). Table 13.2 overleaf records the rates of imprisonment for those countries included in this volume.

As Walmsley points out, these figures should be used with some caution. The figures do not always relate to the same date. Some include those on remand, others do not. Some include juveniles, when held under prison administration, and others do not. Nevertheless, they make an initial and important point of wide global variation. Walmsley's figures of course do not distinguish between juvenile and adult populations. The United Nations' surveys on the operation of criminal justice systems, carried out by its Office for Drug Control and Crime Prevention, have attempted to provide rates of youth/juvenile imprisonment per 100,000 of the population. These are the only global data sets of juvenile incarceration that are available. The most recent, the 8th survey, was sent to 191 countries in 2003; there were 65 replies (United Nations, 2005). Data collected from the 5th, 6th, 7th and 8th surveys dating back to 1994 provide a picture of

Table 13.2   World prison populations circa 2003–2004

	Total	Rate per 100,000 Population
USA	2,085,620	714
New Zealand	6,802	168
England and Wales	75,320	142
Scotland	6,742	132
Netherlands	19,999	123
Australia	23,362	117
Canada	36,389	116
Italy	57,046	98
France	55,028	91
Belgium	9,245	88
Finland	3,719	71
Japan	73,734	58

Source: Derived from World Prison Population List (6th edition) (Walmsley, 2005) Studies, 2004.

an incarceration rate of 21.57 juveniles per 100,000 population in South Africa and 17.71 in Scotland, but an almost absence of juvenile custody in Japan (0.04/100,000) and in Belgium (0.02/100,000). (see Table 13.3 opposite)

It should be noted that some states, such as Australia have no entry in this particular data set presumably because they either do not regularly collect such data or have always declined to respond to the UN's surveys. We need also to be clear that the term 'juvenile' is differentially applied. For example, in Japan the data includes all those under 20 years of age; in Scotland the data refers to those mostly aged between 16 and 21; in Canada, England and Wales and the USA 'juvenile' only refers to those under the age of 18. It is also interesting to note that the USA's rate of juvenile incarceration is recorded as having been reduced from 38.44/100,000 in 1997 to 6.21/100,000 in 2002 (this may be because the count was restricted to state prisons and private facilities and excluded 'residential custody' at the later date). There are other reasons why caution is advisable. What is classified as penal custody in one country may not be in others though regimes may be similar. The existence of specialised detention centres, training schools, treatment regimes, reception centres, closed care institutions and so on may all hold young people against their will but may not be automatically entered in penal statistics (Muncie and Sparks, 1991). As a result, only guarded comparisons can be made, though from a European point of view it does seem to indicate a generally more tolerant penal climate than that found in North America, Russia or South Africa.

More regular data of young people in European prison populations has been collected by the Council of Europe for the past 20 years. These sources report that in September 2002 England and Wales held 2,754 under 18 year olds in prison, compared to 688 in France, 183 in Scotland, 105 in Belgium, 101 in the Netherlands and just 17 in Finland and 13 in Norway. The corresponding figure for

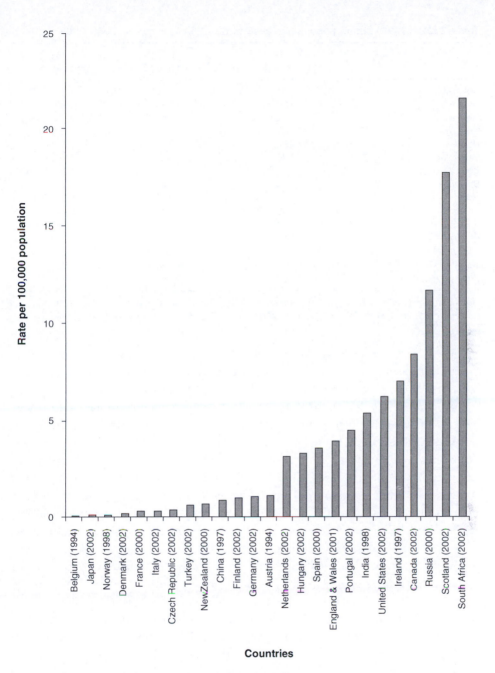

Table 13.3 Total convicted juveniles admitted to prison: selected countries 1994–2002

Source: Derived from the 7th and 8th United Nations Surveys of Crime Trends and Operations of Criminal Justice Systems, 2002, 2005

juveniles held in residential custody, state prisons and private facilities in the USA in 2000 was 110,284 (International Centre for Prison Studies, 2004). The percentage of under 18s in total national prison populations in these selected countries

Table 13.4   Under 18s in prison: selected European/USA comparisons 2000–2002

	September 2000	September 2002	% of prison population
Denmark	11	12	0.3
Spain	136	***	0.3
Finland	11	17	0.5
Norway	15	13	0.5
USA	110,284	***	0.5
Netherlands	87	101	0.6
Italy	***	240	0.8 (12/04)
Belgium	97	105	1.1
France	730	688	1.3
Germany	843 (03/01)	***	1.4
Austria	***	114	1.5
Portugal	***	289	2.1
Scotland	164	183	2.8
Turkey	1,929	2,237	3.7
England and Wales	2,480	2,754	3.9

Sources: Derived from Penological Information Bulletin, Council of Europe no. 23/24, 2002; no. 25, 2003; Council of Europe SPACE 1, 2003; World Prison Brief, accessed 2005.

ranged from 3.9% in England and Wales to 0.3% in Denmark. All countries, except France and Norway, for which the relevant data is available, reported increases in these penal populations between 2000 and 2002 (see Table 13.4)

Just as significantly these figures again throw up some remarkable divergences. From an English point of view it suggests a closer affinity in European terms to Turkey than to nearer (geographically, politically, culturally) neighbours, and in global terms implies something of a 'pernicious transatlantic punitive emulation' of the USA (Goldson, 2002: 396). Yet these statistics provide some basic comparisons only. They tell us nothing, for example, of the gender or 'race' composition of this particular age group. To address such questions, statistical measures, even when reliable, are of only limited value. As Pease (1994: 125) has argued, on their own they are particularly 'useless for all practical and intellectual purposes' in helping to assess national differences in processes of penal severity or leniency. Either might be present with or without high penal populations (for a discussion of the methodological difficulties involved in comparing relative states of harshness and leniency see Nelken, Chapter 11 of this volume). What is required, as all the chapters in this volume have revealed, are detailed analyses of the politics of policy formation in different jurisdictions.

Repenalisation

To test the proposition of repenalisation we need to track shifts in incarceration rates over the long term. Walmsley (2005) found in his world prison population list of 211 countries, that 73% had recorded *increases* in their prison populations over the previous five years. However, there are no comparable worldwide statistical time series records for under 18s. The closest data set can be derived only for parts of Europe by figures collected on under 21 year old populations by the Council of Europe between 1992 and 2002. Even then there are some notable absences, such as Germany and Denmark for which there are no records over this period. There are no figures for Greece beyond 1996. For Austria there are only figures for 2002. Nevertheless, significant increases in the numbers of under 21 year olds in prison are noted in the Netherlands (+54%), Norway (+38%) and England and Wales (+ 37%), but conversely Italy (–44%), Northern Ireland (–40%) and Finland (–20%) have all recorded significant decreases (Muncie, 2006). If these figures are to be trusted then half of Europe is witnessing some form of youth repenalisation while the other half is pursuing reductionist programmes.

As the chapters in this volume have revealed, the reasons for these dramatic divergences are rooted in a complex of contrasting penal cultures. Certainly international research has consistently found that there is no correlation between custody rates and crime rates. However, the unequivocal message coming from Europe and most Western societies is that over the past 20 years there has been a dramatic shift in juvenile justice policy involving a diminution of discretional welfare interventions in favour of various justice-based principles and procedures. This, it is claimed, is a key driver of more punitive approaches to young offenders and underpins processes of repenalisation. This shift has also been explained with reference to the burgeoning of neo-liberal economics, political conservatism and the import of penal policies particularly from the USA (Wacquant, 1999; Garland, 2001; Simon, 2001; Pratt et al., 2005). Driven by fears of immigration and an assumed 'new tidal wave of juvenile violent crime', ethnic groups in particular have been increasingly identified as a threatening and permanently excluded 'underclass' about which little can be done but to seek their neutralisation and segregation. There has been a notable swing to the right in many Western, particularly European, countries, with far right parties, fuelled by fears of crime and immigration, claiming some success in England and Wales, Austria, Holland, France, Germany, Denmark and most recently Switzerland. In many jurisdictions, juvenile justice is clearly becoming increasingly racialised. Similarly, many initiatives originating in the USA such as zero tolerance policing (France, Belgium, the Netherlands, Australia), parental sanctions (Japan, Canada, New Zealand), mandatory sentencing (Western Australia), dispersal zones (the Netherlands), curfews (Belgium, France, Scotland), electronic monitoring (the Netherlands, Scotland, France, but also Sweden), naming and shaming (Japan, Canada), 'fast tracking' (New Zealand) and risk prediction (the Netherlands, Australia, Canada) have been transferred globally. Elements of all of these continue to have a presence in England and Wales (see Muncie and Goldson, Chapter 3 of this volume). But it appears their effect has not been uniform; in some cases existing more in political rhetoric than in practice (Jones and Newburn, 2002; Newburn and Sparks, 2004; van Swaaningen, 2005). Juvenile justice reform also remains remarkably nationalised, localised and contingent.

Nevertheless the commentaries included in this volume have all detected a growing hardening of (public, political, media) attitudes and criminal justice responses to young people: particularly evident in discourses of accountability and responsibility even if not always reflected in growing rates of incarceration. The only exception is Krisberg's (see Chapter 1 of this volume) account of contra tendencies in the USA which may be beginning to herald a partial retreat from its draconian penal populism of the 1990s and the re-awakening of some earlier juvenile justice ideals.

In England and Wales the numbers of 15 to 20 year olds in prison almost doubled in a decade from some 5,000 in 1993 to nearing 9,000 in 2002. The apparent fall in crime in many US cities has proved to be an irresistible draw for British politicians. Any number of 'zero tolerance' initiatives have targeted anti-social behaviour and incivilities, effectively criminalising non-criminal behaviour. A tough stance on crime and welfare has become the taken-for-granted mantra to achieve electoral success (see Muncie and Goldson, Chapter 3 of this volume).

In the Netherlands there has also been a dramatic reversal in Dutch penal policy from the mid 1980s onwards (see uit Beijerse and van Swaaningen, Chapter 5 of this volume). Once heralded as a beacon of tolerance and humanity (Downes, 1988), the Netherlands has embarked on a substantial prison building programme linked to a tendency to expand pre-trial detention and to deliver longer sentences on conviction (Pakes, 2000; 2004). In 2002, Dutch city councils gave the police new powers to arbitrarily stop and search without reasonable suspicion in designated areas of 'security risk'. The practice has amounted to the criminalisation of poor and black neighbourhoods, targeting in particular Moroccan youth (*Statewatch* Jan–Feb, 2003: 8). For van Swaaningen and uit Beijerse such shifts are symptomatic of a resurgent law and order discourse which prioritises security over justice, as epitomised by the remarkable rise of punitive populism often associated with the right-wing politician Pim Fortuyn (van Swaaningen, 2005). The result is an uneasy mix of punitive and welfare rationales. Between 1990 and 2003 the number of youth custodial places increased from 700 to 2,400.

In France, the right-wing Government of Alain Juppe from 1993 to 1997 reversed its traditional, *Bonnemaison* social crime prevention policy based on conceptions of *solidarity*, instead prioritising a police-led zero tolerance and *disciplinary* approach (See Gendrot, Chapter 4 of this volume). It is a policy that was continued by the left-wing Jospin Government. The socio-economic conditions that produce youth marginalisation and estrangement are no longer given central political or academic attention (Bailleau, 1998). Rather, concern appears directed to migrant children, particularly from Africa, Asia and Eastern Europe, who have arrived in search of political asylum and economic opportunity. Special surveillance units have been established to repress delinquency in 'sensitive neighbourhoods', penalties for recidivism have been increased and the deportation of foreigners speeded up (Wacquant, 2001). With the return to power of the right in 2002 a new public safety law expanded police powers of search, seizure and arrest, instituted prison sentences for public order offences (such as being disrespectful to those in authority), lowered (from 16 to 13) the age at which young offenders can be imprisoned, and introduced benefit sanctions for parents of offending children. A generalised prioritisation of 'security' over social prevention has called into question the continuing ability of French republicanism, traditionally driven by 'progressive centre' notions of legal equality and of social inclusion, solidarity and integration, to ensure more of a lasting rejection of American punitiveness than seems to be politically acceptable in countries such as England and Wales (Pitts, 2001; Rutherford, 2002). This was underlined in 2005 when France's interior minister responded to over two weeks of national disturbances (when an increasingly marginalised ethnic minority youth set thousands of cars alight) by announcing an uncompromising police crackdown. High profile repression was preferred to long term prevention.

Tham (2001) reports similar shifts in the 1990s across many European social democracies, driven by a complex constellation of a break up of social democratic welfare humanitarianism, neo-liberal market reform, fears of illegal migrants, changes in labour markets, the emergence of a new moralism of 'zero tolerance' associated with the disciplinary techniques of the free market and a related lowering of the tolerance level for crime and violence. Governments of all persuasions appear to be increasingly turning to law and order as a means of providing symbols of security and to enhance their own chances of electoral support. But while many countries may have added punitive elements to their legislation in the 1990s, only the Netherlands and England and Wales can claim (on the basis of the Council of Europe's prison statistics) to have witnessed a dramatic US style youth repenalisation. In these jurisdictions in particular there appears little reluctance to locking up young people and to designate such places of detention as 'prison' when doing so. Elsewhere a philosophy of child protection seems to continue to hold sway albeit increasingly tested by new discourses of responsibility. The irony for all though is that during the last decade youth crime rates across much of the Western world have been mostly falling or at least stable.

A future for the 'non-punitive' and decarceration?

It is not difficult to find examples of decarceration in the history of Western juvenile justice. Arguably the most significant was the closure of all juvenile facilities in Massachusetts in the 1970s. In England and Wales the numbers in custody were dramatically reduced between 1981 and 1992 as a result of permissive policy practitioner initiative and magisterial decision-making (Rutherford, 1989). Less well known is that most jurisdictions in Australia have witnessed substantial falls in juvenile incarceration since the 1980s probably as a result of extending diversionary options including the use of youth conferencing. Recent evidence from Canada also suggests a growing decarcerative movement. A number of European countries, such as Italy and Finland, have been able to report significant decreases in their daily count of youth (under 21) incarceration between 1992 and 2002. According to the UN data, such countries as Japan, Norway and Sweden similarly stand out as having been able to keep youth imprisonment to an absolute minimum and as maintaining such toleration throughout the 1990s. Whether politically, pragmatically or economically inspired, a case establishing the damaging effects of custody on children (and the wider community) has repeatedly been made and acknowledged. The willingness and ability to act on this knowledge, however, remains piecemeal.

Finland made an explicit decision some 40 years ago to abandon its Soviet style tradition of punitive criminal justice in favour of decarceration and diversion (see Lappi-Seppälä, Chapter 12 of this volume). As a result, the young offender prison population has been reduced by 90% since 1960. There has been no associated rise in known offending. This was achieved by a long-term programme of applying indefinite detention to a small number of violent offenders and by suspending imprisonment for a majority of others on the condition that a period of probation was successfully completed. Immediate 'unconditional' sentencing to custody is now a rarity. Prison home leave, early release and family visits are commonplace. There are no specific juvenile courts but 15 to 21 year olds are only imprisoned for the most exceptional reasons. The voluntary acceptance of mediation can be used as grounds for the waiving of sentence (Lappi-Seppälä, 1998, 2001). This dramatic shift has been facilitated by a conscious effort on the part of successive Finnish governments to formulate a national identity closer to that of other Scandinavian states. Certainly it has been made possible by an insistence that elites and experts are better placed to formulate and decide penal policy rather than the whims of public opinion and party politics. Finland's experience seems to show that high incarceration rates and tough penal regimes do not control crime. They are unnecessary. Decarceration can be pursued without sacrificing public safety. Indeed something of a consensus appears to exist in Nordic countries (Iceland, Norway, Sweden, Finland, Denmark) that 'forward looking' social and educational measures together with mediation take precedence over prosecution and punishment. Compliance with the UN Convention of the Rights on the Child also results in juveniles not being incarcerated with adults and because of an absence of prisons dedicated to juveniles most do not endure penal custody at all (Nordic Working Group, 2001: 147–148).

The case of Italy deserves comment as it currently appears at the forefront of youth penal reductionism in Europe (see Nelken, Chapter 11 of this volume). This has been accounted for by the introduction of new penal laws in the late 1980s which explicitly stressed penal leniency for this age group in order to not interrupt educational processes and personal development. It is backed by a widespread cultural attitude which prioritises the Church and the family (rather than formal juvenile justice) as the key agencies of social control. Diversion takes precedence over formal early intervention. In particular, avoidance of conviction and refusal of punishment is facilitated through the mechanisms of *irrilevanza* (insufficient seriousness), *perdono* (judicial pardon) and *messa alla prova* (pre-trial probation for all offences). As a result, young people tend to be incarcerated only for very few serious violent offences and only when the conditions of *messa alla prova* have not been met (though this may be differentially applied to immigrants and gypsies). As Nelken notes, this means that many serious offences do not even end up with a conviction, let alone a prison sentence. Gatti and Verde's (2002: 312) data shows a marked decline in the numbers of juveniles entering penal institutions in the late 1980s but some increase during the 1990s following the introduction of reception centres. Nevertheless, the daily average of juveniles placed in *prigione scuola* in 1998 was just 176. More fundamentally an Italian cultural tradition of familial control has been traditionally linked to something of a 'benevolent tolerance' and subsequently low levels of penal repression (Nelken, 2002, 2005). The 'cultural embeddedness' of Catholic paternalism (compared, for example, to US evangelical Protestantism) may not determine penal policy but provides the parameters in which differential readings of the purpose and meaning of punishment become possible (Melossi, 2000). Young people in trouble with the law are more regarded as in need of help and support than requiring of retribution, denunciation or indeed punitive responsibilisation. Moreover, as Nelken (2005: 231) argues, juvenile justice procedures in Italy tend to be based more on principles of what is philosophically defensible rather than because they can be 'scientifically' shown to work as in more supposedly pragmatic cultures such as England and Wales.

Similarly Japan's often assumed non-punitiveness (at least in terms of custody rates – see Table 13.2) has been accounted for in the context of a tradition of 'maternal protectionism' and a culture of 'amae sensitivity' which prioritises interdependence over individual accountability. The juvenile offender is deemed as much a victim as a criminal (Morita, 2002). But Japan also appears to be facing a renewed politicisation of juvenile crime, evident in amendments to the Juvenile Law in 2000 and further proposals in 2005 in which principles of child protection have been challenged by those of a resurgent penal populism. Of most significance has been a lowering of the age of criminal responsibility from 16 to 14 and a generalised introduction of a moral rhetoric of responsibility, guilt and condemnation into juvenile justice discourse (Fenwick, 2004 and see Fenwick, Chapter 10 of this volume).

Experiments in restoration and mediation

There has been a substantial growth in interest in restorative justice and victim-offender mediation across Western jurisdictions in the past 20 years and restorative models have penetrated most juvenile justice systems. In contrast to processes of 'adulteration' and 'repenalisation', contemporary juvenile justice reform also appears informed by contra penal trajectories such as those derived from the import of family group conferencing pioneered in New Zealand, Australia and North America. Within restorative justice the talk is less of formal crime control and more of informal offender/victim mediation and harm minimisation.

These initiatives in part draw upon notions of informal customary practices in Maori, Aboriginal and Native American indigenous populations. Both the United Nations and the Council of Europe have given restorative justice their firm backing. Community safety, reparation, community work, courses in social training and so on, together with compliance with United Nations conventions and Council of Europe recommendations, have all been advocated as means to achieve participative justice and to reduce the recourse to youth imprisonment. The Council of Europe has recommended to all jurisdictions that mediation should be made generally available, that it should cover all stages of the criminal justice process and, most significantly, that it should be autonomous to formal means of judicial processing. The European Forum for Victim–Offender Mediation and Restorative Justice was established in 2000. Across many parts of Africa, Stern (2001) records renewed interest in solidarity, reconciliation and restoration as the guiding principles for resolving disputes rather than the colonial prison. The Child Justice Bill, under consideration by the South African government since 2000, is particularly influenced by a recognition of children's rights coupled with application of the ideals of restorative justice (Skelton, 2002; van Zyl Smit and van der Spuy, 2004). In 2002 the UN's Economic and Social Council formulated some basic universal principles of restorative justice, including non-coercive offender and victim participation, confidentiality and procedural safeguards. It is clear that restorative justice is no longer marginal but a burgeoning worldwide industry with local projects proliferating across much of Europe, Africa, Canada, the USA and Australasia (Justice, 2000, Miers, 2001; Tickell and Akester, 2004).

The key issue remains of how far restoration can work as a radical alternative in those instances when it appears to be simply co-opted into systems that are otherwise driven by punitive, authoritarian rationales. As has been repeatedly pointed out, there is a clear danger that any form of compulsory restoration may degenerate into a ceremony of public shaming and degradation, precisely because the underlying intent is simply to reinforce (Western-inspired) notions of individual responsibility rather than develop those of social justice for indigenous and non-indigenous populations alike (see, in this volume, Bradley, Tauri and Walters, Chapter 6; Cunneen and White, Chapter 7; and Smandych, Chapter 2). Further, international evaluation research has cast some doubt on whether restorative justice 'works' to reduce recidivism. The results tend to be mixed, but with some reductions in re-offending for young violent offenders. All of this encourages significant scepticism and ambivalence towards the claims made for restoration and its future potential to overhaul the injustices of retribution (White, 2000, 2002; Daly, 2002).

Protecting children's rights?

The 1989 United Nations Convention on the Rights of the Child (UNCRC) established a near global consensus that all children have a right to *protection*, to *participation,* to *personal development* and to basic material *provision.* It upholds children's right to life, to be protected in armed conflicts, to be safe-guarded from degrading and cruel punishment, to receive special treatment in justice systems and grants freedom from discrimination, exploitation and abuse. The only UN member states that have not ratified are Somalia and the USA (Somalia has had no internationally recognised government since 1991, the US has claimed that ratification would undermine parental rights). The UNCRC builds upon the 1985 USA Standard Minimum Rules for the Administration of Youth Justice (the Beijing Rules) which recognised the 'special needs of children' and the importance of dealing with offenders flexibly. It promoted diversion from formal court procedures, non-custodial disposals and insisted that custody should be a last resort and for minimum periods. In addition the Rules emphasised the need for anonymity in order to protect children from life-long stigma and labelling. The Convention cemented these themes in the fundamental right that in all legal actions concerning those under the age of 18, the 'best interests of the child shall be a primary consideration' (Article 3.1). Further it reasserts the need to treat children differently from adults, to promote their dignity and worth with minimum use of custody and that children should participate in any proceedings relating to them (Article 12). In 1990 the UN guidelines for the Prevention of Juvenile Delinquency (the Riyadh guidelines) added that youth justice policy should avoid criminalising children for minor misdemeanours. The International Covenant on Civil and Political Rights, expressly outlaws capital punishment for under 18s and promotes rehabilitative interventions. The European Convention on Human Rights first formulated in 1953, provides for the due process of law, fairness in trial proceedings, a right to education, a right to privacy and declares that any deprivation of liberty (including curfews, electronic monitoring and community supervision) should not be arbitrary or consist of any degrading treatment. Collectively these Conventions and Rules might be viewed as tantamount to a growing legal globalisation of juvenile justice (Muncie, 2005).

Many countries have now used the UNCRC to improve protections for children and have appointed special commissioners or ombudspersons to champion children's rights. A monitoring body – the UN Committee on the Rights of the Child – reports under the Convention and presses governments for reform. Yet, Human Rights Watch (1999) and Amnesty International (n.d.) have noted that implementation has often been half-hearted and piecemeal. The UNCRC is persuasive but breach attracts no formal sanction. Millions of children worldwide continue to live in poverty, have no access to education and are routinely employed in armed conflicts. Child trafficking and forced labour are rife. Street children on every continent continue to endure harassment and physical abuse from the police and many others work long hours in hazardous conditions in flagrant violation of the rights guaranteed to them under the Convention. Countries give lip service to rights simply to be granted status as a 'modern developed state' and acceptance into world monetary systems. The pressure to ratify is both moral and economic (Harris-Short, 2003). It may be the most ratified of all international human rights directives but it is also the most violated. Abramson's (2000) analysis of UN observations on the implementation of juvenile justice in 141 countries notes a widespread lack of 'sympathetic understanding' necessary for compliance with the UNCRC. Describing these obligations as being largely received as 'unwanted', he notes that a complete overhaul of juvenile justice is required in 21 countries and that in others torture, inhumane treatment, lack of separation from adults, police brutality, bad conditions in detention facilities, overcrowding, lack of rehabilitation, failure to develop alternatives to incarceration, inadequate contact between minors and their families, lack of training of judges, police, and prison authorities, lack of speedy trial, no legal assistance, disproportionate sentences, insufficient respect for the rule of law and improper use of the juvenile justice system to tackle other social problems, are of common occurrence.

Thirty-three countries continue to accompany their ratification with reservations. For example the Netherlands, Canada and the UK have issued reservations to the requirement to separate children from adults in detention. In the English case this has long rested on an inability to fund suitable places for girls and young women. The UK has also reserved its option to deploy children in active military combat. It is the only state in Europe that extensively targets under 18s for recruitment into the armed forces. Similarly those jurisdictions that have introduced schemes to enforce parental responsibility, curfews and anti-social behaviour legislation (most notably in England and Wales, France and the USA), would again appear to be in contempt of the right to respect for private and family life and protection from arbitrary interference (Freeman, 2002). More seriously, many of the principles of restorative justice which rely on informality, flexibility and discretion sit uneasily against legal requirements for due process and a fair and just trial. Indeed the UN Committee on the Rights of the Child report on the UK in 2002 expressed concern that the UNCRC has not been incorporated into UK domestic law. The low age of criminal responsibility, the increasing numbers of children in custody at earlier ages, for lesser offences and for longer periods, the lack of separation of female juveniles from adults in prison, the retention of 'reasonable chastisement' as justification for the corporal disciplining of children, the resistance to grant child refugees a right to humanitarian assistance and a general lack of a rights based approach to youth policy have all come under stringent attack (Paton, 2003). It was only in 2002 that the UK reluctantly, after a High Court challenge to comply with the Human Rights Act 1998, accepted that the welfare of children applies as much to those in prison as elsewhere.

In many countries it seems abundantly clear that it is possible to claim an adherence to the principle of universal rights whilst simultaneously pursuing policies which exacerbate structural inequalities and punitive institutional regimes. 'Cultural difference' and the absence of localised human rights cultures preclude meaningful adoption of international agreements (Harris-Short, 2003).

It is undoubtedly the case that the core business of juvenile/youth justice systems worldwide is to process those children who are routinely exposed to poverty, abuse, inequality, ill health, poor (or lack of) housing and educational disadvantage (Goldson, 2000). Or as Amnesty (n.d.:4) have put it: 'when children come into conflict with law, it is most often for minor, non-violent offences – usually theft – and in some cases their only 'crime' is that they are poor, homeless and disadvantaged'. Further, some have argued that processes of repenalisation and adulteration suggest an acceleration of the governance of all young people *through* the motifs of crime and disorder (Simon, 1997; Muncie and Hughes, 2002). As the chapters in this volume attest, such analysis resonates with developments in many Western societies. New sets of juvenile justice laws are being put in place which mark a retreat from welfare and a dual commitment to severely punish the 'persistent offender' while attempting to prevent offending by pre-emptive early targeting of 'at risk' populations. Ironically compliance with the UNCRC is often stated as a key driver of such reforms. Similarly a growing interest in restoration is being used as an alternative to rehabilitation. The emphasis appears now to be one of *punitive responsibilisation*.

However, while there is clearly some evidence to support this thesis (as expressed by new discourses of responsibilisation as well as custodial increases), there remain marked and significant global variations in policy, extent of adherence to UN Conventions and resort to custody. National difference seems to be explicable primarily in the extent of a political willingness to sustain welfare protectionism or to subsume juvenile justice within alternative forms of conflict resolution. A cultural and political sensibility that imprisoning young people is not only harmful but also self-defeating would also appear crucial. Some of the key drivers of a reductionist and decarcerative policy seem to lie in restatements of a 'children first' philosophy: an ability to pardon and to protect but above all in the wholesale removal of the issue of juvenile crime for the purposes of media and/or political gain. In policy terms this involves removing all children from prison administration establishments, a greater commitment to suspending sentences and employing inclusionary and participative community based interventions, such as mediation, as direct alternatives to custody. Acknowledgement of, and full adherence to, the spirit and principles of the UNCRC would also appear to be pivotal. However it is explained, it is clear that locking up young people is driven by something other than crime, or, as has been most recently assumed, by increases in violent crime. The use of custody appears politically and culturally, rather than pragmatically, inspired. For some countries, prison seems to 'work' at a political and symbolic level even when it is a demonstrable failure. To understand why, we need to look more closely at what drives the recurring punitive mentality in 'cultures of control'. What appears lacking in those countries witnessing penal expansion is a wholesale depoliticisation of the youth crime issue.

Neo-liberal economics, conservative politics, policy transfer and international conventions are undoubtedly creating some standardised and homogenised response to youth offending. But youth justice is also significantly localised through national, regional and local enclaves of difference (Muncie, 2005). Pressures towards adulteration, zero tolerance and repenalisation are mediated by distinctive national and sub-national cultures and socio-cultural norms (O'Malley, 2002). As Tonry (2001: 518) has argued, the best explanations for penal severity or leniency remain 'parochially national and cultural'. In such countries as Australia, Canada, Italy, and France it is also difficult to prioritise national developments above widely divergent regional differences, most evident in sentencing disparities. In Canada, juvenile justice appears more resistant to punitive challenge in Quebec than, say, in Saskatchewan. In the Netherlands the new dispersal zones in Rotterdam may have no equivalence in other major Dutch cities, such as Amsterdam. Such sub-national divergence is also apparent in the USA where there is no uniform juvenile justice system but 50 different state systems each with their own distinctive history, laws, policies and practices. While overall the USA still incarcerates to an extent unknown elsewhere, custody rates in states such as Maine and Minnesota are much closer to a European average than in other US states such as Texas and Oklahoma. In Australia, too, state variance in sentencing is remarkable, with Victoria recording a detention rate of 13.2 juveniles per 100,000 population compared to 103.5 in the Northern Territories (see Cunneen and White, 2002, and Chapter 7 of this volume). Pursuing such an argument further, once it is recognised that differences *within* nation state territories may also be greater than some differences *between* them, then taking the national (let alone the international and the global) as the basic unit for understanding policy shifts and implementation becomes questionable (Stenson and Edwards, 2004; Crawford, 2002; Edwards and Hughes, 2005). Moreover, a renewed emphasis on local political cultures and governance may well open up an 'implementation gap' in which spaces for re-working, re-interpretation and avoidance of national or international trends can be forged.

Modern juvenile justice appears as ever more hybrid: attempting to deliver neither welfare or justice but a complex and contradictory amalgam of the punitive, the responsibilising, the inclusionary, the exclusionary and the protective (Muncie and Hughes, 2002). Within this mix, possibilities for transition and change are forever present. In the USA and Canada we may now be witnessing the beginnings of some exhaustion of extreme penal populism. In Finland and Italy decarceration and tolerance continue to remain in some ascendancy. Coupled to a growing recourse to rights agendas, comparative analysis is capable of not simply revealing difference and diversity but also a wide range of positions from which the logic of the punitive can be disputed and overcome.

References

Abramson, B. (2000) *Juvenile Justice: the 'Unwanted Child' of State Responsibilities. An analysis of the concluding observations of the UN Committee on the Rights of the Child, in regard to juvenile justice from 1993 to 2000*. International Network on Juvenile Justice/Defence for Children International, www.defence-for-children.org

Amnesty International (1998) *Betraying the Young: Children in the US Justice System*. AI Index AMR 51/60/98, www.web.amnesty.org

Amnesty International (n.d.) *Children's Human Rights – The Future Starts Here*. www.amnestyusa.org/children/future

Bailleau, F. (1998) 'A crisis of youth or of juridical response?', in V. Ruggiero, N. South and I. Taylor (eds) *The New European Criminology*. London: Routledge.

Bottoms, A. (2002) 'The divergent development of juvenile justice policy and practice in England and Scotland', in M. Rosenheim, F. E. Zinring, D. S. Tanenhaus and B. Dohrn (eds) *A Century of Juvenile Justice*. Chicago: University of Chicago Press.

Council of Europe (2002) *Penological Information Bulletin*, nos. 23 & 24, December, Strasbourg, Council of Europe.

Council of Europe (2003) *European Sourcebook of Crime and Criminal Justice Statistics*, (2nd edition). WODC: Den Haag.

Council of Europe (2003) *SPACE1 Annual Penal Statistics 2002* Strasbourg, Council of Europe.

Council of Europe (2003) *Penological Information Bulletin*, no. 25, December, Strasbourg, Council of Europe.

Crawford, A. (2002) 'The governance of crime and insecurity in an anxious age: The trans-European and the local', in A. Crawford (ed.) *Crime and Insecurity: The governance of Safety in Europe*. Cullompton: Willan.

Cunneen, C. and White, R. (2002) *Juvenile Justice: Youth and Crime in Australia*. Melbourne: Oxford University Press.

Daly, K. (2002) 'Restorative justice: the real story' *Punishment and Society*, 4(1): 55–79.

Downes, D. (1988) *Contrasts in Tolerance*. Oxford: Oxford University Press.

Edwards, A. and Hughes, G. (2005) 'Comparing the governance of safety in Europe: A geo-historical approach' *Theoretical Criminology*, 9(3): 345–363.

Farrington, D. (2000) 'Explaining and preventing crime: The globalisation of knowledge' *Criminology* 38(1): 1–24.

Fenwick, M. (2004) 'Youth crime and crime control in contemporary Japan' in C. Sumner (ed.) *The Blackwell Companion to Criminology*. Oxford: Blackwell.

Fionda, J. (1998) 'The age of innocence? The concept of childhood in the punishment of young offenders' *Child and Family Law Quarterly*, 10(1): 77–87.

Freeman, M. (2002) 'Children's rights ten years after ratification' in B. Franklin (ed.) *The New Handbook of Children's Rights*. London: Routledge.

Garland, D. (2001) *The Culture of Control*. Oxford: Oxford University Press.

Gatti, U. and Verde, A. (2002) 'Comparative juvenile justice: an overview of Italy' in J. Winterdyk (ed.) *Juvenile Justice Systems: International Perspectives* (2nd edition). Toronto: Canadians Scholars Press.

Goldson, B. (2000) 'Children in need or young offenders?' *Child and Family Social Work,* 5(3): 255–265.

Goldson, B. (2002) 'New punitiveness: the politics of child incarceration' in J. Muncie, G. Hughes and E. McLaughlin (eds) *Youth Justice: Critical Readings.* London: Sage.

Goldson, B. (2004) 'Youth crime and youth justice' in J. Muncie and D. Wilson (eds) *The Student Handbook of Criminal Justice and Criminology.* London: Cavendish.

Harris-Short, S. (2003) 'International human rights law: imperialist, inept and ineffective? Cultural relativism and the UN Convention on the Rights of the Child' *Human Rights Quarterly,* 25(1): 130–181.

Hudson, B. (1987) *Justice through Punishment.* Basingstoke: Macmillan.

Human Rights Watch (1999) *Promises Broken: An assessment of Children's Rights on the 10th Anniversary of the Convention of the Rights of the Child.* www.hrw.org/campaigns/crp/promises

International Centre for Prison Studies (2004) *World Prison Brief.* www.kcl.ac.uk/depsta/rel/icps/worldbrief

Jones, J. and Newburn, T. (2002) 'Policy convergence and crime control in the USA and the UK' *Criminal Justice,* 2(2): 173–203.

Junger-Tas, J. (2002) 'The juvenile justice system: Past and present trends in western society' in I. Weijers and A. Duff (eds) *Punishing Juveniles.* Oxford: Hart.

Junger-Tas, J. (2004) 'Youth justice in the Netherlands', in M. Tonry and A. Doob (eds) *Youth Crime and Youth Justice: Comparative and Cross-national Perspectives,* Crime and Justice volume 31. Chicago: Chicago University Press.

Justice (2000) *Restoring Youth Justice: New Directions in Domestic and International Law and Practice.* London: Justice.

Lappi-Seppälä, T. (1998) *Regulating the Prison Population,* Research Communications no. 38. Helsinki: National Research Institute of Legal Policy.

Lappi-Seppälä, T. (2001) 'Sentencing and Punishment in Finland', in M. Tonry and R. Frase (eds) *Sentencing and Sanctions in Western Countries.* Oxford: Oxford University Press.

Melossi, D. (2000) 'Translating social control: Reflections on the comparison of Italian and North American cultures' in S. Karstedt and Bussman R.-H. (eds) *Social Dynamics of Crime and Control.* Oxford: Hart.

Miers, D. (2001) *An International Review of Restorative Justice,* Crime Reduction Research Series Paper no. 10. London: Home Office.

Morita, A. (2002) 'Juvenile justice in Japan: A historical and cross-cultural perspective' in Rosenheim, F. Zimring, D. Tanenhaus and B. Dohrn (eds) *A Century of Juvenile Justice.* Chicago: University of Chicago Press.

Muncie, J. (2005) 'The globalisation of crime control: the case of youth and juvenile justice', *Theoretical Criminology,* 9(1): 35–64.

Muncie, J. (2006) 'Repenalisation and rights: explorations in comparative youth criminology', *Howard Journal of Criminal Justice,* 45(1): 42–70.

Muncie, J. and Hughes, G. (2002) 'Modes of youth governance: political rationalities, criminalisation and resistance' in J. Muncie, G. Hughes and E. McLaughlin (eds) *Youth Justice: Critical Readings.* London: Sage.

Muncie, J. and Sparks, R. (1991) 'Expansion and contraction in European penal systems' in J. Muncie and R. Sparks (eds) *Imprisonment: European Perspectives.* Hemel Hempstead: Harvester Wheatsheaf.

Nelken, D. (2002) 'Comparing criminal justice' in M. Maguire, R. Morgan and R. Reiner (eds) *The Oxford Handbook of Criminology* (3rd edition). Oxford: Oxford University Press.

Nelken, D. (2005) 'When is a society non-punitive? The Italian case', in J. Pratt, D. Brown, M. Brown, S. Hallsworth and W. Morrison (eds) *The New Punitiveness*. Cullompton: Willan.

Newburn, T. and Sparks, R. (eds) (2004) *Criminal Justice and Political Cultures: National and International Dimensions of Crime Control*. Cullompton: Willan.

Nordic Working Group on Youth Crime (2001) *Youth Crime in the Nordic Countries*. Haaksbergen, Netherlands: De Lindeboom Publishers.

O'Dwyer, K. (2002) 'Juvenile crime and justice in Ireland', in N. Bala, J. Hornick, H. Snyder and J. Paetsch (eds) *Juvenile Justice Systems: An International Comparison of Problems and Solutions*. Toronto: Thompson.

O'Malley, P. (2002) 'Globalising risk? Distinguishing styles of neo-liberal criminal justice in Australia and the USA' *Criminal Justice,* 2(2): 205–222.

Pakes, F. (2000) 'League champions in mid table: On the major changes in Dutch prison policy', *Howard Journal,* 39(1): 30–39.

Pakes, F. (2004) 'The politics of discontent: The emergence of a new criminal justice discourse in the Netherlands' *Howard Journal*, 43(3): 284–298.

Paton, L. (2003) 'Children's rights in the UK: implementing the United Nations Convention on the Rights of the Child' *ChildRight*, 198: 3–6.

Pease, K. (1994) 'Cross-national imprisonment rates: limitations of method and possible conclusions' *British Journal of Criminology*, 34: 116–130.

Pitts, J. (2001) *The New Politics of Youth Crime: Discipline or Solidarity?* Basingstoke: Palgrave.

Pratt, J., Brown, D., Brown, M., Hallsworth, S. and Morrison, W. (eds) (2005) *The New Punitiveness*. Cullompton: Willan.

Rechea Alberola, C. and Fernandez Molina, E. (2003) 'Juvenile justice in Spain: past and present', *Journal of Contemporary Criminal Justice*, 9(4): 384–412.

Rutherford, A. (1989) 'The mood and temper of penal policy: curious happenings in England during the 1980s', *Youth and Policy*, 27: 27–31.

Rutherford, A. (2002) 'Youth justice and social inclusion', *Youth Justice,* 2(2): 100–107.

Schabas, W. (1996) 'Reservations to the Convention on the Rights of the Child', *Human Rights Quarterly*, 18(4): 472–491.

Schaffner, L. (2002) 'An age of reason: paradoxes in the US legal construction of adulthood', *International Journal of Children's Rights*, 10: 201–232.

Simon, J. (1997) 'Governing through Crime', in L. Friedman and G. Fisher (eds) *The Crime Conundrum*. Boulder, CO: Westview.

Simon, J. (2001) 'Entitlement to cruelty: neo-liberalism and the punitive mentality in the United States', in K. Stenson and R. R. Sullivan (eds) *Crime, Risk and Justice*. Cullompton: Willan.

Skelton, A. (2002) 'Restorative justice as a framework for juvenile justice reform: a South African perspective' *British Journal of Criminology*, 42(3): 496–513.

Snyder, H. (2002) 'Juvenile crime and justice in the United States of America', in N. Bala, J., Hornick, H. Snyder and J. Paetsch (eds) *Juvenile Justice Systems: An International Comparison of Problems and Solutions*. Toronto: Thompson.

Stenson, K. and Edwards, A. (2004) 'Policy transfer in local crime control: beyond naïve emulation' in T. Newburn and R. Sparks (eds) *Criminal Justice and Political Cultures: National and International Dimensions of Crime Control*. Cullompton: Willan.

Stern, V. (2001) 'An alternative vision: criminal justice developments in non-Western societies' *Social Justice*, 28(3): 88–104.

Streib, V. (2003) *The Juvenile Death Penalty Today*. www.law.onu.edu/faculty/streib

Tham, H. (2001) 'Law and order as a leftist project? The case of Sweden', *Punishment and Society*, 3(3): 409–426.

Tickell, S. and Akester, K. (2004) *Restorative Justice: The Way Ahead*. London: Justice.

Tonry, M. (2001) 'Symbol, substance and severity in western penal policies', *Punishment and Society*, 3(4): 517–536.

United Nations Office for Drug Control and Crime Prevention (2002) *The Seventh Survey on Crime Trends and the Operations of Criminal Justice Systems*. www.odccp.org/odccp/crime-cicp-survey-seventh.html.

United Nations Office for Drug Control and Crime Prevention (2005) *The Eighth Survey on Crime Trends and the Operations of Criminal Justice Systems*, www.unodc.org/pdf/crime/eighth survey/8pct.pdf

van Swaaningen, R. (2005) 'Public safety and the management of fear', *Theoretical Criminology*, 9(3): 289–305.

van Zyl Smit, D. and van der Spuy, E. (2004) 'Importing criminological ideas in a new democracy: recent South African experiences', in T. Newburn and R. Sparks (eds) *Criminal Justice and Political Cultures: National and International Dimensions of Crime Control*. Cullompton: Willan.

Wacquant, L. (1999) 'How penal common sense comes to Europeans: notes on the transatlantic diffusion of the neo-liberal doxa', *European Societies*, 1(3): 319–352.

Wacquant, L. (2001) 'The penalization of poverty and the rise of neo-liberalism', *European Journal on Criminal Policy and Research*, 9: 401–412.

Walmsley, R. (2005) *World Prison Population List* (6th edition). London: International Centre for Prison Studies.

White, R. (2000) 'Social justice, community building and restorative strategies', *Contemporary Justice Review*, 3(1): 55–72.

White, R. (2002) 'Communities, conferences and restorative social justice', *Criminal Justice*, 3(2): 139–160.

Index